Praise for

COMMUNICATION R$_X$

"This book provides a blueprint for almost all interactions in healthcare, not just between patients and clinicians, but also among colleagues. *Communication Rx* is a must-read for anyone who is interested in improving quality and safety—and that should be everyone!"

—DONALD M. BERWICK, MD, MPP, President Emeritus and
Senior Fellow, Institute for Healthcare Improvement

"An unrivaled collection of thought leaders together in one foundational resource on patient-centered communication. Improving how we communicate in healthcare is critical to advancing patient safety, quality, and experience. Now, the professional men and women of the ACH, who represent the best and brightest in the industry, have come together to deliver the most up-to-date and comprehensive piece of work yet that advances this critical work. This book is a must-have reference for healthcare leaders, providers, patients, and families."

—JAMES MERLINO, MD, President and Chief Medical Officer, Strategic
Consulting, Press Ganey Associates, Inc.; former Chief Experience
Officer, Cleveland Clinic; and author of *Service Fanatics*

"At a time when technology has created virtual worlds; when it is possible to finance a house, talk across continents, or see unfiltered news images with one mouse click, the encounter between patients and physicians in one another's presence remains sacrosanct. The authors of *Communication Rx* have given us one of the best and most comprehensive evidence-based guides to navigating the intricacies of this relationship to date. It is the best prescription I can think of for unlocking the healing potential of the patient-clinician relationship."

—RICHARD M. FRANKEL, PhD, Professor of Medicine,
Indiana University School of Medicine

"No one should be practicing medicine or running a department or a healthcare system without mastering the tools and skills in this compact, beautifully written book on communicating with patients, families, and our colleagues in healthcare."

—DOUGLAS STONE AND SHEILA HEEN, coauthors of the
New York Times bestselling *Difficult Conversations*

"Change will only come when everyone in the healthcare workforce has developed solid communication skills and the ability to deal effectively with differences. This wonderful book provides practical guidance on how to enhance your communication skills and how to work well with others. Essential reading for our times."

—ELLIOTT S. FISHER, MD, MPH, John E. Wennberg Distinguished
Professor of Health Policy, Medicine, and Community and
Family Medicine, Geisel School of Medicine, Dartmouth

"When my work in healthcare started to focus on management and leadership, my late father gave me one book, *Language in Thought and Action* by S.I. Hayakawa. I think *Communication Rx* is the sequel that Hayakawa might have written if he had plunged into exploration of the application of his ideas in healthcare. In it, true experts describe the fundamental skill sets for effective communication with patients and among clinicians. It is more than a book about how to talk and how to listen; it is a manual for developing relationships that can adapt to the pressures and unpredictability of medicine."

—THOMAS H. LEE, MD, Chief Medical Officer, Press Ganey Associates,
Inc., and author of *The Epidemic of Empathy in Healthcare*

"An engaging and evidence-based book on the necessity of communication in healthcare to reduce the epidemic of suffering, this guide to improving healthcare communication is a must-read for caregivers who want to make a difference in the lives of the patients they serve."

—CHRISTINA DEMPSEY, MSN, MBA, CNOR, CENP, FAAN, SVP,
Chief Nursing Officer, Press Ganey Associates, Inc.,
and author of *The Antidote to Suffering*

"Whether you're a clinician interested in improving your communication with patients, a teacher seeking to arm your students with useful tools and techniques, or a healthcare executive intent on improving your system's patient survey results, this well-written and practical book will be an indispensable companion."

—ROBERT M. WACHTER, MD, Professor and Chair, Department
of Medicine, University of California, San Francisco, and author
of the *New York Times* science bestseller *The Digital Doctor*

"Communication is easily the most powerful tool in the medical armamentarium, yet attention to this in training programs has been scant. *Communication Rx* provides direct and practical skills for both clinicians and teachers. It is an invaluable resource for medical professionals across the healthcare spectrum, and a welcome addition to the medical canon."

—DANIELLE OFRI, MD, PhD, author of *What
Patients Say, What Doctors Hear*

"This remarkable, well-edited text reminds us all of the importance of effective communication and provides the reader with specific recommendations on how to hone those critical skills that facilitate the building of meaningful relationships. This resource not only offers practical guidance on how to listen more effectively and thereby improve the quality of care, it also serves to remind us of the joy that is possible in caring for others."

—MICHAEL C. BENNICK, MD, MA, AGAF, FACP, Associate Chief of Medicine, Medical Director of the Patient Experience, and Chairman, Patient Experience Council

"Composed of brief readable chapters richly illustrated with vignettes, *Communication Rx* offers practical guidance across a wide range of topics, ranging from the timeless fundamentals of communication and relationship skills to current state-of-the-art topics such as electronic records and culture and diversity. What's more, it goes well beyond patient-clinician relationships to look at communication on healthcare teams and organizational culture. This book is the new reference standard for relationship-centered care."

—ANTHONY SUCHMAN, MD, MA, Founder and Senior Consultant, Relationship Centered Health Care

"At a time when clinician burnout is on the rise and patient frustrations with our debilitated healthcare delivery system continue to escalate, Chou and Cooley provide a timely and comprehensive guide that can turn the tide. By helping clinicians enhance their communication skills, the stronger patient-clinician relationships that ensue will lead to better care and more joy in practice. This material is essential for the toolbox of every clinician, leader, and learner in healthcare."

—VIVIAN S. LEE, MD, PhD, MBA, former CEO, University of Utah Healthcare, and former Dean, University of Utah School of Medicine

"Drs. Chou and Cooley have assembled a remarkable group of recognized communication experts to address a clear deficit in modern medicine: the underutilization of the power of effective, intimate connection between provider and patient. Through a series of insightful and delightfully true examples, they weave an accurate accounting of how optimal communication can result in both enhanced patient outcomes and increased professional satisfaction, a true win/win. I know of no other book that addresses the incredible potential of patient-centered communication more cogently. As a healthcare executive, I see great value here for patients, physicians, and healthcare leaders alike."

—HOWARD B. GRAMAN, MD, former Chair, Board of American Medical Group Association, and former CEO, PeaceHealth Medical Group

"Experience equals quality for patients. Good communication allows for greater trust and better relationships between patient and providers. In today's world of increasing transparency where every experience is shared, it is critical that providers have the skills they need to build and maintain that trusting relationship with their patients. The concepts and skills described in this book establish an excellent foundation for interpersonal communication improving patient outcomes and provider wellbeing."

—SARA LASKEY, MD, VP and Chief Experience Officer, MetroHealth
System, and Executive Board Member, The Beryl Institute

"Excellent resource for all Experience leaders and a must-read for all clinicians. This book is a perfect reminder that we treat human beings, not diseases, and effective communication is the key to all human interactions. It's a step-by-step guide to deal with all kinds of communication challenges with practical tools, deeply rooted in scientific principles."

—ALPA SANGHAVI, MD, Chief Quality and Experience
Officer, San Mateo Medical Center

"Patients, providers, administrators, and our entire healthcare team benefit when communication is done in the service of our interpersonal and interprofessional relationships. Our clinicians and administrators have found great value in the skills and training outlined in this book. Local expert trainers—both clinicians and nonclinicians—have been critical to the success of our communication program and to the value we are realizing as more and more colleagues adopt these evidence-based skills."

—ANGELA HOCHHALTER, PhD, VP Patient Centered
Care Redesign, Baylor Scott & White Health

"Relationship-centered communication (RCC) is the cornerstone for my interactions with patients and colleagues. In the clinical setting, it's the framework for all I do, shaping my communication with patients, their visitors, and the interdisciplinary care team. RCC imbues all my teaching with house officers and medical students. It is gratifying to see UCSF trainees embrace these simple, profoundly effective skills. As the physician lead for patient and staff experience at Zuckerberg San Francisco General, we have developed a core team to spread RCC across the organization to providers, staff, and volunteers, convinced that it will enrich all who touch our campus."

—JEFF CRITCHFIELD, MD, Chief Medical Experience Officer,
Medical Director, Risk Management, Zuckerberg San
Francisco General Hospital and Trauma Center, and Professor
of Medicine, University of California, San Francisco

"We know from surveys that our patients are concerned that clinical providers may not be meeting their expectations with regard to certain items that are important to them during their clinical encounters. These include understanding and acknowledging the patients' goals for treatment, appreciating the impact of their suffering on their personal lives and emotions, and imparting empathy. In addition, there is the perception that the explanations of the diagnosis, evaluation, and treatment plans for their disorders could be improved. One of the key factors contributing to these concerns is the absence of formal patient- and relationship-centered communication education during medical school and postgraduate residency training. The ACH has for many years focused its activities on developing evidence-based training curricula to improve this communication process for our clinicians, and their efforts have been successful in enhancing the skills of those who have participated in these training programs. Within our own system, the initial results for our faculty have shown an impressive improvement in patient survey responses. This book further enhances the mission for effective physician-patient communication by providing a rich source of information on this very important subject. An extensive panel of experts share the evidence that forms the basis for the valuable educational initiatives provided by the ACH."

—DAVID B. SCHWARTZ, MD, FACOG, FRCOG, FCOG (SA),
Director of Clinical Affairs, Special Programs, Office of the Dean,
and Clinical Professor of Obstetrics and Gynecology, Maternal
Fetal Medicine, University of Maryland School of Medicine

COMMUNICATION

Rx

COMMUNICATION

Rx

Transforming Healthcare Through
Relationship-Centered
Communication

Edited by
**CALVIN CHOU, MD, PhD and
LAURA COOLEY, PhD**

New York Chicago San Francisco Athens London Madrid
Mexico City Milan New Delhi Singapore Sydney Toronto

1 2 3 4 5 6 7 8 9   LCR   22 21 20 19 18 17

ISBN: 978-1-260-01974-2
MHID: 1-260-01974-8

eISBN: 978-1-260-01975-9
eMHID: 1-260-01975-6

Library of Congress Cataloging-in-Publication Data
Names: Chou, Calvin L., author.
Title: Communication Rx : transforming healthcare through
   relationship-centered communication / by Calvin L. Chou and Laura Cooley.
Description: New York : McGraw-Hill, [2018] | Includes bibliographical
   references.
Identifiers: LCCN 2017023809 | ISBN 9781260019742 (hardback) |
   ISBN 1260019748 (hardback)
Subjects: LCSH: Communication in medicine. | Physician and patient. | BISAC:
   BUSINESS & ECONOMICS / Business Communication / General.
Classification: LCC R118 .C46 2018 | DDC 610.1/4—dc23
LC record available at https://lccn.loc.gov/2017023809

McGraw-Hill Education books are available at special quantity discounts to use as premiums and sales promotions, or for use in corporate training programs. To contact a representative, please visit the Contact Us page at www.mhprofessional.com.

To my parents, Chris and Shu-fen, who taught me how to listen and how to strive toward unconditional positive regard

—CLC

To my parents, for teaching me to work with dedication and to live with compassion

—LAC

CONTENTS

PART III

PRACTICAL APPLICATIONS OF THE SKILL SETS

PART IV

INSTITUTING COMMUNICATION INITIATIVES

ACKNOWLEDGMENTS

T hough they are too numerous to name individually, we are indebted to all who have created, led, and contributed to the community of ACH faculty and faculty-in-training over the past 40 years: it keeps on giving and makes us all better. The times we have spent during our winter faculty development courses and summer ENRICH courses have showed us how to, and occasionally how not to, be present and as personally mindful as possible in diverse, matrix-laden, family-aware groups infused with Rogerian ideals. Specifically, the faculty development leaders in recent years whose facilitation examples have allowed us to pursue the work that we outline in this book include Amina Knowlan, Charlie O'Leary, Gerald Boyd, Maysel Kemp White, Tony Suchman, Joanne DeMark, and Ted DesMaisons. We also appreciate all of our institutional partners throughout the country, including those who have partnered with us in train-the-trainer programs and who provide ongoing inspiration, community, and mutual learning.

For this book, we give special appreciation to the entire team at McGraw-Hill, and particularly Casey Ebro, who approached us with the idea for the book and responded to our requests and questions throughout the process with uncommon alacrity; Carol Chou and Sally Fortner, who provided the comprehensive literature review reported in Chapter 1; and Krista Hirschmann, Jenni Levy, Tim Gilligan, and Alpa Sanghavi, all of whom read portions of the book and provided invaluable feedback.

PREFACE

*There is a direct link between the quality of your
communication and the quality of your life.*
—J. Stewart[1]

(Laura Cooley) will always remember the day when I truly realized
the value of authentic communication and relationships in healthcare. My father was too weak from the cancer, chemotherapy, and
radiation, and their side effects, to even walk into the clinic that day. It
was hard to believe that only two years prior he had been a healthy 63-
year-old man who was hiking and gardening regularly.

When the oncologist, Dr. Brown, finally rushed in (after failing to
greet my mother or me), he stood over my father's wheelchair, reviewed
the chart, and abruptly flipped my father's hands over to inspect the
raw burns on his palms from the chemo. He then made yet another
recommendation for chemo. We sat quietly. My father raised a couple
of simple questions about his side effects and the new chemo, doing so
haltingly, as the recent development of a brain metastasis had impaired
his speech.

As Dr. Brown scribbled a few notes in silence and edged his way
toward the door, I cleared my throat and halted his departure. I had
prepared several delicate questions about life expectancy and choices.
As my questions began to flow, Dr. Brown scanned our faces and eased
himself onto a stool. He leaned in and proceeded to have a direct and

honest conversation. In the next few moments, we learned that my father might expect about three to six months of low-quality life. As Dr. Brown delivered this devastating news, paradoxically, his humanistic side emerged. He sat quietly for a few moments, offered his sincere condolences, and then departed gently. As my family wept together, the nurse provided a calm, comforting presence, and stayed with us until we were ready to exit the exam room.

Those final moments of clear and compassionate communication allowed my family to digest the somber news and make more informed decisions in the direction of palliative care. My father died only three weeks later. I was so grateful for the opportunity to engage in a conversation that honestly prepared us for the inevitable future. Until that moment, my parents had not fully realized that there were alternatives to the aggressive treatment offered. I was saddened by the thought that we would have missed that communication opportunity had I not insisted. What happens to other patients and families? How many other opportunities are missed?

I believe that most healthcare clinicians truly want the best for their patients. I believe Dr. Brown did, too. I wish that he and other clinicians could regularly perform the fundamental skills that are essential for communicating effectively and for connecting authentically. Relationship-centered communication has the power to reduce suffering for patients and families like mine, and to reengage healthcare clinicians in the true spirit of caring and healing, even when a cure cannot be found.

* * *

What do we mean by "communicating effectively"? Often, during our workshops, we'll ask people to introduce themselves by sharing something interesting about their name. Our name, the Academy of Communication in Healthcare (ACH), deliberately includes the word *Communication* as a core aspect of not just what we do but who we are—it is literally our middle name! Admittedly, communication is a complicated word even within its own discipline of study. Derived from the Latin words *communis* and *communicare*, meaning "to share" and related to the word *community*, human communication is the use and interpretation of symbols (verbal and nonverbal) to create a shared reality with other people. We deliberately say communication to differentiate our work from technology, referred to as "communications." Though electronic devices certainly permeate our lives, we focus on immediate interpersonal exchanges, rather than those involving organizations or the media. Even with this focus, given the range of symbols in healthcare (jargon, procedures, specialties, stories, and emotion, among many others), health communication is a particularly complex context in which to try to skillfully "share" meaning with other people.

As a reflection of our organizational mission, this book seeks not just to improve communication skills, but through those skills to develop deep and meaningful relationships that facilitate high-quality patient care and renew our joy for caring for others. In this sense, communicating effectively is so much more than the accurate exchange of information; it is about recognizing and strengthening our interconnections as a dynamic, professional system. Extra layers of challenge arise from the understanding that all communication has not only content (the meaning I am trying to share with you) and relationship (who we are to each other given our individual and common experiences) but also situational context (e.g., emergency versus anticipated, electronic versus face-to-face, etc.). We believe, however, given the costly, inefficient, and sometimes heartbreaking consequences of not doing so, that deliberate practice and attention to improving our skills is well worth the effort.

As a nonprofit organization, our dedication to this effort is long-standing. The ACH originated in 1978 as a task force within the Society of General Internal Medicine. At that time, communication was rarely studied in the healthcare setting; best practices were born of physicians' individual experiences, rather than from evidence-based science. The dearth of information and guidance led many founders of the original task force to do seminal research in this area. Such efforts resulted in the task force becoming an independent organization known as the American Academy on Physician and Patient (AAPP) in 1993. Recognizing the explicit exclusivity of that title, and wanting to honor the full scope of systems work we now embrace, members voted in 2006 to change the name to the American Academy on Communication in Healthcare, and more recently, to the Academy of Communication in

Healthcare. Those name changes support an active expansion of our community by inviting the true diversity of professionals and perspectives involved in healthcare to join our mission.

Communication Rx covers selected communication scenarios that commonly arise in healthcare. Many others are detailed in a seminal textbook on physician communication skills,[2] written by early members of the AAPP, giants in the field on whose shoulders we stand. We have purposefully avoided duplicating many of the chapters that to this day remain clear and useful exemplars (e.g., conducting a family interview, using interpreters, conducting a sexual history, and addressing many aspects of psychosocial medicine, including patients with personality styles, alcohol use disorders, and others). Instead, we intend this book to be a resource for a much broader audience, including clinicians in all health professions, leaders and administrators, patient experience specialists, patient advocates, and companies that assist in the patient experience. In fact, as the skills in many cases are generic and transferable, we think their application goes well beyond healthcare.

We have organized this book into four parts to address different aspects of communication skills training and its applications. Part I (Chapters 1–2) provides an overview of the importance of communication skills, the research that supports the influence of communication on healthcare outcomes for both patients and clinicians, and the relationship between communication skills and patient experience.

Part II (Chapters 3–5) delves into the three evidence-based, fundamental skill sets that we teach in our courses. Because the evidence has accumulated relatively recently (in the past couple of decades), many practicing clinicians may never have undergone specific training in these fundamentals. If professional baseball players, who are paid much more than most clinicians, can do fielding drills before every game, clinicians—whose collective outcomes, we might argue, are more consequential to society—can also continue to work on their fundamental skills.

Part III (Chapters 6–15) shows how the fundamentals apply to almost every interaction involving communication in healthcare. This part begins with a chapter addressing common, as well as advanced, communication challenges that clinicians face (Chapter 6). Mostly, the same fundamental skill sets apply in the latter cases, along with extra finesse and self-awareness. Advanced applications in communicating with patients include working with the electronic health record (Chapter 7), motivational interviewing (Chapter 8), and shared decision-making (Chapter 9). We then offer applications of the skills to interactions with colleagues and team members, with chapters on feedback (Chapter 10), coaching (Chapter 11), teamwork (Chapter 12), and communication challenges with colleagues (Chapter 13). We address more systemic and societal factors in chapters on culture and diversity (Chapter 14) and communicating through hierarchy (Chapter 15).

Finally, Part IV (Chapters 16–18) addresses how health systems can adopt these ideals of communication. We include a chapter on teaching the skill sets (Chapter 16), which, as you will see, also incorporates the fundamentals from Part II. Chapter 17 discusses train-the-trainer programs that institutions may find helpful to jump-start and sustain communication skills improvement initiatives. Chapter 18 considers the institutional context in which change might take place and describes implementation methods and common pitfalls. Video examples for much of the content in this book can be found in the ACH's online learning resource, *DocCom,* and numerous textbooks on fundamental communication, among them *Smith's Patient-Centered Interviewing.*[3]

The authors of these chapters are current participants in or graduates of the ACH Faculty-in-Training Program,[4] a relationship-centered distance learning community where expertise grows through iterative and deliberate practice fostered by safe and appreciative feedback. Authors are predominantly physicians from both the inpatient and outpatient worlds, with essential contributions from a midwife, a physician assistant, a marriage and family counselor, and health communication educators and scholars. As you glance through our affiliations, you'll see that we represent 16 institutions across the United States and Canada. We absolutely welcome feedback on the book, particularly feedback that is honest, kind, and intended to improve the work in healthcare to which we are all committed.

In whatever capacity you give care to our patients, join us on this journey through fundamental and advanced skills in healthcare communication to better serve our patients, our colleagues, our institutions, and ourselves.

THE LANDSCAPE

Building the Case for Communication and Relationships

(Calvin Chou) paused and shook my head as I previewed the chart of my new patient, Mr. Johnson. He was an Army vet and former line cook in his early 60s and had been on disability for many years for chronic lower back pain. He was treated with high-dose opiates until his urine tests turned positive for cocaine a year ago. His primary care physician at the time referred him to a pain management clinic, and opiates were quickly tapered. Mr. Johnson wasn't happy about this. He had transferred to two different clinicians in the past year. I know and trust both of them, and I could see they'd had a rough time. Both had refused to give Mr. Johnson more opiates. Both had documented similar endings to their visits (and to the relationships): "patient got up, interrupted me, yelling epithets, and walked out, slamming the door behind him."

Patients like Mr. Johnson once made me extraordinarily anxious. Clinical training generally does not teach us how to treat Mr. Johnson. My usual approach would have been to firmly state, with full justification, that opiates are not an option. The patient would leave the visit angry, and even though I would know I'd done the right thing, I would still feel terrible. Now, having developed a reputation for being a "communication expert" (a castle in the air, if ever there was one), I am often asked to see "difficult" patients. I don't jump for joy about these visits, but I do feel more confident than I used to. I no longer expect that I will just get my way because I'm the one with clinical training. But when I rely on a toolbox of communication skills, including listening, empathy, and compassion, patients can leave the encounter with some hope, and I can derive some satisfaction from the visit.

Where did I get this toolbox? As a pre-med student in college in the early 1980s, I had only the vaguest notion of what becoming a doctor really meant. My parents were immigrants and didn't work in healthcare, so what little I knew came from television: reruns of "Marcus Welby, MD," or summers guiltily spent indulging in episodes of "General Hospital." The contrasts couldn't be sharper. Dr. Welby seemed like a kind, wholly trustworthy, humanistic physician who listened to his patients and tried to do right by them, whereas the doctors on "GH" found themselves repeatedly embroiled in scandal, intrigue, and bizarre plot lines. Still, I actually learned a lot by observing how the doctors and nurses seemed to really care about their patients and each other (when they weren't being kidnapped or framed for murder). What a disappointment it was that the mad preparation for medical school consisted wholly of studying biology, chemistry, and physics rather than perfecting the finer points of humanism. The application to medical school seemed to depend wholly on test grades and scores, with no mention of the storied and elusive skills of "bedside manner." I saw some classmates who were admitted to prestigious medical schools, but I wondered, given my observation of their interpersonal interactions, how they would enact the full range of physician skills as seen on TV—let alone in real life!

There was a bright spot in my training: in residency, when I was on outpatient-based months, we attended a weekly 90-minute seminar called "Medical Interviewing and Psychosocial Aspects of Medicine." This was something I hadn't explicitly learned about in medical school. That seminar focused less on the content and knowledge learning in medicine; instead, it emphasized how clinicians can communicate with patients to convert all that knowledge into effective treatment plans.

Clinicians have more than 200,000 patient interactions (e.g., outpatient appointments, emergency department visits, interactions on inpatient rounds) during their careers—and that doesn't include telephone calls or secure messaging.[1] Clinicians also have innumerable meetings and conversations with colleagues and interdisciplinary teams. Yet, like me, most clinicians received little or no formal training in what might be seen as the most common procedure that all clinicians perform. Would you trust a surgeon who told you, "I haven't had any formal training for this procedure, haven't observed any experts, nor have I been observed and received feedback, BUT over the course of time, through trial and error, I think I've found what works for me"? That is essentially how physicians were "trained" in communication skills for decades.

In the 1970s the concept of "patient-centered care" emerged. This model shifted control of medical decisions toward the patient. It's your body: you should be involved in the decisions about your care. Research has confirmed the value of a patient-centered orientation: we must know what is important to patients and what they understand. This does not mean, however, that the patient is always right, according to the customer service mantra. Effective communication, in the context of a patient-clinician relationship, is not the same as customer service in a retail business. Patient-centeredness research examines how the clinician cares for and shares power with the patient in an encounter, not whether the clinician completely cedes control to patients. Testing, diagnoses, and treatments should not be solely up to the patient to decide because clinicians bring expertise that patients need—and want—for the best care. It's not safe to give Mr. Johnson any opiates, as much as he might want them.

So the pendulum is starting to settle in between patient and clinician. This approach is known as *relationship-centered care* (RCC).[2] RCC acknowledges the clinician's expertise as well as the patient's perspectives and preferences; it focuses on the space between patient and clinician, not exclusively on one person or the other. In fact, RCC brings all the relationships in healthcare together—patients, clinicians, team members, and families—to improve the quality and safety of healthcare and well-being. As a result, RCC requires that clinicians bring not only their knowledge base but also their genuine personhood into each patient encounter. It turns out that, contrary to the supposed ideals of my medical training, clinicians are not Spock-like creatures driven only by knowledge and rational thought. We have emotions, which affect patient and clinician alike and must be a prominent—and essential—part of the relationship.[3] Recent research in basic neurological science has shown a physiological basis for empathy, and the healing power of recognizing emotion and providing compassionate support.[4] Emotions are also inherently involved in the decision-making process, especially when there is scientific uncertainty. So there is a balance to strike: we can't allow emotions to hijack our work, nor can we ignore them completely. We must cultivate awareness of our emotions and determine how they affect our own behavior, our relationships with our patients, and the decisions we make. Unfortunately, in the fast-paced and pressured practice of clinical medicine, it often seems easier for clinicians to remain more task-oriented and to minimize these emotions during the course of our typically hectic days. That stance runs risks, not only of sealing us off from the fulfillment of our relationships and the power of RCC, but also of misdiagnosis, poorer outcomes, and burnout.[5]

A hallmark of RCC is the interpersonal interactions and strong communication skills that allow clinicians and team members to connect with patients and the emotions they invariably bring. Though our training may have favored hypercerebral types who could name dozens of items on a differential diagnosis for blood in the urine, our system has evolved. Medical knowledge is just one of at least six areas required by medical school and residency training accreditation agencies for clinical trainees to demonstrate full competence in healthcare practice. The areas of interpersonal communication and professionalism both figure prominently in those mandated competencies. The medical marketplace has also changed. Patient satisfaction measures have existed for many years, but only recently have patient experiences of care become an important metric for healthcare systems and a basis for reimbursement.

RCC has contributed to moving medicine out of the paternalistic model of the past century. It is the right way to practice. In addition, over the past three decades, patient-clinician communication has become a prominent field of scientific research. Despite the details of legislation and political uncertainty that always exist, data about the positive effects of relationship-centered communication skills in healthcare continue to burgeon. What's more, relationship-centered communication skills are completely transferable to relationships in one's professional and personal lives: they are people skills, not just healthcare skills. This book focuses on practical strategies that are based on the extensive underlying research.

Effective Communication Leads to Better Outcomes

Overall, effective communication leads to increased satisfaction, increased trust with the clinician,[6] improved overall health status, and functional and psychological well-being.[7]

Effective communication leads to improved outcomes in specific diseases. There is a reduced risk of coronary heart disease.[8] Mortality from myocardial infarction decreases, because of effective communication with patients[9] as well as improved systems communication.[10] Hospital readmissions due to congestive heart failure also decrease.[11]

Effective communication leads to better outcomes in chronic illness. Patients of physicians with high empathy scores, measured by a validated scale, were significantly more likely to have good control of diabetes and cholesterol.[12] Effective communication also improves patients' ability to more effectively manage chronic diseases such as high blood pressure, diabetes, and HIV.[13] Symptoms improve for patients with irritable bowel syndrome and chronic constipation.[14] Patients with medically unexplained physical symptoms (the kind that lack easily biomedically solvable diagnoses) whose clinicians use effective communication skills have significant increases in satisfaction with their clinicians and their relationships with their clinicians.[15]

Effective communication improves outcomes after surgery. The incidence of serious postoperative outcomes, such as cardiac arrhythmia[16] and delirium,[17] decreases. Also, patients who perceived their trauma surgeons as being more empathic had better medical outcomes after hospitalization.[18]

Effective communication improves cancer outcomes through increased adherence to cancer screening,[19] improved cancer survival,[20] reduced suffering from cancer,[21] and better care at the end of life.[22]

Effective communication results in improved pain outcomes. Patients report better pain control[23] and improved response to pain management modalities such as acupuncture.[24]

Finally, effective communication reduces healthcare costs. Increased patient-centeredness is associated with reduced costs for diagnostic testing.[25] Clear communication with family members about decisions at the end of life decreases ICU admissions and unnecessary ventilation and resuscitation efforts.[26]

A recent review found that the patient-clinician relationship has a beneficial effect on overall healthcare outcomes with an effect size approximately equal to that of taking a daily aspirin for five years to prevent heart attacks.[27] What's more, unlike aspirin, good patient-clinician relationships do not cause GI bleeding!

Faulty Assumptions: "I Already Communicate Well"

There is more work to do, however. The literature also shows that clinicians do not communicate as effectively as they think. There are systemic factors that interfere with the way that most clinicians would like to practice optimally. Even so, there is still a gap between what we think we're doing and what we're actually doing.

We do not elicit the full spectrum of patient concerns at the outset of the encounter, so we wrestle with "doorknob" questions that make us less efficient.[28] We redirect patients after 18–23 seconds of listening to them speak, and rarely allow them to return to their thoughts.[29] We unreliably seek patients' perspectives on their illnesses and inadequately address their emotions.[30] We incompletely attend to cultural differences.[31] We use incomprehensible jargon and don't confirm that our patients understand their diagnoses and treatment plans.[32] We do not effectively involve patients in decision-making or when we obtain informed consent.[33]

We can measure the negative process outcomes of our ineffective communication. Outpatients do not return to clinicians with poor communication skills.[34] Readmission rates for inpatients are higher in cases of inadequate communication.[35] Worst of all, from the clinician's perspective, perceived failures in communication, or patient experiences of humiliation from poor communication from clinicians, even nonverbal ones, are associated with more malpractice claims.[36]

Communication Skills Can Be Taught . . . and Learned

There is good news. Clinicians with more effective communication achieve benefits beyond individual patient "satisfaction." (See Chapter 2 for further discussion.) We all have challenges in our daily practices (difficult conversations, dissatisfied patients) that leave us feeling unsettled and dissatisfied with how we have performed. Learning to communicate more effectively with patients helps us not only make more accurate diagnoses and enhance adherence to treatment but also helps us increase our own well-being and resilience.

Clinicians who use communication skills such as agenda-setting for a clinical encounter,[37] motivational interviewing,[38] or specific communication skills for managing patients with dementia[39] report increased satisfaction with their encounters and decreased frustration and burnout. Clinicians who participated in a mindful communication program had higher well-being and attitudes toward patient care.[40] Clinicians who underwent a daylong communication skills course showed higher patient experience scores, increased empathy scores, and lower burnout scores when compared with those who did not.[41]

Finally, contrary to widely held assumptions, clinicians practicing in diverse settings (primary care, inpatient, surgical, subspecialty) can improve fundamental as well as advanced communication skills,[42] using motivational interviewing,[43] shared decision-making,[44] crosscultural communication,[45] and end-of-life communication.[46] It's tempting to offer a "quick fix" to help clinicians with low patient experience scores. But as chief medical officers and patient experience staff have begun to discover, it is not enough to attend a 30- to 60-minute lecture to acquire proficiency in these skills. Learning skills is not the same as learning a concept. Whether you were on the football team or in the marching band, you know that skill improvement and achieving mastery require deliberate practice and feedback.[47] No one would ever expect a proceduralist to attend an hour-long lecture, or even a half-day seminar, and then be able to do a new procedure with complete proficiency. With communication skills, clinicians must also take into account the complex needs, desires, histories, approaches, stories, assumptions, and psychology that every individual patient brings to a relationship. This work is challenging, to be sure; we all view the way we communicate as strongly personal, and feedback about communication may feel more like an attack than a gift.

Therefore, in order to effectively teach skills for lasting benefit, trainers must not only explain concepts but also facilitate skills practice and become experts at giving feedback. Studies also show that effective training processes result in persistence of learned skills over time. Data on effective communication skills programs show that they typically last for one entire day, focusing on applying learnings to clinical practice and on learners' goals and needs. Skills-based exercises, including role-play, in small groups or in individualized coaching work better than isolated didactic presentations; specific feedback on communication skills is the most important element that contributes to heightened patient experiences of care.[48] ACH faculty have found that when we teach these skills in these ways, the vast majority of clinicians find not only that these skills are helpful to their everyday practices but also that the programs inspire renewed energy and dedication to their careers.

Conclusion

Returning to Mr. Johnson, the veteran with back pain and an unhealthy relationship with opiates, suffice it to say that it was not a perfect interaction, nor does it have a storybook ending. By carefully using the skills outlined in this book, particularly the fundamental skill sets in Chapters 3–5, we had some successes. Even though I did not prescribe opiates, Mr. Johnson did not fly off the handle, and in fact, at the end of the visit, he stuck out his hand and calmly said, "Thank you."

I performed no magic on him during our encounter. In retrospect, the main magic I did was on *myself*, by resisting the urge several times to emphasize my superior knowledge, which I think would have been a relationship-breaking move. Instead, I used every single clinical skill I know and remained aware of my emotions. I was noticing the patient's frustration and disappointment as well as my own, knowing that because I was systematically approaching the visit, I could validate his experience. I could offer emotional support . . . but not opiates.

While communication skills training is not a panacea, it can reliably improve quality of care, outcomes, and patient experience. As recent technological advances drive people toward interacting with devices rather than directly with others, interpersonal communication skills have never been more important in healthcare. In the high-stakes setting of health, well-being, and wellness, a trustful, caring relationship between patient and clinician leads to better outcomes for both. We invite you, your colleagues, and your institution to join with us in our efforts to transform healthcare through effective communication.

CHAPTER 2

Communication and Patient Experience

Suffering . . . is real for our patients . . . We will not rest until
we have done all we can to alleviate their suffering.
—*Thomas H. Lee, MD*[1]

Most of us would agree that the highest calling of medicine is to relieve suffering. To accomplish this, clinicians and health systems must look beyond medical interventions and instead prioritize truly caring for patients. By "caring," we do not mean that clinicians should simply be nicer so that patients feel happier, or that every hospital should offer Ritz Carlton-style amenities. Rather, it means we must build healing relationships that promote partnership, empathy, respect, and understanding. It means we must realize that patient experience correlates with quality, safety, and patient loyalty. It means our health systems must embrace the human experience as central to their missions. On the flip side, we need to acknowledge that when communication fails to build connections—when patients experience their care as rushed, impersonal, and unfeeling—we may unwittingly deepen their suffering rather than relieving it. The good news is that communication skills can be taught and learned, and leading edge health systems can adopt relationship-centered care as the norm rather than the exception.[2] In this chapter, we describe key elements of the patient experience of care, and we highlight the links to communication. We use specific examples to illustrate the core principles of relationship-centered communication and describe practical considerations for one-on-one interpersonal encounters with patients and families and colleagues within the context of a healthcare team.

The Patient Experience Challenge for Leaders

Let's begin with the challenges faced by Dr. Ahmed, CMO of a large health system. Dr. Ahmed is accountable for improving patient experience at his hospital. In each batch of patient experience surveys, he sees that the percentage of "top box" scores is disappointingly low. Dr. Ahmed is baffled. His hospital is fortunate to have great clinicians with the finest technical skills and resources. Still, patients report that something is missing in the human dimensions of care. Dr. Ahmed is concerned that if the scores fall any lower in the competitive market, they could threaten the hospital's reputation, ranking, and value-based reimbursement. He understands that focusing on patient experience is good healthcare and good business, but he must admit that patients and families in his hospital don't consistently feel cared for. Gazing at the scores on his computer screen, he wonders what he and the health system can do to improve them.

Patient experience scores, like the ones Dr. Ahmed reviews each week, provide a window into patient perspectives on the care we provide and they receive. Standardized national patient surveys like the Consumer Assessment of Healthcare Providers and Systems (CAHPS) family of surveys ask patients to evaluate communication skills by exploring if clinicians listen carefully, treat patients with courtesy and respect, and explain things in a way patients can understand.[3, 4, 5] These questions do not merely measure patient satisfaction: they ask whether specific types of communication did or did not happen during an encounter, be it a clinic visit with one clinician or a hospitalization with multiple clinician interactions.[6]

In our experience reviewing years of comments on this set of communication questions, a common theme emerges. In both the positive and negative comments across the spectrum of clinical settings, what patients repeatedly note is their perception of whether the clinicians and staff show that they care. The clearest way of showing caring is through intentional and effective communication.

The Pitfalls of "Patient Satisfaction" for Clinicians

When busy clinicians are asked to improve patient satisfaction or experience scores, we often go on the defensive, questioning the metrics and survey data that generated the low scores. Many of us resent checking more boxes and adding yet more tasks to already overstuffed agendas. Rightfully, we push back against providing care that is inappropriate just to make patients happy. The term *experience* has been adopted as a replacement for *satisfaction* in an effort to place additional focus on quality and safety elements, rather than merely aiming to satisfy patients.

Even clinicians who believe the validity of the scores may feel that patient complaints link to systems failures and difficult personalities rather than our own skills. We frequently complain that our busy schedules simply don't provide enough time to communicate well. As a CMO, Dr. Ahmed is acutely sensitive to these concerns and wants to ensure that his efforts to improve patient satisfaction will not be viewed as rubbing salt into the wounds of burnout. At the same time, he hopes that heeding the core principles embodied in these patient experience metrics could help clinicians better communicate the caring he knows they feel, while reconnecting them to purpose in their work and joy in their practice of clinical medicine.

Why Relationship-Centered Communication Drives Patient Experience Improvement

On the other side of the country, an Associate Chief of the Medical Service is rounding with an inpatient medical team, checking in on patients and making decisions about care for the day. Mr. Perez, admitted five days prior with a difficult problem of unrelenting abdominal pain and diarrhea, reflects to his team of doctors:

> It's the little things you do here that make a difference. It's
> the smile and wave when you walk by my room. It's when
> you take the time to sit down to speak with me, not at me.
> This is the best hospital I've been to.

As many health systems have shifted attention to the patient experience of care as a component of the value provided to patients, the "secret sauce" of how to improve that experience has often seemed elusive. Yet here, in the middle of a busy morning of the hustle and bustle of admissions, discharges before noon, computer clicks, and notes written, Mr. Perez poignantly tells his doctors the answer. What transcends it all is how they relate to him. In a world where many things can be automated and systematized to get the best and most reliable outcomes, the interpersonal relationships in healthcare still rely on our own mindset and communication skills. Were the interactions respectful, caring, and compassionate? Were the patient's and family's goals and values acknowledged and included in decision-making? Was information conveyed with clarity?

Patient experience extends across the entire continuum of care, and every interaction counts. Each interaction conveys what the health system, patients, and clinicians value most. For clinicians, the challenge is to acquire and intentionally practice relationship-centered communication, starting with the very first moment of each encounter.

Patient Reflections on Communication Skills

When asked to comment about perceptions of their doctors, patients can describe what it looks like when communication works well:

> Dr. Li is wonderful, very caring, and kind. Whenever I talked,
> she moved her hands from the keyboard and turned her
> head and her body toward me and away from the computer.
> She not only was listening but showed me with her body
> language that she cared and that what I had to say, no matter how trivial, was the most important thing to her in that
> moment. Absolutely exceptional care!

> Dr. Moor was the first clinician to actually listen to my symptoms and not treat me like I didn't make sense. That alone greatly increased my trust and confidence in him.

And conversely, patients can describe what it looks like when communication fails:

> I know that Dr. Hall is a smart doctor and she knows her stuff, but she spends most of her time looking at the computer. I do not feel she is a poor clinician by any means. If she had focused on what I was most concerned with during the visit, I would have been very happy. But all of what I wanted to address seemed to be pushed to the side.

Whether a clinician hears and validates patient concerns or dismisses them can make all the difference in whether the patient feels cared for. Equipped with this knowledge, the case for strengthening evidence-based communication skills among our clinicians grows.

Which Communication Skills Matter?

The way many of us routinely approach medical care can unintentionally result in poor experiences for patients. We clinicians often go about our work of diagnosing and trying to help our patients as efficiently as we can, often unintentionally missing what is most important to the patient. Too often, we focus on what we think the patient needs or wants without asking to make sure we are on target. As a result, all of our care and attention can be misdirected, causing frustration across the board. We must change our mindset from just "What is the matter with you?" to *What matters most to you?* This simple, profound shift conveys respect for the patient's role and perspective in his or her own health. It also helps us deepen our understanding of our patients.[7] It's important to emphasize that clinicians need not choose between building relationships and our commitment to biotechnical excellence: the approaches are complementary. Furthermore, there is growing evidence that skilled communication along with active patient engagement improves diagnostic accuracy, promotes shared decision-making, reduces the use of unnecessary and often costly tests, and may even lead patients to choose management plans with greater value and lower cost.[8-9]

Communication Skills That Work: Agenda Setting

Dr. Williams, a busy obstetrician/gynecologist, was disheartened that despite his best efforts, patients rated his communication skills below those of his colleagues. He began to dread each quarterly review of his patient experience surveys. In retrospect, Dr. Williams realized that his communication skills must not be as good as he thought they were. He and his patients experienced a turning point after he attended a communication skills workshop where he learned how to elicit a patient's full set of concerns and set the agenda early in a clinic visit (see Chapter 3).[10] Prior to adopting this approach, he entered each exam room with a defensive mindset, worried that the patient would have more complaints than he had time to cover. His practice was simply not to ask, and his patients felt he was rushed and not interested in hearing their concerns. With agenda setting, all of that changed. Dr. Williams discovered that when he and his patient co-created a game plan at the beginning of the visit, he no longer felt pressured to cover everything. He was less defensive, listened better, and felt on more equal footing with his patients regarding expectations for their visits. His scores improved, and he went back to enjoying practice.

Dr. Williams's experience demonstrates that learning a new communication skill can change a clinician's mindset and improve the experience of his patients. Hearing the patient's list of concerns went from a dreaded burden and time sink to a means to build connection and make the most efficient use of limited time. The experience of both patient and doctor was improved. Dr. Williams noticed improvement in his own sense of efficacy and "joy" in doctoring; he became a champion of communication skills training for his multispecialty group.

Communication Skills That Work: Showing Empathy

Health problems and medical care nearly always bring up emotions. Emotions are typically related to fears, uncertainty, and perceived or actual threats to one's identity, livelihood, or function. When we focus exclusively on biomedical care, we fail to address these emotions, which deeply affect patient experience.[11] In a study looking at the use of empathic statements with hospitalized patients, only a third of physicians used an empathic statement in response to emotion expressed by the patient. Meanwhile, each empathic response was independently associated with a significant decrease in patient anxiety and more positive patient impressions of the physician.[12]

Learning how to show empathy is something that can benefit all clinicians. We must learn how to listen for and recognize emotion in another and express that recognition. We can do so with brief statements of partnership, emotion, acknowledgment, respect, legitimization, or support (see Chapter 4). As a result, we increase our effectiveness and patients and families internalize our support. When the medical condition or its impact cannot be "fixed," this ability to provide empathy becomes a cornerstone of the care. The following example shows the power of empathy in affecting the patient experience.

> Mr. Walker hadn't eaten for nearly 24 hours, and he was getting angrier by the minute. His endoscopy had been cancelled the day before due to a high volume of emergency cases. The orders read "NPO," so he hadn't received a dinner or breakfast tray. At the time of rounds, he still didn't know if he'd be having an endoscopy that day and had already made two calls to the patient relations office to complain about his care. He vented his anger and frustration as soon as the care team entered his room.
>
> Rather than reacting defensively or attempting to mollify Mr. Walker, the rounding physician intentionally chose to convey empathy for the patient's predicament. "Wow—you've had a terrible 24 hours! I can only imagine how frustrated, angry, and hungry you are. I think anyone would

be at least as frustrated as you are. I apologize that you've
been left in the dark about when the endoscopy will be
done, and I appreciate your hanging in there with us. I don't
personally do the procedure, but I can promise that I'll do
my best to find out when it's scheduled. I'll be back with
you in a few minutes to let you know. I suspect that not
knowing what's causing your blood loss makes the waiting
even worse for you. You want answers."

Mr. Walker replied, "Yeah—you got that right."

With Mr. Walker, the clinician repaired their relationship by expressing empathy, legitimization, apology, appreciation, support, respect,
and partnership. After this exchange, Mr. Walker called patient rela-
tions to "cancel the complaint." His concerns had been heard and acted
on. In this case, empathy benefited the patient, and the hospital's service
excellence department had one less complaint to manage. This is what
we mean by the "secret sauce" of relationship-centered communication.

Communication Skills That Work:
Understandable Explanations

Relationship-centered communication is not only critical in primary
care, where relationships develop over time. In brief or episodic interactions like emergency department visits and procedural disciplines
where the stakes are high and time is short, these skills may be even
more important.

Dr. Anderson, a senior anesthesiologist, reported the following vignette. For years, he used a standard "spiel" with patients prior
to induction that covered pretty much everything he thought was
important for them to know. He'd end by asking, "Do you have any
questions?" This interaction always felt rushed, but he accepted that
as the reality of anesthesia practice. After attending a communication
skills workshop and learning how deeply patients appreciate having
their concerns heard, Dr. Anderson tweaked his approach. He decided
to reverse the order of his pre-anesthesia routine. He now begins by
pulling up a stool and asking for the patient's list of concerns about the

anesthesia (see Chapter 3) before giving his spiel—which he then tailors according to the patient's concerns (see Chapter 5). For example, when asked up front about his fears regarding anesthesia, a patient told Dr. Anderson that his biggest worry was that intubation would leave him with no voice, preventing him from singing with his church choir at a big event in two weeks. The beauty of the new approach is that Dr. Anderson not only heard about the patient's concerns but he also had time to specifically address them during an encounter that lasts an average of four minutes. In terms of the CAHPS question, Dr. Anderson truly "explained things in a way that the patient could understand."

Intentionally addressing items of importance to patients ensures that their concerns are heard and addressed. The end result is a more efficient encounter, a deeper connection, and a sense of effectiveness and meaning for the clinician that might otherwise be missed in simply going through the motions.

Communication and Systems Design

Relationship-centered communication can have a transformative impact on how team members provide care. When members of a team prioritize relationships with patients, families, and other team members, all parties benefit, including the health system itself.[13] On the other hand, when medical teams fail to make authentic connections with patients, they often experience their care as fragmented, poorly coordinated, and confusing. Another factor that can influence patient experience is how we structure our medical rounds. If, rather than seeing inpatients separately, doctors and nurses choose to routinely conduct rounds together, it's far easier for them to be on the same page when responding to patient concerns and questions. Structured interprofessional bedside rounding (SIBR) is most effective when the opinions of the patient and every team member are valued and everyone knows that his or her voice is heard. To make rounds run smoothly and optimally, team members agree to a choreography that guides how they respectfully enter the room, greet the patient and family, make introductions, set an agenda, make a personal connection, use the computer, and invite participation.[14-15]

Why go to all of this effort? SIBR has been proven to enhance patient experience.[16-17] Seeing their clinicians working together helps patients gain confidence in their overall care and decreases concerns about whether "the right hand knows what the left hand is doing."[18] While doing rounds together, we can engage patients further using relationship-centered communication skills such as empathy; asking about the patient's ideas, concerns, and expectations; and conducting teach-back during every encounter. Especially in complicated cases, care decisions evolve during bedside discussions with outcomes that are tangibly better than the starting points. Let's look at an example of how a team's relationship-centered communication can improve patient experience during the discharge process.

Sarah was nearing the end of a complicated two-week hospitalization. She and her husband, Dave, were anxious to get home but worried about how things would go without the support of the nurses, doctors, and the rest of the team. The medical team told Dave and Sarah to expect discharge SIBR rounds on the afternoon before Sarah left the hospital. Rounds would include her physician, charge nurse, bedside nurse, case manager, and pharmacist. This interaction took less than 15 minutes and concluded with Sarah and Dave summarizing their understanding of the plan (see Chapter 5). Sarah's and Dave's unique ideas, concerns, expectations, circumstances, and resources provided a foundation for shared decision-making.

The following morning the team members asked, "So, what did you think of SIBR?" The discussion continued:

> SARAH (LOOKING AT DAVE): Dave and I were just talking about that before you came in. Dave called it NASCAR rounds, didn't you, Dave?
>
> PHYSICIAN: NASCAR rounds—that sounds like it was pretty hectic.
>
> DAVE: No, hectic is not at all what I meant. "Thorough" would be a better word. Everyone we needed was there. It was crowded but efficient—like a NASCAR pit crew. We really felt like we were part of the team. I can't tell you how much that means to us.

SARAH: Yes. We felt like you guys really know me—not just my medical problems—but me as . . . well, as me, and that you're taking me into account in the plans.

DAVE: I'm a planner so I appreciated when you guys asked what concerns we have about going home. That hit the mark better than asking if we have any questions. It got us thinking more concretely.

For Sarah and Dave, interprofessional bedside rounds and relationship-centered communication led to a "top box" patient experience and improved the quality and safety of her discharge plan.

Conclusion

Our conversations with patients and the broader design of our everyday work provide great opportunities to revisit our communication approaches in an effort to convey greater compassion and caring. With small adjustments and mindful awareness of the perspectives of the patients and families, it becomes natural to build relationship and create connection. Strengthening our understanding of where our patients are allows us to meet them there more effectively, where we can help the most. The ripple effects of relationship-centered communication reach both individual clinicians and interdisciplinary teams and help everyone work toward the common goal of enhanced patient experience. We often find that clinicians welcome rather than resist opportunities to deepen their connections with patients because it makes their work more effective and meaningful. Stronger relationships serve as the antidote to the discord and burnout that ensues when we do not attend to these core principles. It is this attention to relationship, beginning with how we are together one-on-one, that stimulates culture changes in organizations to alleviate suffering so that all patients can authentically feel our caring.

PART II

THE FUNDAMENTAL SKILL SETS

CHAPTER 3

Skill Set One: The Beginning of the Encounter

Let's start at the very beginning! A very good place to start.
—"Do-Re-Mi," *The Sound of Music*[1]

(Auguste Fortin) recently went to the dermatology clinic at my HMO to have a worrisome mole looked at. I was sitting on the exam table, naked except for my underwear and a paper sheet, when the dermatologist startled me by walking briskly in and asking, "Where's the mole?" It felt odd to be examined by a stranger whose name I didn't even know.

In recent years, heightened awareness about the power of the first impression has permeated popular and academic literature. Within even the first few seconds of an encounter, a person makes an unconscious judgment about the person they are meeting, a judgment that will likely affect all future interactions. Therefore, the clinician's first impression represents a highly important opportunity. It seems obvious that we should introduce ourselves to patients and families and make an effort to start each encounter warmly and professionally. When we're busy or stressed, we often forget this fact and neglect initial formalities. The effort we put in when we initially meet our patients is critical. We meet patients for the first time when they may be confused

27

or medicated. They can be with different people when we subsequently see them. The focused attention we give our patients and those who accompany them will affect their initial impression of us, which will make a lasting impact on how they feel about us. This brings us to the first of three key components of beginning the encounter.

Establish Rapport

Establishing rapport may seem like the easiest part of the encounter, but it's too often forgotten. When one of our students went to the hospital with appendicitis, he was irritated when his entire surgical team barged into his hospital room at 5:30 a.m. the next day without knocking, flipped on the lights, and proceeded to examine him without introducing themselves or making any small talk. Taking time for each person on your clinical team to introduce themselves to each person on the patient's team, including loved ones who are present, can go a long way. Even small talk (about the weather or flowers in the room) can also help the patient feel comfortable. Let's not discount the rapid rapport-building and trust that can come from a genuine gesture of greeting[2] (handshake, fist bump, or whatever fits your style). Other simple acts that make a big difference for patients include sitting when talking to them[3] and acknowledging the discomfort they often feel when naked, cold, hungry, waiting, and under bright lights in our clinical settings.

Elicit the List of *All* Concerns

Once we have done all these small and simple things to optimize rapport, we're ready to start talking about the clinical issues for which the patient is seeking care. Again, though, the typical way of doing this may not suffice. Here's an example: A 63-year-old man with ankylosing spondylitis (a form of arthritis that can weaken the bones in the spine) presented to the emergency department (ED) with excruciating sudden-onset neck pain. The ED doctors evaluated him and were concerned he had a broken neck, so they ordered x-rays of the painful area. These did not reveal a fracture, so the patient was diagnosed with "musculoligamentous neck pain" (basically, strained muscles). Because his pain didn't improve with medications, he was admitted to the internal medicine service for inpatient pain management. The hospitalist physician met the patient upstairs on the hospital ward and corroborated the established history. But he also obtained an additional piece of information: the patient reported that, "whenever I lean forward, my head feels like it's going to fall off my neck and I have to catch it with my hand." This is a rare and worrisome complaint. The attending asked for the patient to undergo further imaging immediately that revealed an unstable neck fracture at a level just below where the prior imaging ended. The patient was taken urgently to the operating room for surgery and, after extensive physical therapy, has now returned to his baseline.

How did several very skilled clinicians miss a crucial and game-changing concern from the patient? Most likely, their conversations with the patient matched what usually happens when clinicians assess their patients,[4] which would have been something like this:

> CLINICIAN: Please tell me what brought you in.
>
> PATIENT: I have this terrible neck pain.
>
> CLINICIAN: That sounds bad. Tell me, when did this start?

The clinician thus launches into focused closed-ended questioning regarding the patient's pain. Though clinicians ask very specific (usually yes/no) questions when taking a history, it's very unlikely anyone would think to ask, "Does your head feel like it's going to fall off your neck when you lean forward?" And some patients (this one included) don't necessarily realize that symptoms are linked; this patient didn't think to describe this sensation when describing his pain. So the standard approach to building the history can leave gaps. We need a better way to elicit the various concerns affecting the patient. Fortunately, such a way exists. Imagine if, after the initial rapport-building phase, the conversation went like this:

> CLINICIAN: Now, I heard a little about why you came in today, but I always like to hear it myself in the patient's own

words. Before we delve into the details, let's make a list of all the concerns that you have.

PATIENT: Well, it's really this bad neck pain.

CLINICIAN: Sounds horrible. We'll talk about that neck pain shortly. What else is on your mind?

PATIENT: Hmmm . . . well, my wife went home to get some rest but is really worried; I'd like to update her.

CLINICIAN: Yes, we definitely want to make sure your wife is updated; we'll make plans for that. What else?

PATIENT: Umm . . . this is going to sound weird, but I have this scary sensation whenever I lean forward that my head is going to fall right off my neck. Like I have to reach up and catch it with my hand.

CLINICIAN: Wow, I can imagine how scary that must be. We'll certainly talk about that as well. What else?

PATIENT: I think that's it.

We can clearly see the value in eliciting all the patient's concerns in the above scenario. But when we try to apply this concept to routine encounters with patients, many of us hesitate. How, after all, can an extremely busy clinician possibly elicit *all* of a patient's concerns? Seems completely impractical, right? Fortunately, we've tested this out. In our own practices, it's taken a little bit of getting used to, but this approach has actually *saved* us time in the long run. How's that? Eliciting all concerns before hearing the story of any one concern helps clinicians be more efficient by decreasing "doorknob concerns"—issues the patient raises as the clinician has a hand on the doorknob, trying to leave. Furthermore, most patients do not have as many concerns as clinicians fear they will, and eliciting the full list can actually help save time by adding organization to the encounter. We have seen firsthand how this actually makes a clinician more efficient in their work.

This is important beyond just saving time, though. Obviously, as the case described demonstrates, eliciting the full list of concerns can have a dramatic effect on the patient's outcomes. Even in less high-acuity settings, though, eliciting all concerns can be extremely valuable. Studies show that patients often do not state their most pressing concerns first and that sometimes the last issue the patient brings up is the most important one.[5] Hearing all our patients' concerns up front actually improves diagnostic accuracy.

Clinicians understandably worry about the time required to elicit patients' full lists of concerns. This is especially true when we are seeing patients in the emergency department where only the most urgent concerns can be addressed, or as subspecialty consultants where the reason for the consult is often quite specific. It is important to understand that eliciting a concern does not mean you have to "own" it. Just hearing the concern and saying, "I'd like to address that at a future time" is often sufficient. In many settings, clinicians find that patients bring up concerns that may not be best addressed right then. Still, acknowledging the concern is important. For a subspecialist in surgery, for example, this might sound something like, "Thanks for mentioning the cough. I am not an expert in that area, so, if it's OK with you, perhaps we can address the other concerns you mentioned and then I can send a message to your primary care clinician to address the cough with you soon."

Clinicians still get to ask their familiar questions to obtain a full history later, so they don't need to feel that they must get those details now. To keep the patient from going into detail with each item mentioned at this stage, clinicians can say, "Before we get into details today, I'd like to hear a list of all the concerns you want to make sure we address." Eliciting all the patient's concerns doesn't take long, but it helps the patient feel heard and gives us valuable information to guide the rest of the encounter and, in some cases, help determine acuity.

A complexity occurs in settings where multiple people are present on behalf of the patient, for example, in pediatrics. As easy as it might feel to concentrate on only the parent in that situation, it is still valuable to elicit a list from both parent and patient (as long as the patient is verbal!) so that everyone has a chance to be heard. Again, this may feel unnatural and concerning to you, because you might worry that your entire encounter might be spent eliciting a list. First, this rarely happens, and second, the small amount of time spent up front will pay dividends in avoiding doorknob questions from family members when you are trying to move to the next encounter. If there is more than one person accompanying a patient, this is family meeting territory, when designating a spokesperson for the people present on behalf of the patient can simplify the list elicitation step.

Negotiate a Shared Agenda

Once the list is complete, we can move on to negotiating a shared agenda. We find out what the patient wants to focus the encounter on and may add other topics as well. Then we can propose an agenda and check that plan with the patient.

Unfortunately, the typical encounter often skips this task. Many of us have a tendency to address the first topic mentioned without knowing if it's clinically the most important one or most important to the patient. Continuing with the neck pain scenario, a suggested way to create a road map and thereby avoid this issue might be:

> CLINICIAN: OK, how about we start by discussing the neck pain and then get into the scary sensation of your head falling forward? After we talk about what we should do next, then we can map out a plan for how best to update your wife. Does that work for you?
>
> PATIENT: Yep, sounds good.

Developing an agenda helps keep us on task while letting the patient know what to expect, which alleviates anxiety. And, as you can see, it doesn't take long. It's also totally appropriate for us to add our own items to the agenda that the patient hasn't mentioned.

> CLINICIAN: I'd also like to talk about a lab abnormality we noticed that might affect our treatment.

In our experience, we have found that with dedicated practice this initial step can be as short as 90–120 seconds. If patients prepare a list of concerns beforehand, it can take even less time; a glance at the patient's list on a piece of paper or their device is all you need. Clinical team members in inpatient and outpatient settings can assist by reminding the patient in advance of a clinician's visit to prepare the list. These adaptations make the beginning of the visit relationship-centered. Patients take charge of their health, and clinicians can thereby move more efficiently with the work.

Conclusion

To recap, the initial part of the encounter happens in three parts:

1. Establish rapport.
2. Elicit the list of *all* concerns.
3. Negotiate a shared agenda.

In addition to saving time, we have also outlined how engaging in these steps improves relationships with patients. Using the same skills in various contexts can lead to improved relationships with colleagues, trainees, supervisors, administrators, and even spouses (though that is beyond the scope of this book). For example, when touching base with a nephrology consultant, asking first about her recent trip abroad can build a great personal connection and rapport. Then you can elicit the full list of concerns and develop an agenda to ensure you discuss everything on her mind regarding your patient's kidneys, not just the one consult question with which you called.

Similarly, if you mentor a trainee or junior colleague, spend a brief moment eliciting his or her full list of concerns to ensure that you spend your time together addressing topics that are most important to you both. This strategy will lead to more fruitful mentorship sessions, as opposed to a disorganized approach where you often end up spending the entire appointment talking about the first item that comes up. There are very few occasions in healthcare settings when these three deliberate actions of developing rapport, eliciting the list of all concerns, and negotiating a shared agenda do not lead to more effective discussion. You'll get weird looks if you try to use this at the supermarket checkout, but in pretty much every interaction with substantive information to be exchanged, it will produce positive results.

CHAPTER 4

Skill Set Two:
Skills That Build Trust

One afternoon, a young woman came to my (Matthew Russell's) outpatient practice with signs of an upper respiratory infection: runny nose, mild fever, cough, and scratchy throat. After examining her, I confirmed the diagnosis and started talking with her about over-the-counter medications that could provide some relief. The young woman didn't take kindly to my suggestions. No matter what I offered—even recommendations such as gargling with salt water—she frowned. At one point, she was looking at me so doubtfully that I began to wonder if I had a poppy seed or piece of spinach in my teeth. I finally asked her, "Am I missing something?"

She replied, "Well, I have AIDS."

This patient had visited our practice before, and I hadn't seen anything in her chart about an HIV infection. I hastily stammered, "Oh, my God, I'm so sorry. I did not know this." I frantically scanned her problem list on the electronic health record again but found nothing. "It's not on your problem list," I told her.

"Well, don't I?" she asked.

Now I was completely baffled. I asked her a few more questions before I was able to put the pieces together. Before coming in, my patient had done a web search on her symptoms. Apparently, one of the top items that came up was the signs and symptoms of acute HIV infection. With this in mind, I explored for any potential risks or exposures and found none.

I reassured the patient that she was not infected with HIV but was dealing with a simple viral infection from the common cold. I also encouraged her to avoid using search engines as diagnostic tools. As you can imagine, she left the visit much relieved.

What would have happened if this same patient was stony-faced without body language that clued me in to the fact that there was something I was missing? What if I wasn't tuned in enough to read her body language? She easily could have left my office still convinced she had an acute HIV infection!

In medical school, I was taught the importance of finding the patient's "hidden concern." As a student, I thought of it as a needle in the haystack—a rare unicorn that only the most accomplished diagnostician could discover. After my interaction with the young woman in my practice, I realized that the hidden concern was not a rare breed but in fact something that could accompany even the simplest symptoms and interactions.

When we are able to build strong relationships with our patients, we can support them effectively through life-threatening illnesses, prolonged illnesses, and acute emergencies. At times our relationships are brief (e.g., in the emergency department), while others may span many years (e.g., in primary care). This chapter describes concrete skills to help clinicians give as much attention to patients' perspectives and emotions as we do to the biomedical details. This approach suggests that clinicians use these relationship-centered skills before even beginning to explore symptom details, diagnosis, or treatment options.

Relationship-Centered Skills: "Don't Just Do Something, Stand There!"

To engage in relationship-centered communication, we must first acknowledge and embrace the personhood of each participant. When we use these skills, we are able to provide a richer experience for the patient and the clinician: the skills enhance rather than interfere with the scientific approach to illness. Healthcare interactions are often filled with complex concepts and strong emotions—a breeding ground for relationship challenges. When we make a point to establish a resilient relationship prior to encountering these challenges, it allows us to more effectively navigate through them.

To get a better understanding of what this looks like, let's go back in time to my bright-eyed, bushy-tailed early days in medical school. The first instructor in my patient communication course was a family physician who had a knack for breaking down complicated concepts so they were easy for both students and patients to understand. We joked that she could tell us all to go to hell and we'd look forward to the trip. Years later, I realize that what she was so wonderful at doing was connecting with people. She was able to be fully present and attentive to what was being said. It wasn't just nodding and eye contact. There was genuine interest and facilitative questions that helped to flesh out each story in more detail. By the time we would get to a physical exam, both the patient and the student observers would feel at ease and confident about her level of competence.

So, what is this special magic that some clinicians have and the rest of us struggle to obtain? If we are to be "scored" on our ability to communicate, we want to get an A. As overachieving clinicians, we all want to be at the top of the class! But for many of us, relationship-centered communication is not something that comes naturally. We may ask ourselves if we will ever be able to gain the skill sets to communicate competently or if we're doomed to interactions that focus more on technology than the humanness of our patients.

In this chapter we describe four specific skills that help develop robust and trusting human connections. They may feel counterintuitive at first, but these sturdy bonds can actually increase the effectiveness of data gathering and treatment planning.

These four trust-building skills are:

1. Ask open-ended questions and listen actively.
2. Elicit the patient's ideas and expectations.
3. Respond with empathy.
4. Transition to further data gathering.

In this book, we emphasize the value of using these four skills to build trust before we get technical. We may think of symptom elaboration, data gathering, diagnosis, and so on as our real work. Instead, following this approach allows patients to gain trust in us and in our abilities first, which enables us to get more accurate details when we begin gathering information. We achieve optimal results when we continue to respond to all of our client's concerns throughout an encounter with empathy.

FIRST SKILL: ASK OPEN-ENDED QUESTIONS AND LISTEN ACTIVELY

A concerned mother enters an office carrying a one-year-old who is awake but lethargic. "My son won't eat. He's very listless. This scrape has not healed for many days. He is very ill." Coming to the rescue, the clinician thinks: *I'll decide who is ill here!* This take-charge attitude can instantly alienate the mother and set her even more on edge. She may feel more worried because she doesn't know if the clinician will value her knowledge of her son and the details of the past few days.

In early training, we learned the basics of asking patients open-ended questions to hear their medical stories. Some of us may have even learned additional nonverbal techniques such as making good eye contact and leaning in to show interest. But as healthcare has become busier, time with the patient shorter, and use of a computer continuous, these interpersonal skills can easily fall by the wayside. Now, most clinicians worry that asking open-ended questions, eliciting patients' perspectives, and responding with empathy will take too much time. When our progress slows, we risk decreased productivity and harassment from "the institution," for not accomplishing our "real" clinical objectives. When we are face-to-face with our patients and they are in the midst of a long explanation of their clinical histories, many of us are thinking: *Just the facts, please! I need to click these boxes and solve your problems in the 10 minutes we've been allotted.*

And if there is a strong emotion, difficult news, or questions to be answered? Many of us don't even want to go there—we feel we don't have time to deal with it. Life is busy for everyone, and people seldom disrupt their lives to visit a clinician for nothing. Even those coming in for a routine follow-up usually have questions, concerns, or symptoms that are confusing, disquieting, or even frightening. As a result, patients want to feel confident that the clinician is emotionally invested in their problems. They want respect, attentiveness, and the freedom to express themselves. Patients are also looking for reassurance of the clinician's technical expertise. They need relationships where they can express their ideas about what might be going on, their feelings and concerns about possible outcomes, and their expectations for the clinical encounter that day. Every patient has feelings that range from worry about the seriousness and treatability of the problem to concern about whether the clinician will show caring, kindness, and respect. They hope to be free from worry about clinicians' potentially negative responses such as discounting, criticism, belittling, and rejection.

Let's go back to the example of the mother with the one-year-old. Instead of taking charge immediately, why is it important to begin with an open-ended question? First, open-ended questions leave control with the patient, who can decide what to say next about the situation. Imagine how the encounter might unfold if this clinician uses the four trust-building skills listed earlier (page 37). First, he or she would elicit and set the agenda to begin with the child's trouble feeding (see Chapter 3). Then the clinician would simply say, "Please tell me all about your son's eating." The open-ended request gives the mother an opportunity to offer details about her son's symptoms or to share her distress. Either way, the clinician offers an invitation for the patient to place trust in the relationship. In addition, open-ended questions signal that the clinician will seek active participation from the patient throughout the encounter. Now it is the patient's turn to choose what to focus on.

Let's say that the mom not only talks about her son's symptoms, saying, "He won't even drink water," but also shares her distress and ideas. "My husband is even more worried than I am . . . a friend's child who started this way had pneumonia. Do you think it's pneumonia? Do you think he'll need antibiotics, or maybe surgery?" These types of responses about symptoms, ideas, feelings, and questions are typical responses to an open-ended question. In these types of interactions, the patient feels in control. While clinicians may fear that patients will launch into long, time-consuming responses, data affirm that patients seldom speak for more than 90 seconds when an invitation is extended.

For those of us who have been trained to lead with multiple clinically appropriate questions, this relationship-based strategy represents a paradigm shift. It's easy to talk about it, but to accomplish this change successfully requires sustained effort. In this strategy, we actively listen to our patients, regardless of the subject matter. When our patients pause, we then explicitly show that we heard what the patient said. Verbal skills that demonstrate active listening include continuers ("uh-huh," "go on," "I see"), echoing statements (using the patient's words), short requests ("tell me more"), and short summarizing statements. Active listening is one way we can affirm that we heard what the patient said. This simple act allows the patient to relax into the relationship, laying the groundwork for the trust that must develop for successful care.

SECOND SKILL: ELICIT THE PATIENT'S IDEAS AND EXPECTATIONS

As soon as some details of the initial story emerge, we must continue to explore our patient's ideas and expectations. Sometimes, as above, the ideas and expectations have already arisen. Other times, we will need to ask explicitly: "What ideas do you have about what is going on?" "What were you hoping might happen as a result of your visit here?"

Again, clinicians worry about opening Pandora's box with these questions. On the contrary, there are two good reasons to ask them up front. First, this inquiry and your empathic response represent more tools to develop trust. Patients appreciate the opportunity to reveal more about their concerns, and usually only briefly add information that gives us a much deeper understanding of where they are coming from. This information can be very useful in expanding your own reasoning process and in framing your treatment plan (see Chapter 5).

Second, knowing the patient's expectations for the visit (if there are any) makes the end of the visit easier for the clinician. The patient-clinician relationship cannot be a poker game in which the patient reveals his or her cards only at the end. If the mother in the ill-child case does not state her expectation for a chest x-ray, for example, the clinician may complete the evaluation and recommend fluids and acetaminophen for a common cold. If the mother then asks, "What about a chest x-ray?" the clinician, thinking the visit has concluded, now has to backtrack and spend time dissuading the mother from her expectation, and, in doing so, likely will communicate annoyance at the disruption. Asking expectation questions up front is mutually beneficial: patients can express their ideas and expectations explicitly, and clinicians obtain a fuller picture—one that facilitates better treatment.

THIRD SKILL: RESPOND WITH EMPATHY

Asking the right questions is not enough. In order to continue building trust and strengthen the relationship, we can go further by recognizing the emotions that patients express and responding to those emotional cues. Of course, it is also important to reassure patients that we will attend explicitly and carefully to the clinical data in a few moments.

No matter how rational and reasoned we can be when our minds are clear, human beings are ruled by emotions. Patients almost always have emotions accompanying their symptoms, illnesses, ideas, and expectations. So, recognizing emotion by attending to nonverbal expressions of empathy and statements of feeling in the patient's narrative is the first step to helping and healing. Clinicians can also either ask directly about the patient's emotions and/or make hypotheses about those emotions and check those hypotheses with the patient.

Once elicited, by working hard to detect when patients reveal emotions, clinicians must respond to them with an empathic statement or a knowing gesture, posture, or facial expression. Failing to communicate empathy at those moments has the effect of erecting a communication barrier. Patients describe that barrier as "the clinician did not listen to me," and this may be the crucial reason for excessive tests, missed diagnoses, inappropriate treatments, poor adherence to recommendations, and low scores on clinician evaluations by patients.[1, 2, 3, 4]

At a basic level, empathy refers to trying to imagine another person's emotional state. We can never know precisely what it feels like to be another person, but our willingness to imagine it matters strongly in clinical settings. It helps us feel a sense of partnership with patients when facing the challenges of their experiences. On the other hand, merely feeling empathy for someone's distress can weigh us down even further—the concept of "mirror neurons" suggests that when we see someone in pain, the area in our *own* brain that feels emotional pain is activated.[5] Instead of succumbing to this potential weight, however, making empathic responses allows us to feel *with* the patient, to show caring concern, and to offer help.[6]

41

Let's return to the example of the mother with the ill child. When she first voices her concern, a very simple empathic response such as, "I see you are very worried," or "What you described would concern any parent," would demonstrate attention to her distress in the moment. The empathic statement helps to build the beginnings of a relationship. The mother remains the expert on her child instead of feeling dismissed and left to cope with more stress.

When I (William Clark) entered medicine, I wanted to relieve suffering by being a good detective, making diagnoses, and providing treatments. I always conveyed kindness and patience, but as my expertise developed, I could feel that something was missing. My patient relationships seldom went beyond the detective phase. Through my own curiosity and a lot of feedback—some of which was not easy to hear—I discovered that I could be a better clinician by learning and practicing skills that demonstrated clearly that I cared about the patient and his or her emotions, and not just about the disease. I came to realize that strong emotions are a natural human response when facing unknown and potentially life-changing circumstances. I understood that strong emotions caused by dramatic events in the patient's life may be present in even the most routine clinical encounter (like the first patient in this chapter who thought she had AIDS). I became able to more often acknowledge patients' feelings and respond with empathy, eventually internalizing this foundational aspect of effective healing relationships. I went beyond detecting to connecting.

Beloved ACH colleagues and I codified this idea and suggested effective and simple statements of empathy that we described in the mnemonic PEARLS: Partnering with the patient, naming the Emotion, Appreciating patients' strengths or character (or "Apologizing" for the situation), voicing Respect (for courage, for persistence, etc.), Legitimizing understandable feelings, and offering ongoing Support to show empathy and attention to the human elements of the interaction.

These concepts are not unfamiliar or original to ACH, but collecting them into a teachable framework (PEARLS) was essential for my learning. Complex clinical situations or interactions that involved strong expressions of fear, anger, or sadness had previously left me at a loss for words, so I would ask the next clinical question. The mnemonic helped broaden my awareness of opportunities to respond more empathically. As I embraced PEARLS-type statements, I could feel the relationship-enhancing effects for myself and my patients. Responding with empathy in these moments also emerged as very helpful in my detective work of diagnosis and treatment. When we fail to elicit and respond to emotions, we are at great risk that patients will feel invisible, perceive us as unconcerned, cooperate only poorly with the rest of our work on their behalf, and report a less positive experience.

Examples of PEARLS

PARTNERSHIP: "Let's work together on this."

EMOTION: "I imagine how frustrating this is for you." "You seem upset." "You look concerned." "I heard you say you are irritated."

APOLOGY: "I'm sorry to keep you waiting."

RESPECT: "You have worked really hard in trying to get through this."

LEGITIMIZATION: "Most people in your position would feel this same way."

SUPPORT: "I'm going to stick with you through this."

You can imagine how many of these statements might have a further connecting and trust-building effect with the ill child's mother.

One further possibly surprising item: responding to emotional cues, for example, by using a PEARLS statement, saves time. Surgeons who incorporate even one statement spend 1.5 fewer minutes per outpatient visit than surgeons who don't. Internists spend 2.5 fewer minutes in their outpatient visits.[7] If you consider this, it starts to make sense. We mentioned that patients frequently have strong emotions connected to their symptoms. If the clinician neglects to address these emotions, patients will continue to state their emotional concern until either the clinician finally uses a PEARLS statement, or in the worst possible outcome, the patient gives up.[8] We have repeatedly seen how deepening connections through PEARLS improves diagnosis, builds trust, and saves time.

FOURTH SKILL: TRANSITION TO FURTHER DATA GATHERING

Once the clinician provides space for concerns to be expressed and addressed with empathy, everyone is well prepared for a transition to gathering more clinical data and providing information about the illness process. A transition statement can be as simple as: "I'd like to ask you more detailed questions about what's been going on, examine you (or your child), and make a plan. Does that sound OK to you?"

Typically, implementing the skills in this chapter requires only a couple of minutes. This exploration helps patients feel that we are on their side, strengthens the relationship, and allows space for patients to simultaneously share their worries and momentarily put them aside. The focus on relationship building as a prelude to clinical data collection makes tracking and responding simpler and more effective for both parties. With this activity, the clinician regulates the flow of information without becoming authoritarian or impersonal. Importantly, once we get the clinical details and move to making plans, we can return to previously stated ideas and expectations and further solidify the relationship by referring to them as we wrap up. Better relationships result in better care.

In subsequent chapters, we will show that incorporating elements of Skill Set Two can greatly benefit numerous conversations in the healthcare workplace. These are not just skills for patients, they're skills for everyone.

Conclusion

The components of Skill Set Two are:

- Ask open-ended questions and listen actively.
- Elicit ideas and expectations.
- Respond to emotional cues using PEARLS.
- Transition to further data gathering

Skill Set Two involves delving into the patient's perspective to elicit information about underlying worries, concerns, and sense-making. The one or two minutes spent in this way facilitate understanding of health literacy, beliefs surrounding illness, the role of the patient, and the role of the clinician. By eliciting these beliefs and perspectives early on, the clinician can avoid unnecessary detours, efficiently and effectively establish a diagnosis, compassionately comfort patients, and provide them with the appropriate knowledge, perspectives, and treatments.

CHAPTER 5

Skill Set Three:
Delivering Diagnoses
and Treatment Plans

*The great enemy of communication . . . is the illusion of it.
We have talked enough; but we have not listened.[1]*
—W. H. Whyte

At the end of a busy clinic session, Dr. Brash angrily heads back to his office. He slams down his stethoscope and exclaims, "Why are patients always so noncompliant? Why don't they do what I tell them to do? They just don't want to be helped!"

"Sounds frustrating," says his colleague sympathetically. "What happened?"

"One of my patients, Ms. Jones, clearly has the classic signs of clinical depression and anxiety. She's even having panic attacks. Last visit I started her on an antidepressant, but this time, six weeks later, she hasn't even touched it! I remember I went over all of the reasons she should be on it, and I even went over side effects. How does she expect to get any better if she doesn't take the medication? I just don't get it!"

Faulty Receiver or Transmitter?

When patients don't do what we think we asked them to do, we have a tendency to label them as "noncompliant" or "difficult" patients. We blame them for not following the treatment plan that we feel we clearly laid out for them—in other words, we accuse the receiver of being faulty. Certainly, we could attribute the lack of adherence to Ms. Jones's underlying depression or blame the patient for not doing what she was "supposed" to do.

On the other hand, this may not be completely the patient's fault. For instance, did we discern whether the patient was on board with the plan in the first place? Did the patient even understand what we told her? Did we explore what her concerns might have been about the diagnosis or treatment plan? Despite all of our wishes to the contrary, and as painful as it may be to admit, it is the messenger—or the transmission of the message—that is sometimes to blame.

To address these questions, let's rewind and take a peek into the conversation that Dr. Brash had with Ms. Jones on the first encounter, when he initially raised the idea of prescribing an antidepressant medication. Ms. Jones had presented to the clinic with fatigue, insomnia, poor concentration, and episodic palpitations and chest tightness, sometimes associated with shortness of breath.

> DR. BRASH: Ms. Jones, I'm going to prescribe a medication for you that will help you feel better. It's an antidepressant and should also help with the anxiety. You should start taking half a pill in the morning, and then after a week, as long as you don't have any side effects, you can go up to a full pill. The most common side effect is feeling a little jumpy, which is why I want you to take it in the morning—but this is only at the beginning and it wears off as you continue to take it. Sometimes there's some diarrhea or a little bit of nausea that goes away, and then sometimes some sexual side effects. I'm going to send it straight to your pharmacy so you can start taking it tomorrow, and I'll see you back again in six weeks to see how you're doing. Any questions?

MS. JONES: Uh, I guess not.

MS. JONES (AS DR. BRASH PREPARES TO LEAVE THE ROOM): But what about my heart?

Problematic Signal Transmission

Dr. Brash indeed made a critical diagnosis and covered important aspects of starting a medication, including the dosing, timing of administration of the medication, side effects, what to expect, and follow-up interval. He likely believes that he has done a thorough job explaining to the patient what to do. However, he delivered all of this important information in a download—an all-too-common, and usually ineffective, communication style. It mirrors the educational process of many clinicians, who traditionally have passively sat in auditoriums being lectured at for hours. That is what "education" was. It is no wonder that we think that "educating" patients involves a similar dynamic.

What we emphasize as being important, in addition to how it is taught, has an impact as well. We spend our entire training learning how to make the correct diagnosis and hone our medical decision-making to implement the proper treatment. We congratulate ourselves when we have clinched the diagnosis and consider ourselves smart when we know the appropriate management strategy. In other words, the emphasis is on making sure the content of the message is accurate. And we tell patients everything in the message without thinking as much about how the message comes across.

However, making the correct diagnosis and knowing how to manage the illness, while necessary, is not sufficient. What we sometimes fail to realize is how all of that information lands on the patient. Is the information digestible? Is it something the patient understands? From Ms. Jones's point of view, she was not given a chance to see how her fatigue translated into a diagnosis of depression, and how the medication would help her feel better. Neither did Dr. Brash explore her fears or concerns about starting a medication for depression and anxiety, or her personal thoughts that her symptoms were a sign of a heart attack, though it was clear to Dr. Brash that she was having panic attacks. In the midst of the data download, it's a wonder that the patient returned at all! It's like we learned Morse code to transmit our message, but we didn't stop to check that our patient even knew Morse code. If we know what to put in the message but do not pay attention to how it is being transmitted, the patient's health outcome is ultimately what is adversely affected. If patients don't understand or agree with the plan, then they won't follow through, which is, unfortunately, what happened with Ms. Jones. And we have missed an opportunity to achieve a successful treatment for the patient, despite our brilliant diagnosis and treatment plan.

Strengthening the Transmission with ART

What will maximize a patient's buy-in to the plan and improve the transmission of the message? How can we change the conversations to maximize patient understanding? Instead of a data dump, break the information down into digestible chunks, with frequent check-ins and continued input from the patient. This approach will maximize the potential for the patient to actually follow the correct treatment plan. We often refer to this approach as "chunk and check." One would never think, for example, to eat an entire pineapple in one mouthful: we can only chew and digest smaller chunks.

To operationalize this approach, our colleague Maysel Kemp White coined the "ART" method, which uses dialogue instead of download to convey information to the patient and ensure understanding.[2]

The ART method has three basic steps:

1. **A**sk the patient for his or her perspective about the diagnosis or about symptoms.
2. **R**espond to them with active listening and/or empathy.
3. **T**ell your perspective.

The method can repeat in ART cycles, where a first series of attempts at mutual understanding deepen and repeat. For example, here is what Dr. Brash and Ms. Jones's conversation might look like using ART to share the information about the diagnosis.

DR. BRASH: Ms. Jones, based on your history and exam, I believe that your symptoms are a sign of depression and anxiety. What are your thoughts on that? (Ask)

MS. JONES: I guess I can buy that. But what about my heart? I mean, these chest pains and heart racing are really scary! Is depression and anxiety actually causing these symptoms? Can depression cause a heart attack?

DR. BRASH: I can definitely see why you thought you were having a heart attack. Chest pain, heart racing, and shortness of breath can be very scary. (Respond) I can tell you, though, that you are young and otherwise healthy, and have no risk factors for heart attack. In these circumstances, your symptoms of chest pain and heart racing are a symptom of the anxiety you are feeling and are very typical for a panic attack. (Tell) What do you know about panic attacks? (Ask—beginning of second ART cycle)

MS. JONES: Is that what this is—a panic attack! I mean, I know I'm stressed, but I've never had this kind of reaction to stress. What do I do about it? Are you going to check me into a loony bin?

DR. BRASH: Many people who have never had a panic attack have the same concerns that you do. (Respond) I know you want to feel better, and I want to help you get there. Luckily, we will not have to send you to a loony bin in order to do so! There are a couple of other options to help you get better. (Tell) Would you like to review them now? (Ask—beginning of third ART cycle)

This conversation is more of a back-and-forth dialogue, engaging the patient by recapping the patient's ideas and perspectives and leading to a conversation, rather than a download.

Why would we check in with our patient, when we have already made a diagnosis and treatment plan on our own?

If we know what our patient is thinking, we can get a lot of valuable information about what he or she does not know, and can spend our time filling in gaps in the information or correcting misconceptions rather than spewing information that the patient already has. This allows us to tailor the discussion to what the patient needs or wants to know.

This technique also improves the patient experience because patients feel that the clinician listened and explained things in a way that they could understand. Sharing the plan this way effectively enhances patient buy-in and increases adherence to the medical plan. Because Dr. Brash heard and acknowledged Ms. Jones's concerns about a potential heart attack, she was much more open to the idea that her symptoms were caused by depression and anxiety.

Finally, the clinician will also feel less frustrated, not only from a sense of satisfaction that the patient is getting what he or she needs, but also as a result of an improved connection with the patient. It ultimately might even save time. As is the case earlier in the encounter, finding out up front what the patient is thinking or worrying about—this time regarding the diagnosis and treatment—cuts down on doorknob questions at the end of the visit. It also increases the likelihood that the desired outcome will be achieved because the patient will be on board with the plan and more likely to follow through.

"Treat to Target": Outcome Is Important

At the end of the day, we want our patients to have favorable medical outcomes. Therefore, we must ensure that the transmission of our medical message reaches its target, or the correct diagnosis will be wasted. Although transmitting our messages more effectively may require an investment of time up front, it is all worthwhile when our patients understand, agree with, and follow through with the treatment plan. In comparison, consider how much time (at least six weeks) was wasted on Ms. Jones's treatment when Dr. Brash did not confirm her understanding of the diagnosis, let alone her commitment to the treatment plan.

The same ART cycle can be applied to the remaining tasks of the interaction, which include negotiating and collaborating on the plan. Let's see how the ART cycle is used effectively in this situation.

DR. BRASH: As I mentioned, there are some treatment options, but before I go further, I'd like to hear your thoughts about how best to manage your depression. (Ask)

MS. JONES: I know that some people take pills. But my aunt took "happy pills," and she was a zombie. I don't want to be a zombie. I really want to avoid pills if possible. Do you think I can get better without medications?

DR. BRASH: I can see why you'd be worried about pills based on your aunt's experience, and I hear that you don't want to feel like a zombie. (Respond) I'd like to work with you to figure out a treatment that will make you feel better, not worse. (Tell) Can we talk about your options? (Ask)

MS. JONES: Yes, I want to know what I can do.

DR. BRASH: The options are to take a medication every day for a period of months, or to talk things out with a counselor, or to do both. The score on the test that you filled out tells us that your depression is pretty severe. In these instances, we usually recommend that you take medication to treat your depression. If we were to go ahead with this, we'd be sure to choose one that doesn't make you feel like a zombie. (Tell) What are your thoughts now? (Ask)

MS. JONES: Well, if you put it that way . . . I mean, I really am sick of feeling this bad, and I want to feel better as soon as possible.

DR. BRASH: I can only imagine how lousy you must be feeling. (Respond) And I am hopeful that this will help you to feel better soon. (Tell)

Dr. Brash used three ART cycles to break down the information into smaller chunks that Ms. Jones could digest. He leveraged the ART cycles to elicit Ms. Jones's concerns while he presented his plan. In this manner, he could address her concerns with empathy as they arose and modify his plan in a timely manner based on her input. This approach can also allow Dr. Brash to illuminate Ms. Jones's misperceptions, appease her fears, and improve the chances that she will understand and follow the treatment plan. Because of the ART approach, Ms. Jones was more amenable to the idea of starting a medication. This is because Dr. Brash validated her concerns and expressed a desire to partner with her to make her feel better. Compared to how Ms. Jones was after the data download, she is much more engaged in this process, and Dr. Brash is constantly checking in with her to make sure she is on board.

The ART cycle can be used as many times as needed to review all aspects of the plan and until all of Ms. Jones's concerns have been elicited and addressed.

"Teach-back" to Ensure Proper Two-Way Transmission

ART can even be used to assess the patient's understanding of the plan, which often takes the form of a teach-back. If the patient can teach the plan back to us, then we can check for accuracy and understanding, and correct any errors.

> **DR. BRASH:** I know I did a lot of talking just now. Just so I know I made myself clear, tell me what you will do when you go home. (Ask)
>
> **MS. JONES:** Well, I'm going to start this pill once a day in the morning, but I'm going to take the lower dose for one week, and then I'll start the higher dose if I'm not having any of the side effects that you mentioned.
>
> **DR. BRASH:** That's right. (Respond)
>
> **MS. JONES:** And you said I'm not going to feel better right away, that I have to stick with this for at least a few weeks before I start feeling better. And even if I feel jittery, I should keep taking it. And in the meantime, I should call to set up an appointment with a counselor.
>
> **DR. BRASH:** That's right also. I know you are nervous about this, (Respond) so we will set up a follow-up appointment in a month to see how you are doing. But if you do start

> feeling those side effects we talked about or have any
> questions at all, I want you to give me a call before then.
> (Tell) How does that sound? (Ask)
>
> **MS. JONES:** As long as I can call you if anything goes wrong.
>
> **DR. BRASH:** Absolutely. (Respond)

In this outpatient-based example, imagine the time you might save answering follow-up phone calls from patients because they walked out of your office confused. This approach also strongly benefits our colleagues in inpatient and emergency department settings, who might otherwise field extra questions or pages from ancillary staff because the original plan was unclear. In fact, this approach works very well in many settings and when used by any healthcare clinician. As an example, a few weekends later, Ms. Jones makes a trip to the emergency department because she has had a particularly severe recurrence of palpitations, chest pain, and shortness of breath. The nurse practitioner in the emergency department performs appropriate studies, confirms that the patient does not have a cardiac cause of her chest pain, and relays the diagnosis to the patient.

> **NURSE PRACTITIONER MILLER:** I have all of your studies back,
> including chest x-ray, EKG, and lab work, and I'm happy
> to tell you that you have not suffered a heart attack. Your
> symptoms are most consistent with a different kind of
> attack—a panic attack. Have you ever considered that
> that might be the cause of your symptoms? (Ask)
>
> **MS. JONES:** Actually, my doctor told me the same thing, and
> he started me on a medication, but it's been taking so
> long, and I was worried again about my heart, so my
> mom told me to come in.
>
> **NURSE PRACTITIONER MILLER:** I'm glad you did. (Respond) I do
> think it would be a good idea to treat the anxiety that is
> causing these panic attacks. (Tell) I assume that is why
> you are on the citalopram.
>
> **MS. JONES:** Yes. He did warn me it would take a while to start
> working, but this last panic attack, as you call it, was

worse than ever. He mentioned I could take lorazepam to ward it off when it happened, but I don't want to take that pill.

NURSE PRACTITIONER MILLER: What are your concerns about taking lorazepam? (Ask)

MS. JONES: My aunt took it for a while and it made her a zombie. I don't want that. It seems too strong.

NURSE PRACTITIONER MILLER: I can understand why that would make you want to avoid the medication. (Respond) On the other hand, we need to help you manage the panic attacks when they happen, until the citalopram kicks in. Another option would be to talk to a therapist who can help you with stress management and biofeedback. (Tell) What do you know about managing anxiety using these techniques? (Ask)

MS. JONES: I told Dr. Brash I would call for an appointment with a therapist, but I just haven't gotten around to it yet. I thought maybe the medicine would kick in before then. Do you think that would help?

NURSE PRACTITIONER MILLER: I can see why you wanted to wait to see how the medication would work. (Respond) Yes, I do think it would help, not only with talking through your problems but also specifically with managing the symptoms of the panic attack when they come on. (Tell)

MS. JONES: OK, I will call when I get home.

Here, Nurse Practitioner Miller uses the ART technique to notify Ms. Jones of the diagnosis, explore barriers she has about the proposed treatment plan, and explore potential solutions with her. What's more, ensuring understanding of the plan has been shown to improve healthcare outcomes including blood pressure control, cholesterol control, and diabetes control.[3] The teach-back technique has specifically been shown to be associated with reduced errors in medication dosing.[4] Finally, this type of approach proves more satisfying not only for patients, but clinicians as well, thus achieving a triple aim of patient satisfaction, patient outcome, and clinician satisfaction.[5] On her follow-up appointment with Dr. Brash several weeks later, Ms. Jones reported that she had been taking her citalopram daily, had felt an improvement in her depressive symptoms, and, with the help of a therapist, had learned some biofeedback techniques to help manage her anxiety episodes as they were occurring.

Conclusion

Skill Set Three involves giving information about diagnosis and treatment to a patient in a way that makes it more likely for him or her to buy into and follow through with a therapeutically successful plan. The "magic" used to achieve this important task involves using the ART technique of Ask, Respond, Tell: breaking the information about the diagnosis and treatment plan into digestible chunks and checking with the patient frequently to ensure understanding of and collaboration on a mutually agreed-upon plan. We will see further examples throughout the book about how this fundamental technique can strengthen understanding in such disparate applications as challenging conversations, motivational interviewing, feedback, coaching, and team communication.

PART III

PRACTICAL APPLICATIONS OF THE SKILL SETS

CHAPTER 6

Challenging Conversations with Patients

I n Chapters 3–5 we introduced the fundamental communication skills that foster effective connections and relationship-centered care. Participants in our courses often say that they imagine the skills will be effective with patients that they get along with, but worry that the skills will fall short with the patients who are bringing their experience scores down. Clinicians seem most distressed when they have to break bad news, manage high levels of emotion such as anger or mistrust, and address expectations they can't satisfy. In this chapter, we offer suggestions for how to apply the fundamental skills in the context of these challenging encounters.

All of these situations involve problems that clinicians can't fix. There's no prescription or procedure that will alleviate the grief that comes with a cancer diagnosis or the anger of patients who feel that the medical system has betrayed them. Many of us notice that these conversations distance us from our patients and as a result, we may believe we've failed. Though we truly can't control others (as much as we would like to), we can support patients through these difficult times and enhance our connections by relinquishing control and using the very relationship-centered skills that we've become familiar with.

When Emotions Are Running High

Our core communication skills are invaluable when emotions are running high. Strong emotion can't be ignored. People who are overwhelmed with grief, fear, or anger can't take in new information or form relationships. The emotions must be addressed before anything else can be done effectively. Emotions are contagious; when we encounter someone who is angry, we may feel angry ourselves. Our emotional level will rise in response to theirs. Instead of communicating our distress, we can manage our emotions by cultivating an awareness of our physical responses and choosing words that will express our empathy for the other person.

I (Jenni Levy) met Ms. King when she was admitted to our inpatient hospice unit. She was 38, and she had metastatic cervical cancer. Her partner, Ms. Long, sat by the bed. Ms. Long had supported Ms. King through the terrible six weeks since her diagnosis and planned to be there until the end. Ms. King made it clear to the hospice staff that Ms. Long was to make her decisions when she could no longer do so, and she filled out all the paperwork to make that legally binding. "You'll have a bad time with my parents," she told me. "I apologize in advance."

Ms. King's parents came to visit the next day. They were furious. They did not agree with their daughter's choice of hospice care. They were convinced Ms. Long was influencing their daughter, and they blamed her for what they saw as a late diagnosis. They wouldn't speak to Ms. Long; when they were alone with their daughter, they spoke so harshly to her that the nurse ordered them to leave the room. The nurse, who was so angry and upset that she was in tears, warned me when I arrived. I was apprehensive and took some time to gather my thoughts and catch a few deep breaths before entering the room.

Ms. King's parents were sitting in the family counseling room with their arms and legs crossed, girding themselves for battle. Mr. King stood up and pointed at me when I walked in. "You WILL send our daughter back to the hospital. We are her next of kin. We are legally allowed to make her decisions." Mrs. King nodded. He continued: "She can have more treatment. We will not allow that woman to send her to an early grave."

How would you feel in that situation? I felt angry and defensive. How dare they act so aggressively! My heart was pounding and my mouth was dry. I wanted to scream, "You will not speak to me that way!"—but I knew that would only escalate the confrontation with Mr. King. I took a deep breath and sat down. It's easy to empathize with people who react in a calm, thoughtful manner. How was I supposed to connect with a man who was threatening me? When I don't know what to do next, I have learned to try a PEARLS statement (see Chapter 4). I remembered what other parents had told me about the tragedy of watching their children die, and I remembered the times when my own grief had caused me to lash out in anger.

I looked up at Mr. King and said softly, "I can't imagine how difficult this time has been for you." He dropped the hand he had been pointing at me. "You love your daughter very deeply." He sat down. His wife started to cry. I no longer felt threatened. I was able to see them as grieving parents, and my own anger started to fade.

Over the next half hour, they told me about their only daughter. They talked about her high school soccer trophies, her difficulties in college, her brief marriage to a man they thought was perfect for her. They both cried when they told me how distant they'd been for the last two years since their daughter came out to them and moved in with her partner. If only they'd known . . . if only they'd seen her more often and realized how sick she was, they would have done something sooner. Ms. Long should have done something. This shouldn't be happening.

I listened and reflected what I heard: their love, their frustration, their confusion, their anguish, and their grief. Of course they were angry. Anyone in their situation would be. I realized that I couldn't change their minds about Ms. Long, as much as I wanted to defend her. When we walked out of the room, they both hugged me and then went down the hall to sit with their daughter, peacefully.

Mr. and Mrs. King's outbursts were increasing their daughter's suffering and causing distress for her partner and for my staff. Early in my career, I would have stood up to Mr. King and matched his anger with my own. Years of practicing these skills gave me a better choice. I was able to build a relationship with Mr. and Mrs. King that allowed them to trust me and to express the grief I knew they were feeling—the grief that I suspected was the real cause of their anger. I didn't try to educate them about hospice care or the legal issues of advance directives. I tried not to think of them as unreasonable, demanding, or homophobic; I concentrated instead on their love for their daughter, their sadness, and the regret I heard as they told me their story. When I used reflective listening and PEARLS statements, Mr. and Mrs. King felt understood and were able to move past their own defensiveness. By the end of the conversation, they wanted to feel connected to their daughter again more than they wanted to force her to leave hospice care.

Not all confrontations end this well. When Mr. King stood up and pointed at me as I walked in the room, I wondered if I was in physical danger. I left the door open until he sat down and I felt the tension ease. If he had continued to physically intimidate me, I would have ended the conversation until I could come back with a colleague.

In this case, the cause of the distress was directly related to the work I needed to do with this family. I had to abandon my agenda and spend the entire visit building a relationship and helping them process their feelings. This enabled me to have another conversation the next day, during which we reviewed their daughter's advance directive, and I explained that we were obligated to follow it. If I had tried to have that discussion at our first encounter, it would have exacerbated their anger and sabotaged our relationship. The investment I made in the first half hour I spent with Mr. and Mrs. King paid off for the rest of their daughter's stay in our facility.

When a patient is angry or upset about something outside of the encounter such as family trouble, work difficulties, or frustration with the medical system, you may not feel it's appropriate or necessary to address that in your discussion. The problem may exist outside your exam room, but the emotion comes right in with the patient. If you can identify the distress early in the encounter and provide support and empathy, the patient will feel relieved and the emotion itself may subside, allowing you to move on. If the patient remains angry, anxious, and preoccupied throughout the visit, he or she is less likely to retain any information that you offer and to follow the plan that you develop.

In instances when emotions are running high, practice the following skills:

- Cultivate awareness of your emotions and manage your own distress.
- Safety first; if your physical safety is threatened, walk away.
- Focus on the relationship by using PEARLS statements to express empathy and understanding.
- Be willing to abandon your agenda in favor of support and relationship.
- The primary goal is support of the patient/family member, not getting someone to agree with you.

Breaking Bad News

Ask medical students and clinicians about breaking bad news, and they will respond with stories about cancer, traumatic accidents, and HIV. These are devastating, life-changing diagnoses to be sure. But our patients may have different ideas about what constitutes bad news. The receiver of bad news, not the giver, is the one who will have the emotional reaction. Therefore, though we may have an idea of how a patient might hear it, bad news is defined fully and solely by the receiver.

Mr. Richards was 52 years old when he saw me for the first time. "I've been having a hard time lately," he told me. "My last doctor gave me some really bad news and he was—I don't know, kind of glib about it. I just had the sense he didn't care at all."

"What was the bad news?"

"He told me I have diabetes. My grandfather had diabetes, and he lost both his legs. I'm a healthy guy. I try to eat right, and I work out. I never thought I'd have diabetes. I didn't even know they were looking for that—it was a routine blood test. The doctor just told me, bam, like it wasn't a big deal. I don't even remember what else he said, and I never took the pills he gave me. Since then I've had a hard time sleeping because I'm so worried. I don't want to lose my legs or end up blind or on a kidney machine."

As clinicians, it's easy for us to think of diabetes as routine. We see it all the time. It's a chronic illness. It's so common that most of our patients will know someone who has diabetes. They may be aware of the potentially devastating complications. That can make something we consider a routine diagnosis to be truly devastating news for a patient.

When we use the ART (Ask, Respond, Tell) method (see Chapter 5) to break bad news, we can avoid the trap Mr. Richards's first doctor fell into. We can support the patient through sometimes unexpected emotional responses, so that he or she can process the information we are providing.

I wanted Mr. Richards to know that I heard what he told me about his fear, and I wanted to express my willingness to work with him. After I asked Mr. Richards, "What was the bad news?," I responded with statements of legitimization, apology, and partnership:

"I can see how terrifying it was for you to get that news. I'm sorry to hear that you feel that your other doctor didn't understand you. I hope we can work together so you understand how you can take care of yourself and be as healthy as you can be." He said, "Thanks, Doc," and looked calmer.

Then I addressed the concern he'd expressed. "We have a much better understanding of diabetes than we did in your grandfather's day, and we can prevent a lot of the complications he experienced."

I might have gone on to talk about HgA1c monitoring, oral medications, insulin resistance, reducing carbohydrates, finger-stick glucose testing, and the other details essential to someone with a new diagnosis of diabetes. All the information would likely have been overwhelming to Mr. Richards and might have left him again confused about what he needed to do. We are much more effective when we "chunk and check" by offering small, comprehensible pieces of information and then checking for understanding (see Chapter 5). "We have several medications that can help get blood sugar under control. What do you know about medicine for diabetes?"

That's the Ask for another cycle of ART. In this visit, I wanted to initiate treatment with one medication and refer Mr. Richards to the diabetes educators. The referral required its own ART cycle. At each step, I checked in with Mr. Richards to see how he was responding. He was open to the idea of taking medication and was grateful for the referral. He wanted to learn more about managing his diabetes. He felt calmer with the increased understanding and support. I had a sense that he was much more likely to follow through on the plan (and to sleep through the night again). Providing information in small, manageable chunks using ART, checking understanding, and making empathic statements helped Mr. Richards cope with both the news itself and the emotional turmoil that he was feeling.

In instances of breaking bad news, practice the following skills:

- Use ART (Ask, Respond, Tell) to elicit understanding, express empathy, and deliver information.
- "Chunk and check"—don't overwhelm the patient by downloading data.
- Give the patient only the information he or she needs to get the next step of care; more information can follow later.

Unmet Expectations

Unmet expectations are another type of bad news and can be approached in much the same way. These conversations also require strong attention to the clinician's own emotions and reactions.

Mr. Martin was 34. He worked in construction and had been pushing through his back pain for weeks. The pain was now worse despite chiropractic care and over-the-counter medication, and he came to the office to get an order for an MRI. He had no evidence of nerve impingement on examination and his pain was limited to his lower back, where he had evident muscular spasm and decreased range of motion.

Mr. Martin presented his request for testing as his primary complaint: "I need an MRI." This type of request can also become clear in the second set of communication skills when we ask about ideas and expectations (see Chapter 4).

I suspected that Mr. Martin would be upset with my assessment and suggestions for treatment. I did not believe he needed any imaging, and hearing that would likely be bad news for him. As I transitioned to the close of the interview, I reflected what I'd heard and made a statement of partnership before telling him the bad news:

"The pain is making it hard for you to work and keeping you awake at night. You're worried that you have a slipped disc, and you asked me for an MRI. I really want to work with you to improve your pain. And,

I'm afraid I have some news that might be hard to hear: I don't think you need an MRI."

This was the beginning of an ART cycle. There's a lot more information I could have given Mr. Martin about MRIs and lower back pain. I didn't know what information would be most helpful for him. I knew that if he was angry that I wasn't ordering the test, he wouldn't really hear anything I said. And he was angry.

"You're just trying to save the insurance company money. Do they pay you more if you say no?"

That insinuation made *me* angry, but striking back at him wouldn't help. I tried to speak to the concern that I thought might lie under his accusation, using a reflective statement. This was the Respond portion of this cycle of ART: "You feel really strongly about getting that MRI. It's very important to you."

"I know I need an MRI to check out my discs."

I wanted to tell Mr. Martin that MRIs are only necessary to guide operations. Before I did that, I responded, using legitimization. My Tell was very brief and was followed by another Ask: "Lots of people want an MRI for their backs, and with all the football players getting MRIs every time they turn around, I can understand why." (Respond) "MRIs are crucial for people who need back surgery." (Tell) "Do you think you need surgery?" (Ask)

"I sure hope not. Do you think I need an operation?"

"No, I don't. I didn't find any evidence of nerve damage when I examined you. You have a lot of muscle spasm, and I think that's causing most of your pain. The MRI won't tell us anything about that, and it wouldn't change the treatment I'm going to suggest."

Mr. Martin still wasn't happy about my answer, but he knew I understood his concern, and he was starting to trust our relationship. He sighed and asked, "What kind of treatment is that?" I began the next ART cycle: "I'd like you to see a physical therapist. What do you know about PT?" He said, "I know it usually hurts more after you see the therapist! My wife had PT for her shoulder. It helped, but she was in a lot of pain for a while." I responded to this concern: "Anyone would be worried about pain after that experience." I went on to explain: "Sometimes PT does cause discomfort; the therapists can offer you ice or heat to help with that, and I can give you some anti-inflammatory medication as well."(Tell) "Have you ever taken that kind of medication?" (Ask) He agreed to try an anti-inflammatory medication and a course of physical therapy, with the understanding that if he didn't feel better, he would come back and we could discuss the MRI again.

Participants in our communication courses tell us that patients in pain and patients requesting pain medication have a particularly troubling subset of unmet expectations. Clinicians understand the need for caution in prescribing opioids; they also understand that most of their patients are actually having pain and they want to help. They also want to reduce the risk of diversion and addiction.[1] Patients in pain, like patients who are angry, have difficulty processing information. As noted in Chapter 1, the combination of an anxious clinician and an angry and uncomfortable patient makes for a very challenging encounter.

The core relationship-centered skills will help build a connection with patients through the interviews. Using reflective listening and PEARLS statements to show that you understand the patients' concerns will help them trust you and increase their willingness to try opioid-sparing alternative treatments. Understanding their concerns and validating their distress does not mean that you will accede to their requests. You can hold your professional boundaries and express your compassion simultaneously.

No approach can guarantee a positive outcome; some patients will not be willing to take "no" for an answer. In such instances, there is little value in repeating the discussion.

When I saw Ms. Allen, she started the visit by requesting a refill of the Percocet she'd received from her previous doctor. I identified her concerns about her back pain and the impact of the pain on her ability to function at work and at home. I did not believe Percocet was appropriate: "I can see that you're suffering. I know you've gotten Percocet before." (Respond) "Unfortunately, I'm afraid I have some news that might be hard to hear: I can't give you another prescription." (Tell)

She replied, "I want my Percocet. There isn't anything else that works."

"Sounds like you're convinced that's what you need, and you're understandably upset. I know we need to address your back pain so you can work and take care of your kids. I've had success with other approaches and I'd like to work with you."

Again, she said, "It's just the Percocet. That's what I need."

"I'm sorry, I wouldn't be doing my job if I gave you an inappropriate medication. If you'd like to discuss alternatives, I'm happy to do that."

Her response: "I want Percocet."

"I'm very sorry I won't be able to help you then. If you change your mind, I'll be happy to see you again."

This was not a satisfying encounter for either of us, although I knew I was doing the right thing. When we build strong relationships and attend to the emotional needs of our patients, we can provide better, more compassionate, and more efficient care. We cannot satisfy every patient in every situation. A relationship-centered approach will improve the overall experience for both the patient and the clinician, so these difficult encounters occur in a different context and are easier to cope with.

Unmet expectations combine bad news with high emotions. When we use a relationship-centered approach throughout the interview, we have a better chance of a successful negotiation at the end. Using ART, chunk and check, and repeated PEARLS statements can help you maintain a connection with the patient and hold to appropriate practice.

In cases of addressing unmet expectations, practice these skills:

- Identify expectations early in the interview.
- Plan the approach for the delivery of bad news.
- Use ART to hear the patient's perspective and respond with empathy (PEARLS) while explaining your thought process.
- Move to conclude the conversation if agreement is not possible.

The Distrustful Patient

If there ever was a time in the United States when doctors were universally regarded as wise and benevolent, that time has passed. Many of our patients have had painful or even harmful encounters with the medical system. People of color and other members of marginalized populations are treated differently by many clinicians (see Chapter 14).[2] Patients with obesity feel stigmatized and marginalized as well, and many of our patients have difficulty navigating the increasingly complex American healthcare system.

We expect patients to trust us as a matter of course and often feel angry and hurt when they do not. These encounters can be managed using the approaches we have discussed for other challenging encounters. We can build relationships when we maintain an awareness of our own emotional responses and keep our focus on the patient.

Ms. Williams came to see me after her insurance changed, and she could no longer remain with her longtime primary care physician. She made it very clear that she was not happy about the shift: "Dr. Robinson has been taking care of me for 20 years. He knows me. And he's a lot older than you." Dr. Robinson, I knew, was also African American, like Ms. Williams. I am white.

Ms. Williams had dutifully brought her medication list and her pill bottles to the appointment. I was concerned about her blood pressure medications; even though she was taking four medications, her blood pressure was still too high, and she had signs of early damage to her kidneys.

From the outset of the interview, I was careful not only to ask her about her entire list of concerns but also to ask what she valued in Dr. Robinson and other clinicians she had seen before. She said, "I want someone who listens and who understands me." I said, "I certainly hope I can be like that for you."

I then asked her about her expectations for the appointment. She said, "I need refills on my pills, and I don't want you to mess with them. It took Dr. Robinson a long time to get this straight." I responded, "Sounds like you two worked together to get something that worked for you. I know we're just meeting for the first time, and that it's hard to lose Dr. Robinson, with whom you've had a long relationship. I will work hard and hope to gain your trust." She seemed to soften.

I continued to identify Ms. Williams's ideas and expectations and to respond to her emotional cues. I was careful and thorough with the physical exam, and explained each transition. As always, I asked for permission before touching her and continued to use PEARLS statements and reflective listening throughout the visit.

At the end of the visit, I started an ART cycle by asking, "What's it like to take all these pills?" She said, "It's a lot to swallow, but I know it's important. My mother had a stroke." I responded, "The idea of having a stroke is pretty scary." Ms. Williams nodded. I went on to tell her, "I'm concerned about your blood pressure today; it's a bit higher than I'd like to see it. I know this is the first time we're meeting. I'd like to get some more information." I started another ART cycle by asking, "What would you think of requesting your records from Dr. Robinson, and coming back to see me in a couple of weeks?" She said, "Well, Dr. Robinson only needed to see me every four months, but I guess I could come in sooner." I gave her a month's worth of refills, had her sign a records release, and scheduled a three-week follow-up appointment. It wasn't ideal; she was still taking insufficient medication. With distrustful patients, it can take longer to build a relationship, and we may have to accept some short-term compromises in the interests of better long-term outcomes.

On Ms. Williams's second visit, her blood pressure was still too high. She seemed a bit more comfortable with me. When I came into the room, I asked after the grandchild she'd had with her at the first visit, and she showed me pictures of his school play. We were making progress with the relationship. I showed her the sheaf of records I'd received from Dr. Robinson and told her I'd looked through them to see what other medicines she'd taken, and what her blood pressure had been. She was pleased with my follow-through, and my attention to Dr. Robinson's opinion. I asked her, "What would it take for you to be comfortable changing some of the medicines?" She paused and looked at me. "I guess I'd need to understand exactly why you wanted to do that." I nodded and responded with two PEARLS statements: "Of course you would. I respect how much you care about doing the right thing for your health, and I want to work with you." I moved on to the Tell: "You are taking two pills that work similarly. I'm proposing that we stop the losartan and increase the dose of this one, the lisinopril. What would you think of that?" She said, "Well, I guess it would be good to not take as many pills." She agreed to make the change "on a trial basis," and we scheduled another three-week follow-up. Her blood pressure was improved on the third visit, and she said, "I guess you know what you're doing, Doc." If I'd made that change on the first visit, she would have been less likely to take the medication I'd prescribed. I took a little longer to get her blood pressure under control, but in the process I laid the groundwork for a long-term trusting relationship.

With a distrustful patient, it is particularly important to make sure you follow through on any commitments you make. Be prepared to offer early follow-up in person or by phone, and continue to use excellent relationship skills each time you see or speak to the patient. As you demonstrate that you are respectful and reliable, you will have done everything you can to lay the groundwork for trust.

When trying to build trust with a mistrustful patient, practice the following skills:

- Focus on respect early in the interview.
- Elicit and respond to the patient's concerns with PEARLS.
- Incorporate the patient's perspective into the plan.
- Be scrupulous and consistent about follow-up.

Conclusion

In our most difficult patient encounters, we feel disconnected from the patient; we ourselves are anxious, angry, and sometimes afraid. Our emotions often mirror the patient's. We must be compassionate with ourselves as well and ensure that we have the opportunity to process our distress with friends, colleagues, or other sources of support.

To help support patients through challenging situations, we can employ relationship-centered skills to overcome distrust and unmet expectations, support patients through the delivery of bad news, and provide compassionate care when emotions run high. When we focus on the relationship, everyone benefits.

CHAPTER 7

The Skill Sets and the Electronic Health Record

uriel Hampton walks nervously into Dr. Kumar's family practice for what she fears will be bad news. She nervously sits on the chair in the exam room. Prominently placed on the table next to her is a large computer screen with a keyboard. The medical assistant walks into the room and sits down to turn on the computer.

Computers have made their way into all parts of the medical system: emergency departments, ambulatory surgical centers, and inpatient acute care units. Electronic health record (EHR) management systems may vary, but one fact holds true across settings: when clinicians are physically with patients, most of them are face-to-face not with the patient but with the computer screen, clicking and typing.

In recent decades, the computer has emerged as the "third person" in the patient-clinician interaction, vividly impacting the patient experience.[1]

Our entire society is now a cyber culture in which computer screens have changed the patterns of daily human interactions. We are all familiar with the many technologies people use to communicate with each other such as e-mail, texting, and Twitter. In 2009, the U.S. government invested more than $30 billion to increase the use of electronic health records.[2] As of 2016, hospital and physician practices combined with federal money have spent an estimated $3 trillion on developing and implementing this technology.

Promise of the EHR

We can easily acknowledge the many advantages of EHRs, including accessibility and legibility of documentation. Studies show that EHRs can improve patient care, safety, and quality of care. Electronic patient records are much more accessible than paper records. Updated medication and allergy listings have improved safety of care in inpatient and outpatient settings. Patients appreciate the e-prescribing feature, which means getting medication more easily and in a timely manner. Research shows us that reminders for health screening have also improved in many practices. Disease-specific programs are now being evaluated, with improvement in the outcomes of some chronic diseases such as asthma, hypertension, and diabetes.

There is no question that the EHR is a permanent part of the exam room and hospital encounter for patients and will continue to enhance aspects of patient care. Yet implementation of the EHR occurred quickly, and in many cases, with little thought given to the dynamics of dyadic clinician-patient communication patterns. Most clinicians train to use the EHR from a technical standpoint and learn what buttons to press while giving only minimal attention to integrating the human dimension of the clinician-patient relationship into the computer-assisted medical visit. This chapter provides a perspective on the EHR from the viewpoints of both the patient and the clinician. It then outlines a model that empowers clinicians to remain relationship-centered while effectively managing the EHR.

Patients' Perspectives

Let's go back to the example of Ms. Hampton, the nervous patient who is now sitting in the exam room with a technology-absorbed medical assistant. How does she view the computer-patient-clinician triad? Perhaps this is best explained in a picture drawn by a seven-year-old child published in the *Journal of the American Medical Association* in an article titled "The Cost of Technology."[3] The crayon drawing of an office visit depicts a mother holding a baby while the physician faces the computer, hunched over the keyboard, with his back to the patient.

As clinicians, we frequently walk into exam rooms and go to the computer first. Too often, we appear to concentrate more on typing than we do on speaking with the patient. Researchers estimate that clinicians spend at least 25 percent and as much as 40 percent of their time gazing at the computer screen.[4] This same study showed that a lack of eye contact between the patient and the clinician is associated with decreased patient satisfaction.

Ms. Hampton is 82 years old with multiple health issues, including arthritis, high blood pressure, and diabetes. Like many older patients, Ms. Hampton is at high risk for social isolation and depression. Treating Ms. Hampton involves not only addressing her diseases but also understanding her psychological issues, thoughts, and behaviors. For example, we know that depression in patients with coronary heart disease is independently associated with increased cardiovascular morbidity and mortality.[5] When Ms. Hampton comes to our practice and we fail to make eye contact with her because we are preoccupied by the EHR, we may miss critical nonverbal cues she gives us. Furthermore, when we focus on the screen, we miss opportunities to respond with empathy to these sensitive social or emotional aspects that affect her health and wellness (see Chapter 4). Unfortunately, patients with three or more chronic conditions are half as likely to receive treatment for their depression during a visit to a clinician's office that uses EHRs compared with patients who visit paper-based practices.[6]

Additional factors, such as literacy levels and socioeconomic status, can influence how EHR use impacts patients. For example, Ms. Hampton raised six children and left high school early to work in order to help support her family. She presently has poor eyesight and a ninth-grade reading level. Research conducted in safety-net clinics showed that there was lower patient satisfaction in outpatient settings where there was high EHR use.[7]

The EHR also adversely affects interpersonal patient interactions in the inpatient setting. Dr. Abraham Verghese wrote eloquently about how medical practitioners doing hospital rounds are more focused on discussions about the "iPatient's" results than on examining actual patients and listening to their concerns.[8] Healthcare team rounds now often occur in conference rooms where clinicians talk about patients and their x-ray reports, lab values, and consultant opinions with only brief bedside encounters. We observe a detachment of clinicians from patients and a diminishment of the potentially powerful therapeutic presence provided by a strong patient-clinician relationship.

Clinicians' Perspectives

We know that patients feel separated from clinicians who rely heavily on EHRs. Many clinicians also express dissatisfaction with the increased burden of EHR documentation. Clinicians complete an estimated 200 clicks during a typical outpatient visit. In one study, physicians spent approximately 53 percent of their time on direct clinical face time with patients and 37 percent on the EHR and deskwork. In addition, physicians noted spending one to two hours a day beyond office hours on EHRs.[9] This correlates with a study showing that the prevalence of physician burnout was significantly higher among physicians who used EHRs than among those who did not, independent of their reported satisfaction with the technology itself.[10]

There are more concerns than just with the increased time spent on documentation and order entry. When we are simultaneously typing, interviewing, and developing a diagnosis, what happens to our cognitive processing abilities? Let's compare a clinician who is seeing a patient while simultaneously typing to another common multitasking event: texting or talking on the phone while driving. Research has shown that texting and driving causes a 23-fold increase in crashes; using a cell phone and driving reduces the brain activity toward driving by 37 percent.[11] For pilots in the aviation industry, errors are more likely with increasing numbers of complex tasks.[12] Although there are now some data on types and frequency of errors with the use of the EHR, we are still learning about this topic.[13] When we begin to recognize the cognitive impairment that EHRs can cause, we may want to dispense with them altogether. But this may not be advisable, given the many benefits EHRs provide. The question becomes: How can we decrease this risk while improving patient-clinician interactions? Part of the answer lies in decreasing communication barriers imposed by the EHR and learning skills for managing the relationship *while* using technology.

Models of Relationship-Centered Care with the EHR

Currently, we can implement strategies to strengthen the patient-clinician relationship while using the computer during the encounter. These steps can relieve some of our documentation burdens and provide improved patient experiences.

As of now, there are no consensus "best practice" statements for how to integrate use of the EHR into the office setting. We formulated a research-based model that embeds discreet EHR-related skills into relationship-centered interactions with patients.[14] These steps maximize benefits of the EHR while intentionally equipping clinicians with skills to mitigate the ill effects of the screen gaze and multitasking linked to EHR use.

Let's go back to the example of Ms. Hampton and identify how the EHR can improve her care without taking away her personalized experience or creating an overwhelming burden of documentation for Dr. Kumar.

SETUP

Ms. Hampton sits in one of two chairs, with a computer screen on the sidewall between the chairs and an exam table nearby.

If we take some time to think about the setup, we can arrange our exam rooms to specifically accommodate the patient-clinician-computer triad. It's important that both the patient and the clinician are able to easily see the screen. We can achieve this by using a mobile computer/movable screen, or rearranging the room so both parties can see a fixed screen. What's critical is that the setup encourages patient participation by allowing the patient to join in or initiate discussion while looking at, pointing to, or highlighting items on the computer screen. In this way, clinicians will never be gazing at a screen with their backs to patients, inadvertently sending a strong message of exclusion.

PREVIEWING AND PREPOPULATING THE CHART

Dr. Kumar has previewed the EHR before entering the room. In Dr. Kumar's office, the medical assistant has undergone training with the

EHR and sits down with Ms. Hampton to type in the reason for the visit, review the medication list, update allergies, and record health maintenance information. Dr. Kumar confirms the accuracy of the information by showing Ms. Hampton the lists or verbalizing them when he is in the room.

It's true that previewing a patient's chart will add extra time to the beginning of a visit. But when we skip this step in the name of time management, inadequate preparation can come back to haunt us: our visits tend to be less organized and less satisfying to both parties, and ultimately tend to take longer.[15] When quickly previewing the patient's EHR, we gain familiarity with the patient, the most recent clinical notes, laboratory results, and medications. In an office setting, other members of the team could potentially perform some of these tasks and help patient flow.

GREETING

Dr. Kumar enters the room after knocking and says, "Hello, Ms. Hampton! It is so nice to see you today." (Handshake) "I hope you did not have trouble getting here today. Did your daughter bring you?" (Pause for patient response) "I'm going to sit down at the computer and log in while we talk."

In the first two minutes of a medical encounter, the patient is deciding whether or not to trust and respect the clinician (see Chapter 3). Social psychologists tell us that people look for both features of warmth and competence upon meeting someone new.[16] Therefore, when entering the patient's space, it's always appropriate to extend a greeting. There may be cultural variations of what this entails: in U.S. culture, we often shake hands. Greetings do not take long (15–20 seconds, typically) and should be done before turning to the computer. The introduction continues with some nonclinical small talk to establish a human connection. In addition to the usual greeting and introduction phase (see Chapter 3), we recommend explicitly introducing the computer in an effort to help the patient understand why it is being used during the visit. Although this practice may become obsolete as computers become more commonplace in the exam or hospital room, this step remains valuable for reducing communication barriers caused by the use of the EHR.

SETTING THE AGENDA

Dr. Kumar works with the computer right away by using summarizing statements and briefly touch-typing the agenda as it is created. Dr. Kumar first asks for the patient's concerns, which include elevated blood sugar, some fatigue, and the need for prescription refills. Then Dr. Kumar adds his own agenda items, which may include the arthritis pain and a flu shot for today's visit. Dr. Kumar maintains eye contact with Ms. Hampton when not typing and pauses to allow time for Ms. Hampton to respond.

Agreement on a visit agenda between patient and clinician helps in both outpatient practice and inpatient settings (see Chapter 3). In our example, Dr. Kumar forms a relationship with the patient as he collaborates on the agenda, while simultaneously managing the computer. This step may seem awkward at first, but can ultimately lead to improved satisfaction and time efficiency.

OPENING THE HISTORY OF PRESENT ILLNESS

After creating an agenda, Dr. Kumar explores the first topic. While Ms. Hampton speaks, Dr. Kumar makes periodic eye contact, nodding his head and looking at the computer occasionally while typing. Dr. Kumar explains his use of the computer with statements such as, "I'm looking up your lab results." Lastly, Dr. Kumar provides a brief verbal summary of what he typed so that Ms. Hampton knows he was listening.

Real-time typing helps save clinicians time. Doing this while minimizing screen gaze is challenging. Often clinicians use scribes, dictation programs to minimize typing, or master touch-typing skills. The clinician must use eye contact to observe for a patient's potential emotion or distress. If we are always gazing at the computer, we can miss this key aspect of relationship building. Active listening skills—including continuers, echoing statements, short requests, and short summaries (see Chapter 4)—can all accompany typing on the computer. We can also use signposting, where we tell the patient what we are doing as we transition to the computer to type or look up data points. When Dr. Kumar says, "I'm looking up your lab results," he is still attending to Ms. Hampton while letting her know that he is making a shift to the computer. Finally, Dr. Kumar reads back what he has written and then turns and looks at Ms. Hampton to ensure accuracy and demonstrate active listening.

BUILDING THE RELATIONSHIP

Ms. Hampton has known Dr. Kumar for a long time and confides in him today that she feels sad and alone. She is tearful as she relates this to Dr. Kumar, who moves his chair away from the computer and closer to Ms. Hampton in order to look at her directly. Dr. Kumar will type this part into the EHR after the visit or while Ms. Hampton is getting onto the exam table.

Empathy given both verbally and nonverbally is therapeutic and improves patient satisfaction and adherence (see Chapter 4). Conversely, the EHR has been shown to obstruct connections with our patients and negatively impact emotions. When a patient opens up and begins talking about something emotional, research has emphasized that we can make a strong connection with our patients and show support by removing our hands from the technology, pushing the monitor away, and moving our bodies and eyes toward the patient to offer our undivided attention.[17]

SHARING DECISION-MAKING AND INFORMATION

As the visit comes to a close, Dr. Kumar turns the computer screen to Ms. Hampton. On the screen is a graph showing that her HbA1C has increased slowly over the past year. They strategize on how to control her blood sugars and discuss increasing her medication.

The computer can help provide additional educational support for the treatment plan. It is important that we verify literacy, primary language, and visual acuity to optimize computer use. Examples of what the EHR can provide at this stage include preloaded patient handouts (or website references) and information about community support services, medication side effects, and follow-up appointments. Prepopulating the computer using commercial and public sources will make this step more efficient. When we reposition the screen closer to patients and point to relevant areas, they can learn important medical facts while gaining a feeling of collaboration. In this mode, we can also use the computer to decide on a treatment or care plan. Research has shown that when we involve patients in treatment planning, it improves their adherence and outcomes (see Chapter 5).

CLOSURE

As Ms. Hampton and Dr. Kumar arrive at a plan for the next visit, Dr. Kumar asks Ms. Hampton to state what she understood the plan to be, and Dr. Kumar types Ms. Hampton's words into the after-visit summary. As the clinician visit ends, Dr. Kumar introduces a medical assistant to review the written information about diet and to reinforce the goals that Ms. Hampton and Dr. Kumar have discussed. Dr. Kumar leaves the room and takes about four minutes to complete the visit note. He then previews the next patient's chart, and the cycle repeats with the goal of maximizing patient care and lessening the burden of documentation.

There are three major goals in closing the visit: checking understanding, arranging follow-up, and providing support (see Chapter 5). The computer is useful in providing clear follow-up instructions, printouts of disease management information, information on medications, and referrals. All of this information can be easily printed and handed to the patient by the clinician or someone on the staff team. In addition, some organizations provide follow-up support with patient care portals for communication via the EHR. Communication on portals can include the patient's follow-up questions or concerns, important health information, and copies of test results.

The Future

In order to improve healthcare experiences for patients and clinicians alike, it is critical that we teach trainees and experienced clinicians relationship-centered communication strategies to manage computer use. The EHR comes with obstacles. Overcoming them requires a commitment to more research (such as time-and-motion studies to evaluate the effectiveness of interventions), use of scribes or advanced care teams in redistributing the work of the EHR, and innovations in improving technology platforms that decrease the burden of documentation for the clinician.

Conclusion

The strategies discussed in this chapter are concise, skills-based, and supported by research. They include: ensuring proper setup of the exam room, previewing the chart, greeting the patient before going to the EHR, minimizing screen gaze during the encounter, intentionally turning to the patient during emotional or complicated interactions, and when possible, using signposting or nonverbal cues to stay connected with the patient during the interview. At the end of the interview, steps to simplify closure and document clear follow-up include sharing on-screen information with the patient and preloading disease and medication information. These skills will help clinicians manage computer technology while simultaneously engaging in more meaningful face-to-face time with patients.

CHAPTER 8

Patient Engagement and Motivational Interviewing

Think about a New Year's resolution or any behavior that you have considered changing (or someone has suggested that you consider changing) over the last year. What is it? Time management? Driving habits? Organizing finances? Exercising more regularly?

Whatever that behavior is, pause now and think through the overall situation for a minute as if you were explaining it to a good friend. What's going on? What problems is the behavior causing? What have you tried?

The situation is likely complicated, and you might have some mixed feelings about it. You would like to do things differently, but where to start? What to do? Or maybe you know what to do, but the effort of adjusting just isn't a priority right now. Your situation might not be a life-or-death health issue, but we're guessing that it impacts the quality of your life to some degree, or you wouldn't have thought of it.

Now turn your mind to someone close to you—a family member, friend, or colleague—whose behavior you wish would change. Maybe it's unhealthy, unsafe, or just generally annoying.

Given the other person's behavior or your own, which one do you think you have a better chance of influencing?

We're going to assume you said your own—if you didn't, this might be a long, tough chapter for you. And yet, even as the person in the driver's seat of your own behavior, you recognize how challenging change is.

Have you ever heard of motivational interviewing (MI)? It is an evidence-based skill that engages people in their own health. Motivational interviewing asks you to humbly set aside your expert role and knowledge in order to explore problems and activate change from the patient's viewpoint. In this sense, MI facilitates a human-to-human connection through reflective listening, and guides the patient in devising his or her own plan, rather than relying on you to problem-solve. We will review the basic elements of MI with the hope that you will finish the chapter with enough direction and inspiration to start practicing these skills, if even just for yourself!

Motivational Interviewing

Most of us have endured years of training, testing, and expense to assure competence. Yet how often have you had the following conversation?

> YOU: Mr. James, have you ever considered cutting down on or quitting smoking?
>
> MR. JAMES: No.
>
> YOU: Well, if you don't stop, you increase your risk for heart attack, cancer, and stroke. You don't want that, do you?
>
> MR. JAMES: Heavens, no! Thank you so much for caring enough to say something. That information really scares me. I want to quit right away. How can you help me?

If only people were so malleable! Other people don't change when, how, and why we want them to. They change when, how, and why *they* want to. And if it's not a change they're interested in making, they generally don't appreciate our years of experience, brilliant advice, and hearts of gold. A consultant for organizational change once said, "People don't resist change. They resist being changed."[1] That's why the very first thing we need to do is take off our clinical hats and set our agendas aside. This first step is absolutely the hardest part.

Motivational interviewing requires different skills than what our data-driven, "I know the answer" training conditioned us for. Specifically, MI is "a collaborative conversational style for strengthening a person's own motivation and commitment to change."[2] This style of conversation, like all communication, relies on both context and content. Here, the context refers to leveling the relationship through a collaborative stance and recognizing that the other person must generate his or her own solutions, no matter how informed and well-intended your suggestions might be. In other words:

> Acknowledging a person's freedom of choice typically
> diminishes defensiveness and can facilitate change. This
> involves letting go of the idea and burden that you have to
> (or can) make people change. It is, in essence, relinquishing
> a power that you never had in the first place.[3]

It is not uncommon for clinicians to nod politely at these principles and then wrestle terribly with their egos and training, realizing that neither offers much value to patients who just need to have the right conversation to figure things out for themselves. Let's face it: we all want to feel helpful and appear competent. With MI, we still can, but in a different, more satisfying way for both clinicians and our patients.

The content in an MI conversation, on the other hand, acknowledges that specific phrases and strategies make a difference in guiding and promoting change. The next two sections review context and content more fully, referring to them in the MI language of "spirit" and "technique."

SPIRIT

We've all seen kids offer forced apologies that sound like the most hate-filled, annoyed "I'm saw-REE" ever. That's what this section is about. When we have an MI conversation, the spirit of the approach must be congruent. Motivational interviewing is not so much a series of guided conversational techniques as it is the spirit of "we're in this together, and I'm right here with you." Without the spirit of MI backing our comments, the techniques below could easily morph into benevolent manipulation or, worse, a really insincere playground reconciliation. The good news is, like many things, the more we mindfully embrace the spirit of MI, the more intuitive and comfortable it feels.

According to authors William Miller and Stephen Rollnick, four interrelated attitudinal elements are necessary for MI "spirit." These essential elements are: collaboration, acceptance, compassion, and evocation.[4]

Often, when the clinician despairs with, "I don't know what to do! They need X and I'm trained in Y," *collaboration* is the solution. Since our patients are the experts of their own experiences, we don't have to know how to fix their problems. Our role is to support them to figure out how to fix it for themselves.

Acceptance, which acknowledges the person without judgment, does not always come easily. For instance, due to my own experiences, I (Krista Hirschmann) find myself having a strong internal reaction toward parents who smoke in front of their children. While I may not accept that behavior, I can accept a stressed, working mother trying to relax her nerves in the fastest, most convenient way possible.

Miller and Rollnick define the third element, *compassion*, as preparing to do what is in the best interest of others and not ourselves. The demands of the healthcare system and the experiences we witness sometimes place extreme stress on our ability to care compassionately for others and can lead to "compassion fatigue."

The fourth element, *evocation*, recalibrates our compassion by drawing out the good reasons people have for "bad" behavior. Or, in less judgmental language, we all have good reasons for sustaining our current choices. The next section describes some basic ways to accomplish evocation.

Collectively, these four elements comprise an authentic stance that will best position us to be fully present and supportive listeners, while positioning our patients for success. Not to worry, though, if our MI spirit is more "saw-REE" and less "rah-rah-sis-boom-bah." Self-acceptance and self-compassion are a terrific place to start—and sometimes that takes some time.

TECHNIQUE

Given that MI originated within the mental health and recovery field, it's no surprise that the full technique embraces robust and unhurried reflective discussion. It's also no surprise that the time to do so is what most clinicians don't have. This section on technique provides an overview of the core skills associated with MI, as well as a distilled strategy to use in the busy office setting.

The Core Skills

In addition to embracing the intended spirit of MI, there are four steps, or stages of conversation, to negotiate with the patient. They are: engage, focus, elicit, and plan. The advantage of recognizing each distinct step is that the process can be divided into discrete conversations over the course of several office visits.

The first step, to **engage** the patient, relies heavily on using open-ended questions to encourage talk that is important to the other person's experiences. When we welcome the person to share, new issues often come to light and offer insight into the situation.

Typical open-ended questions for MI include:

- "What are your thoughts on X?"
- "Tell me more."
- "What's a typical example?"
- "Please share a time you tried to change your behavior."

Responding to the answers is its own subset of active listening skills. Recall from Chapter 4 that active listening means that although we may be speaking at times, our comments do not introduce new information or ideas. Rather, our responses demonstrate and confirm our ability to listen with an "inner ear," or to what the person is saying both on and below the surface. Doing so helps check any assumptions we might have, as well as making the other person feel heard and validated, thereby strengthening the relationship.

Simple reflection skills help us understand what we are hearing, while helping the patient process the information. A reflection might sound like: "You said changing behavior has been frustrating for you." In addition, intermittent affirmations and empathy acknowledge the emotional dimensions of the conversation. Such statements include:

- "That was a hard time for you."
- "Many people face that challenge. You're not alone."
- "You did the best you could."

Finally, summaries are simply a collection of reflections strung together at the end of the engagement process. These reflections pull the story together, confirm the listener has heard correctly, check to make sure that the story is complete, and ensure that the speaker appears engaged and ready to transition to the next discussion. A summary might state:

> You've shared several reasons why you'd like to quit smoking, particularly with babysitting your grandchildren, and also how hard it is for you. You've tried several times, quit for a week or two and then fallen back into old patterns, afraid of putting on extra weight. You are willing to try again, but are not sure of the best strategy to use.

This method of asking, listening, responding, and summarizing mirrors the ART (Ask, Respond, Tell) process we introduced in Chapter 5.

Once we engage a person to this point, the second step is to **focus** the conversation on a particular issue. Avoid trying to tackle multiple behavior changes (e.g., diet, exercise, and smoking) in one session. Even with smoking, focusing could mean just exploring options to quit and not actually quitting. Whatever the exact focus, we can move to the third stage and **elicit** solutions to develop a plan that must come from the person and not from us, unless we ask permission to offer a suggestion. For instance:

- "What strategies have you thought about trying?"
- "There are a few other options you haven't mentioned. Would you be open to hearing about them?"

Whatever ideas we elicit, we can **plan** (the fourth stage of conversation) for change by setting small, manageable goals that can be quickly and easily accomplished. This will build confidence and self-efficacy for the patient.

A Distilled Strategy

If the longer conversation just outlined is not possible due to time constraints, consider the following technique, which is a modified approach that still embodies the spirit of MI and introduces the strategy of engaging first through **conviction**, followed by building **confidence**. (Note that the approach encompasses skills from Chapter 5.)

To demonstrate, let's return to the example of the grandparent who continues to smoke. You could start the conversation like this:

"On a scale of 0–10, with 0 being no importance and 10 being the most important thing in your life, how important is it for you to stop smoking?"

This patient is ambivalent and responds, "Maybe 2 or 3."

You respond, "Thank you for your honesty. What makes your answer as high as a 2 or 3? Why not a 0?"

That prompt makes it difficult not to start talking about reasons to quit smoking. This patient might talk about not wanting to smoke around the grandchildren, not wanting to set a bad example for them or affect their health. After encouraging the patient to list the reasons, you can follow with: "So what would it take to move you from a 2 or 3 to a 5 or 6?"

This question helps the patient to think aspirationally, and consider other reasons to quit smoking. Far from being a Jedi mind trick, this process highlights a way for people to think about what is possible, rather than delving into excuse after excuse about why they are entrenched or have decided it's not important.

In many settings, clinicians want patients to stop smoking yesterday. Rather than pressing for behavior change now (which almost never happens), sometimes just getting a patient to think aspirationally unmires them from the tar pit. At this point, after exploring the reasons, you might re-ask the question about importance on a 0–10 scale. Any upward movement is a small victory, provided that you can follow up to reinforce the patient's reasons for change before the inexorable slide back into the pit.

If you have a bit of extra time, and the patient is engaging you, you might ask: "Let's say for a moment that you feel completely convinced that you should stop smoking—you have no doubt that it's important. On a scale of 0–10, 0 being low confidence and 10 being really high confidence, how confident are you that you could quit?"

The patient says, "Probably an 8 or 9."

"You sound pretty confident," you say. "Why as high as 8 or 9?"

The patient responds, "I'm pretty sure it's an oral fixation. If I bought those little precut carrots and put one in my mouth whenever I craved a cigarette, I think I could cut down or completely stop."

You now have a clear map of where the patient stands: not totally convinced about quitting smoking (low on conviction) but confident that it could happen once convinced (high on self-efficacy). The goal is always to increase conviction first, and then confidence, because if it's not at all important to the patient, why waste time trying? The real beauty of this method is that the patient might come up with a solution that you might never have considered, as the patient did in this true, and ultimately successful, example.

If you read nothing else about MI, keep this series of conviction/ confidence questions in mind, as it is the shortest (and quickest) form of MI you could possibly use in an office visit. You might even feel emboldened to use them in administrative meetings, i.e., "How convinced are you that this is an issue of patient safety?" or on the home front, i.e., "How convinced are you that it's important to rinse out the milk jug before tossing it in the recycling bin in a hot garage?"

Quick Recap

"Where are you on the conviction/confidence scale?" Asking what makes it as high as it is allows the patient to draw from past successes and strengths.

"What would have to happen for you to increase your score?"

In short, these questions give you a starting point for understanding your patient's perspective, what it's going to take for him or her to change—whether the patient needs information, support, or both. Motivational interviewing is like looking at a map together with the patient and having the patient (not you) mark the path.

Conclusion

You can only control you. As much as you might want MI to change your patient (or boss or spouse), MI is really meant to change you. If we, as professionals, can't accept and embrace change for ourselves, how can we expect patients to engage in change for themselves?

On that sobering note, what have you just read that appealed to you? What is one thing that you might be willing to try? How can you imagine implementing it within the next two weeks? Obviously, the spirit and assortment of techniques work best as a whole package, but MI is a big proponent of small, manageable changes. How are you willing to slightly pivot your approach with patients?

If you're not ready, that is OK, too. We appreciate you reading this far and considering the material. If and when you are ready to stop merely thinking about that New Year's resolution and to start doing something about it, just keep MI in mind as a guide for supporting your own behavior change—and maybe the behavior of others.

CHAPTER 9

Shared Decision-Making

I n Chapter 8, we talked about motivational interviewing, a process in which we start from a place of knowing what is best for the patient. For example, virtually all clinicians would agree that patients should stop smoking to improve their health. In contrast, in shared decision-making (SDM), there may be more than one right answer. Shared decision-making is the practice of eliciting a patient's informed preferences regarding a screening or treatment decision. Our goal is to help patients choose the answers that will work best for them.

Decision-making is complex. Think about a common decision we make such as buying a car. We usually do research before we go to an auto dealer. We talk to our friends about why they like their cars, do research online about the pros and cons of different models, and brainstorm the choices in our price range. We clarify what we care most about in making our decision. Do we want a hybrid? Do we need a four-wheel drive? What are the safety ratings? How cool will we look driving it? And then we get to test-drive the cars we are considering before making our purchase.

Making decisions about our health is even more difficult than buying a car. Patients are often asked to choose between multiple options when they are reeling from a new diagnosis that can represent bad news. They don't have the detailed information about the choices open to them or the risks and benefits of each. And patients can't test-drive a surgical procedure to see how well it will work for them.

That is why patients and clinicians need to work together as a team. We are the medical experts who know the evidence-based information, and patients are the experts on what matters most to them. Just as figuring out the right car purchase depends on the buyer's preferences, many decisions in healthcare involving screening tests, surgery, and chronic disease management depend on the patient's values and preferences, rather than solely on the clinician's perspective.

How Well Do Clinicians Do Shared Decision-Making?

Clinicians may feel that they're already doing effective SDM, but the evidence documents poor communication, knowledge gaps, and lack of attention to patients' preferences.[1] In one representative study, preferences were elicited from less than a fifth of patients.[2] Clinicians often think that they know a patient's preferences *without* directly asking, but research in end-of-life care, screening, and surgical decisions does not support this contention. In multiple studies, the majority of physicians simply recommended screening tests, rather than educating patients first.[3] When clinicians did attempt to educate, most discussed the pros of screening, and only a small minority presented the arguments against screening. Less than half of patients could correctly answer even one of the five knowledge questions that experts felt were essential in understanding how to make an informed treatment decision.[4] Yet in this era of transactional, rather than relationship-centered, encounters, we often find ourselves saying to a patient, "So you need a colonoscopy and a PSA test. You'll get a note from the gastroenterology clinic, and go to the lab." A lack of informed decision-making is still more the rule than the exception.

A Better Way

Care that incorporates and reflects individual patient preferences, needs, and values is a key foundation of high quality healthcare.[5] Patients who are more engaged in making decisions about their health have better health outcomes and healthcare experiences.[6] As we focus specifically on skills for shared decision-making, it is useful to have a structure like the Three Talk model with its team talk, option talk, and decision talk phases.[7]

SHARED DECISION-MAKING: A MODEL FOR CLINICAL PRACTICE

Although conversations with patients are rarely linear and one may need to go through the different parts more than once, the model shown in Figure 9.1 provides a useful roadmap.

FIGURE 9.1 Three Talk Model

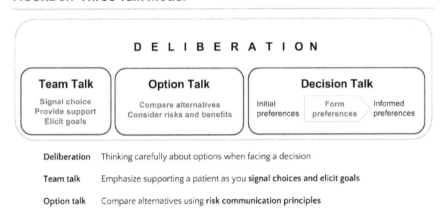

Deliberation	Thinking carefully about options when facing a decision
Team talk	Emphasize supporting a patient as you **signal choices and elicit goals**
Option talk	Compare alternatives using **risk communication principles**
Decision talk	Elicit **preferences** and **integrate** into next steps

Used with permission. ©2017 Dartmouth Shared Decision Making Center.

Team Talk

The team talk phase is where you can invite the patient to be on the same team with you. We know that even well-educated, wealthy professionals are often intimidated in a clinician's office or the hospital. Patients worry their care will suffer if they are not deferential or if they disagree with the clinician. Real teamwork is not possible in such a setting.

With some awareness, though, it's fairly easy to create a collaborative environment. To convey the importance of working together as a team, you might say something like:

> Now that we have a diagnosis, we are facing a decision and need to figure out what to do next. Fortunately, we have options. While I know the science about the options, you

are the expert on what matters to you. Different treatments have different risks and benefits. I want to understand what matters most to you. I need your help in that. Working together, we can make the best decision for you.

Option Talk

During the option talk phase, you will elicit and clarify patients' preferences and explain the benefits and risks of the different options. Once they understand the tradeoffs of the different screening or treatment options, patients often state more clearly what is most important to them. Your job is to understand patients' ideas, values, and unique life circumstances in order to help them make the decision that is best for them. We'll delve more into this more complex phase in the risk communication and decision aids sections below.

Decision Talk

The third phase, decision talk, will take place once a patient understands the pros and cons of the options, and the clinician has heard their informed preferences, as shown in the following case history:

> Ms. Parker was a formerly healthy Army nurse when she was diagnosed with early stage breast cancer. Medical literature confirmed that either a mastectomy or a lumpectomy with radiation would have very similar outcomes for her.[8]
>
> After hearing her options and the risks and benefits of each, Ms. Parker was extremely clear about her choice. She definitely wanted to preserve her breast and chose to have a lumpectomy. I (Nan Cochran) sent a letter to her surgeon clearly explaining her preference to have a lumpectomy. However, he used a paternalistic approach and told her she had to have a mastectomy, which she reluctantly underwent. When I saw her again two months later, she was clinically depressed. She refused to allow her husband to see her disfiguring scar, and they no longer had a sexual relationship. She tearfully complained, "I was mutilated." She felt like her life had been destroyed, because her preferences had not been respected.

Ms. Parker's story painfully describes the "preference misdiagnosis" epidemic,[9] which is unfortunately very common in U.S. healthcare. Key domains of medical professionalism include a respect for patient autonomy and a willingness to be sensitive and responsive to differences in our patients, including the diversity of their values and preferences. Yet in medicine, there is still a widespread assumption that the right decision is a matter of science alone. Instead, we need to ask patients, "What is most important to you in making this decision?" Patients often have *multiple* values, so follow that question with: "And what else is important?"

Decisions regarding a wide range of healthcare issues vary depending on the individual patient's attitudes, life circumstances, and preferences. For example, treatments for hip or knee osteoarthritis are preference-based decisions. Focusing on severe knee osteoarthritis illustrates this point clearly. Patients who want to maintain an active lifestyle or don't want to take medications regularly may be very interested in having a knee replacement to improve their symptoms. Another patient, with equally severe symptoms but who is risk averse or less active, may choose to continue taking medicines and be totally unwilling to consider a knee replacement. If clinicians do not fully elicit patient preferences, or if they fail to inform patients of the pros and cons of each treatment option, patients may feel forced into a decision, like Ms. Parker, that is contrary to their wishes. Clinicians wrongly assume that patients will speak up if they disagree with a recommendation.[10] Patients must be fully informed and engaged in the decision-making process in order to make the decision that is right for them. This is where Option Talk is critical—and why it is not easy.

Risk Communication

Medical research is difficult to translate transparently, especially when working with patients challenged by health literacy. Numbers are rarely discussed with patients. However, when we use qualitative and vague terms such as "infection is rare" or "it is unlikely you will have serious side effects," patients tend to overestimate benefit and underestimate risks.[11] Younger and better-educated patients desire more information and a greater role in decision-making and are more satisfied and adherent when they receive this.[12]

It is critical to provide risk and benefit information to patients in clear, easily understood language. Those challenged by health literacy will understand information better when it is accompanied by graphics and pictures.[13] High-quality decision aids can present medical data in an understandable format using language that is less confusing to patients.

Decision Aids

Decision aids bridge the comprehension gap between patients and clinicians. These are written, video-based, or online tools designed to communicate unbiased, easily understandable, and up-to-date evidence about treatment or screening options to patients. More than 115 trials of decision aids including more than 34,000 patients, addressing 23 different screening or treatment decisions, have consistently demonstrated that these aids provide patients with greater knowledge about treatment options, more accurate risk perceptions, and greater comfort with their decisions. Decision aids also lead to high participation in decision-making and leave fewer patients undecided.[14] An example of a decision aid to treat osteoporosis, authored by the Mayo Shared Decision-Making Center, is depicted in Figure 9.2.[15]

Let's walk through this decision aid together. But before we do, you need a little extra background.

Think about an elderly person you know who has fallen and broken a hip, or one who cannot straighten their back and has to walk with a hunched-over gait. Both of these problems are likely due to osteoporosis, which is a weakening of the bones that is common in the elderly. The reason clinicians want to treat osteoporosis is to reduce the risk of broken bones: half of all elderly people who suffer hip fractures die within one year.

Now consider the case of Ms. Johansson, a 65-year-old woman of Swedish descent who broke her wrist in a fall several years ago. Because of her age and history of a broken bone, she has two risk factors for osteoporosis. This means she is in the "elevated risk" category for another fracture in the future.

In the leftmost panel of Figure 9.2, you can see that roughly 20 percent of women like Ms. Johansson will break a bone over the next 10 years. Clinicians typically look at this information, think the risk

FIGURE 9.2 Osteoporosis Decision Aid

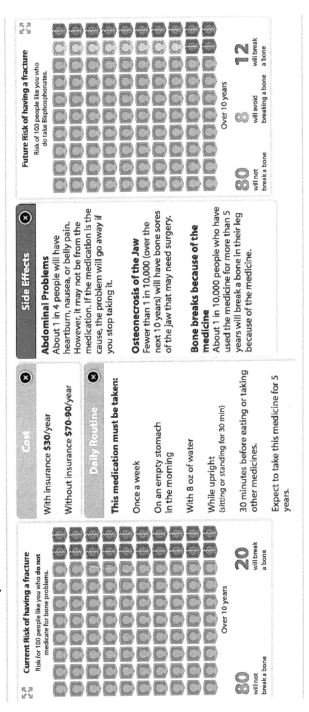

is really high, and try to convince Ms. Johansson she needs to take a medicine to decrease her risk.

A shared decision-making conversation, using the decision aid, would look very different. If clinicians review information on a decision aid that displays treatment options using graphics and pictures, patients understand their risks better. As Ms. Johansson's clinician, you might say:

> "Let's look at the benefits and downsides of taking a new medicine to treat your osteoporosis. The left side of the figure tells us in 100 women just like you who do not take additional medicine, 20 will break a bone due to osteoporosis over the next 10 years, and 80 will not.
>
> "The right side of the figure shows how many people will benefit if they take medication regularly to treat osteoporosis. You can see that in this group, out of the 20 who would have broken a bone, 12 will still break a bone in the next 10 years. So 8 women in 100 will avoid having a fracture." Then pause and elicit questions from the patient.
>
> "We also need to talk about the downsides of medicine for your osteoporosis, since all medicines have side effects. In the middle of this figure are the cost and the most common harms of the medication."

The decision aid does not tell a patient what to do. After reviewing a decision aid, clinicians should routinely ask, "What is most important to you in making this decision?" This is probably the most important question, and it demonstrates the crux of shared decision-making. Our goal as clinicians in these instances is to be agnostic in our recommendations for these decisions to our patients, not to make the final decision for them. Having a detailed understanding of a patient's preferences and life circumstances is therefore essential to help them make the best decision.

Conclusion

This chapter reviewed aspects of team talk, option talk, and decision talk that are important facets of successful shared decision-making. We need to learn to work with patients as members of the same team in order to understand their values and to help inform them to make the best medical decisions possible. We have illustrated the chapter with some important tools, but shared decision-making involves substantially more than just providing decision aids to patients. These tools are only adjuncts to our counseling. Many challenges persist in educating clinicians about using these techniques, and implementation of SDM in typical practice settings remains burdensome despite its clear benefits. Modifying systems of care, developing more numerous and widely available decision aids, and training other team members to help patients with preference-sensitive decisions are all essential steps in working toward providing high-quality care using a relationship-centered approach.

CHAPTER 10

Feedback: A Commitment to the Relationship

E very day of our lives, we give and receive feedback. Reactions to feedback range from joy and pride to disdain and defensiveness. For example, your younger sibling might ask you for advice on a resume she is submitting for a new job. When you offer pointers, she may be very receptive and appreciative of your feedback. Conversely, your partner might offer a backhanded compliment on the dinner you just prepared, and you might retaliate with an off-the-cuff comment on how he or she loaded the dishwasher.

In these everyday settings (as well as in professional settings), how we interact with each other when we give or receive feedback can greatly influence the quality of our relationships. In a healthcare system increasingly driven by outcomes, we risk overemphasizing our ends without nurturing or even examining our means. The process of feedback is core to any system's success. On a human level, providing periodic, authentic, and useful feedback is key to a healthy work and learning environment. Just as reactions to feedback may vary, individuals may also have varied understandings of what feedback means. Some may view feedback strictly as judgmental criticism, while others may see it as an opportunity for growth.

Here, we define effective feedback as specific, nonjudgmental information, comparing a person's performance with a standard, given with the intent to improve performance.[1] We are constantly providing feedback to others, consciously or unconsciously, skillfully or carelessly.

Misunderstandings and conflicts often occur when we interpret other people's actions as implicit feedback on our performance. Being intentional in our feedback conversations is critical to our success as team members, healthcare clinicians, and educators.

You can also think about feedback as a way of strengthening a commitment to the relationship. If I care about a professional relationship (or a personal relationship, for that matter), giving authentic reinforcing and constructive feedback means I am invested in the other person's success. With this in mind, feedback conversations can be transformed from something that we dread into something that deepens our connection with others. In this chapter, we will demonstrate how to use relationship-centered communication skills as a framework for giving feedback that helps nurture relationships in healthcare work environments.

Consider this scenario:

> Mr. Wilson is a medical assistant in a busy ambulatory practice. The practice institutes a prescription-refill workflow where medical assistants triage refill requests and route them within the electronic health record to the appropriate clinicians. Clinicians, who had previously been handling refills, love the new system because it frees up their time for other clinical tasks. Patients love the new system because their prescriptions are available sooner. Mr. Wilson, however, is feeling exhausted. In between rooming patients, he is frantically routing prescription refill requests and falling behind. Meanwhile, Dr. Garcia, who has been working with Mr. Wilson for years, has noticed his declining performance and feels frustrated that she continually has to room patients herself to pick up the slack. They both notice that their social conversations, which used to be quite rich, have become less frequent and are almost exclusively business-related. After a busy clinic where Dr. Garcia roomed two of her own patients, she is feeling particularly frustrated and decides to provide Mr. Wilson with some feedback.

Feedback is often given in reaction to something that has or has not been achieved. In the above scenario, Dr. Garcia is reacting to Mr. Wilson's inability to room patients in a timely manner. Right before the feedback exchange, both the doctor and the medical assistant are feeling frustrated and at odds. As a result of their emotional states, the subsequent feedback conversation may go poorly.

Well before starting such a conversation, the individuals might consider engaging in a more useful form of feedback that prioritizes their relationship while offering an opportunity for a successful dialogue. The relationship-centered model of communication can help to inform a rational approach to hosting such a feedback conversation in three steps that mirror the three fundamental communication skill sets (see Chapters 3–5). We will start by setting up the conversation for success in the context of the relationship. Then we move to observation, where we gather information. Only then do we provide the actual feedback, beginning with reinforcing feedback and moving to constructive feedback. After the feedback exchange, we discuss next steps, which are the new goals going forward.

Setup: What You Put in Is What You Get Out

Before offering someone feedback, we must first establish a relationship with that person and intentionally set up the conversation for success. This may seem like a lot of extra work, but it makes a huge difference in how the feedback is received. If you were to go to dinner with a friend, it would be off-putting if you insisted on going to the restaurant of your choice and then told your friend what food to order. In fact, you probably wouldn't be invited to have dinner again anytime soon. A more relational approach would involve getting your friend's input, discussing your preferences, and perhaps agreeing on entrées to share so you can both sample different menu options. During this process, you might even learn something about one another that you didn't know before. Effective feedback conversations are not all that dissimilar from this scenario. The setup is when we set the agenda for the professional relationship (see Chapter 3) and where preferences and expectations are shared on both ends (see Chapter 4). For this approach to be successful, we must address the potential need for confidentiality and make sure the other person is ready to talk.

Let's go back to our story of Mr. Wilson and Dr. Garcia. Before providing any feedback, Dr. Garcia might first set up the conversation by checking in with Mr. Wilson about how he is handling the recent changes: "It seems like there is a lot going on right now in terms of changes in the clinic. Do you have some time to sit in the break room to talk?" Once they are both seated, she can ask, "How has all this been for you?" She might learn that Mr. Wilson is feeling really stretched thin in terms of his workload. In fact, he is feeling disconnected from the patients, given all of the refills, which is quite distressing to him. In addition, his son is going through a hard time in school because of a learning disability, and Mr. Wilson needs to get home right after his shift to help with some tutoring that his son desperately needs. Given this context, Dr. Garcia could then ask what Mr. Wilson's expectations and goals are for himself in terms of his work. Mr. Wilson shares that he really wants to be more focused on the patients (instead of the refills) because he really enjoys that part of his job. He also states that he wants to leave on time in order to be available to his son. Here is an opportunity for Dr. Garcia to express empathy via PEARLS (see Chapter 4), saying something like: "Sounds like this has been a tough time for you. I really respect your commitment to our patients and your son." Now, having heard Mr. Wilson's perspective, Dr. Garcia can share her expectations of Mr. Wilson: "I also want to run on time and prioritize our patients. I would like to partner with you to find a way to make that happen." By generating a shared understanding and identifying goals upon which both can agree, the ensuing feedback conversation will be grounded in their relationship and shared alliance. The next step, then, is to observe skillfully.

Observation, Part I: You Can't Improve What You Don't Measure

Feedback is based entirely on data. Therefore, honing our observation skills is critical to being effective in our communication. Emotions create intensity that can get in the way of observation. As emotional beings, to paraphrase award-winning novelist Toni Morrison, it's often easier to remember how somebody made us feel than what that person said or did. In delivering effective feedback, it is critical that we focus not on emotions but on specific activities and behaviors we observed. Emotionally, Dr. Garcia is frustrated. She may feel tempted to blame Mr. Wilson for the clinic running behind schedule and could be thinking, *You don't know how to do your job!* The truth is, however, Mr. Wilson knows exactly how to do his job (and is actually quite good at it), but the circumstances have created a difficult situation. If Dr. Garcia leads with judgment and emotion, Mr. Wilson could easily recoil and the conversation could quickly spiral downward. Dr. Garcia's task is to distill what she observed and share that information with Mr. Wilson with as little judgment as possible. This might seem obvious, but it can prove quite challenging in practice and takes some getting used to. For example, instead of focusing on how she feels, Dr. Garcia might simply note that their second patient of the day showed up on time and waited for 15 minutes after being checked in, after which Dr. Garcia went to the waiting room and brought the patient into the exam room herself. This critical step of data-gathering cannot be overlooked, as the ensuing conversation needs to focus, at least initially, on the observed behavior. Once they identify and agree on the behavior, she can discuss the impact of that behavior (how she felt about it), which they can then process together.

Observation, Part II: Believing Is Seeing

You may have experienced the phenomenon where you learn about something new (e.g., a word, book, or TV show) and then suddenly, you are hearing about it all the time, seemingly out of nowhere. Although it may be coincidence, it is more likely that you have been, as neuroscientists describe it, "primed." Consider a medical student who is flagged as "a risk" because he or she comes from an underprivileged background and holds a degree from a college not known for its academic rigor. Undue and constant scrutiny of his or her performance reveals some deficiencies, but nothing that wouldn't otherwise be discovered in other students under the same scrutiny. However, because the observers have been primed, they are only seeing those behaviors in that specific student and not in others. What is seen must be compared to an objective standard that is applied to all.

The opposite is also true with the so-called "halo effect." Observers may come to believe that a trainee is particularly skilled based on initial, often brief, and sometimes biased exposure. When the observer evaluates the trainee, he or she may write up an unduly positive report despite evidence to the contrary. In this instance, the trainee can do no wrong and wears that sought-after halo.

Dr. Garcia would be well-served to notice some of the things that Mr. Wilson is doing effectively. Although she has recently been focusing on Mr. Wilson's lack of efficiency, she could also notice a couple of other things. For example, several of their patients have brought gifts specifically for Mr. Wilson over the holidays because of his relationship with them. Recently, he went to a different floor to bring down a wheelchair for an elderly patient who needed help getting to the lab. These pieces of information are important and will help to continue to build a relationship between Mr. Wilson and Dr. Garcia in the next phase.

Reinforcing Feedback: Without It, Good Performance May Decrease

Everyone loves praise, even if they say they don't—the better if it is specific. There is immense power in being recognized. Giving voice to those behaviors provides important reinforcement as well as implicit respect for the other person. Studies suggest that a 4:1 ratio of reinforcing to corrective feedback is a good benchmark for calibrating how much feedback to provide (in healthy marriages it is closer to 5:1).[2] Instead of singularly focusing on problems in our relationships, we need to give a healthy dose of authentic reinforcing feedback before even a single piece of corrective feedback is provided.

You will notice that thus far, we haven't mentioned "positive" or "negative" feedback. This is intentional. As discussed earlier, divorcing ourselves as much as possible from judgment and judgmental language is critical. If we use the term "negative feedback," one could argue that feedback is something to be ashamed of. Instead, if we focus on actionable behaviors, both parties can move away from judgment and blame to focus on solutions. Conversations can then follow a "keep-stop-start" framework, moving from reinforcing feedback (i.e., keep doing) to constructive feedback (i.e., stop doing) and then to next steps (i.e., start doing).

Additionally, using the ART (Ask, Respond, Tell) skill from Chapter 5 at each stage can be particularly useful.

In the conversation between Dr. Garcia and Mr. Wilson, Dr. Garcia decides first to ask Mr. Wilson what he thinks he is doing effectively. In his typical self-deprecating fashion, because he is having a tough time, Mr. Wilson can't really come up with much that he is proud of and instead focuses on his deficiencies. Instead of allowing the conversation to go straight to constructive elements, here Dr. Garcia can highlight some of the key behaviors that she authentically values in Mr. Wilson's performance. She responds (the R of ART) by saying, "There is actually quite a bit that I can think of that I appreciate about your work." She then tells (the T of ART) her perspective by sharing how much their patients value him as evidenced by their gifts and his commitment to helping those in need. Dr. Garcia is providing a much-needed boost to Mr. Wilson. More important, she is deepening their professional relationship. By simply sharing that she noticed and values these behaviors, she is implicitly stating her alliance with him. Mr. Wilson will be more receptive to the constructive feedback that is coming and will be more likely to view the feedback as coming from a place of shared values rather than judgment.

Constructive Feedback: Courage Is What It Takes to Sit Down and Listen

Having effectively laid the groundwork, now is the time to provide the constructive feedback. Asking for a self-assessment here (as in the prior section using ART) can be very powerful. By starting with an Ask, such as, "What would you like to do differently going forward?," one can understand what level of insight the person has about his or her performance. Mr. Wilson might answer, "I feel badly that I fell behind in rooming patients today, and I know this has happened before. I am sorry about this. I really want to do better." Here, Mr. Wilson is keenly aware of where his performance fell short. Dr. Garcia then can respond (the R of ART again) with something like, "Sounds like you are really struggling with competing tasks in the clinic." Then telling her own perspective (the T in ART): "I agree, let's talk about some possible solutions" before transitioning to next steps.

If, however, this is a blind spot for the other (as is commonly the case), then pausing and asking about intention may be useful before providing the corrective feedback. For example, when asked by Dr. Garcia about what he would like to do differently, Mr. Wilson might answer that he really doesn't see anything wrong with how the clinic session went. Here, Dr. Garcia might ask, "I see. I am curious then what your intention was when you were at your computer, and Mr. Smith was checked in and was waiting?" Here, Mr. Wilson has the opportunity then to share that he was trying to complete needed work on his computer and hadn't realized the patient had been waiting for 15 minutes. At this point, Dr. Garcia can then share how Mr. Wilson's behavior has impacted her (highlighting how his intention differed from its impact on her). "I am hearing that your intention was to address the medication refills. The impact, however, was that the patient got to the exam room with a delay, and as you know, I can get frustrated with delays."

Next Steps: Setting the Next Agenda

Setting the next agenda is the real payoff. Here is the opportunity to set new goals and expectations, just as was done in the setup. As the relationship builds, the goals may become more nuanced, ambitious, and deep. Possibilities may emerge that were not explored or even considered before. Moreover, when new challenges arise, the strength of the relationship will provide greater resilience to navigate those challenges.

Returning to our earlier scenario:

> Mr. Wilson responds to Dr. Garcia, "I am sorry to hear that you were frustrated. I am frustrated, too. I want our clinic to run more smoothly, but I can't seem to find the time to do the refills and room the patients."

Dr. Garcia responds, "That actually makes a lot of sense. I hadn't realized that the clinic leadership was having you do that while you were rooming patients. I'd like to bring this up at our next team meeting to see if we can find a solution. In the short term, do you have any thoughts on how we can make this work better?"

Mr. Wilson replies, "Maybe I can focus on rooming patients initially and only work on the refills if there is a no-show. Then, once all the patients are roomed, I can spend some time getting as many refills as possible done."

"That sounds like a good short-term plan. I will be sure to circle back to you after our next team meeting. In the mean-time, let me know when you need to get home to your son. Know that I am rooting for you and for him."

"Thanks, Dr. Garcia. That means a lot."

Now, they are clear on what their agenda will be for their next encounter and, more important, have deepened their connection with each other.

Conclusion

Skills useful for developing relationships with patients (see Chapters 3–5) also apply to feedback. By using a relationship-centered approach, difficult conversations can be changed into productive, empathic conversations. Our team members and colleagues are our most valuable assets in providing care. Building our relationships with them while continuing to improve the quality of care is key to making a productive and enjoyable work environment.

CHAPTER 11

Appreciative Coaching: "I Want to Be Known as the Clinician Who . . ."

n his *New Yorker* article "Personal Best," surgeon and author Dr. Atul Gawande describes his experience with coaching after he asked a colleague to observe his surgical technique.[1] Any physician—or anyone who knows a physician—recognizes that this is a highly uncommon and unusually humble thing for a practicing physician to do. As physicians, we are trained to appear confident at all times and to never admit errors. Why would we need coaching?

Dr. Gawande notes that because of his Yoda-esque mentor's observations, he made important adjustments for procedures with which Dr. Gawande was already highly familiar. Though his mentor had no training in Dr. Gawande's specialty, he offered some very useful insights into the process of setting up a case, ensuring an optimal surgical environment, and avoiding common pitfalls. Dr. Gawande concludes that "coaching done well may be the most effective intervention designed for human performance." If an experienced surgeon can learn new strategies from a coach for further improvement, imagine what could happen if all clinicians were equally open to feedback. Let's talk about the most common activity in medicine: communication with patients. Although communication happens all the time across every medical specialty, many of us don't give our communications skills or strategies much thought. When we become willing to be coached in better communication practices, everyone benefits.

Core Requirements for a Coach

Some of the most successful coaches in history have not been the most renowned performers. In 2016, Joe Maddon managed the Chicago Cubs to their first World Series victory in 108 years. With a combination of strategic fielding decisions and wacky team-building stunts like making players wear pajamas on airplanes, he pushed them out of their comfort zones and won accolades for his genius and skill. Yet he never made it to the major league as a player.[2]

Similarly, coaches for clinicians in healthcare do not necessarily need to undergo training as clinicians themselves. Mr. Maddon shows us that knowledge, observational ability, and motivational skills can inspire high performers toward even higher accomplishments. Coaches who lack medical training bring a valuable perspective to the table—the patient's perspective. This can be highly beneficial as long as coaches remember that all patients won't necessarily have the same needs and wants as they do.

The recipe for the most effective healthcare communication coaches calls for several important ingredients:

- Empathy and ability to modulate one's own emotions
- Familiarity with organizational change management
- A framework for appreciative coaching

Before we jump right into the framework, let's start with the first two elements.

Empathy and the Ability to Modulate One's Own Emotions

In my (Maysel Kemp White's) training as a family therapist, I learned that I did not have to love the people that I was counseling, some of whom were abusing their children. What I did need to do was develop empathy for them. Over time, I came to believe that people are always doing the best they can with their current resources and limitations. I had to suspend my personal judgments of their behavior, be present for the person who was seeking my guidance, and validate his or her experience. The same is true for those I coach; in order to be effective, I must be present for each learner.

In decades of working with clinicians, coaches have found that essentially all of us as medical professionals hope to be known for our caring toward our patients. We want to do the right thing at the right time. After all, these traits are what drew many of us to healthcare in the first place. When it seems that we are falling short of these objectives, telling us that it seems like we don't care only invites defenses. Coaches need to honor our attempts, while helping us gain the skills to adjust our behavior so that we can effectively express our caring. There may be times when a coach observes a behavior in someone he or she is coaching that feels startlingly unexpected. For example, a coach may notice that a clinician is blithely and unwittingly sharing information with a patient's family without noticing the family's clear evidence of distress. Coaches are most effective when they are able first to understand their own reactions to what occurred, and then share their emotions and perspective afterward in an evenhanded way.

Familiarity with Organizational Change Management

A coach's ability to succeed also depends on the ability of the consulting organization to express its commitment to improvement in a growth-oriented, rather than punitive, way. Few of us are as courageous as Dr. Gawande, who sought his own coach. Healthcare systems commonly send clinicians to a coach when their patient experience scores fall below the institution's average. Even though the intent is to help struggling clinicians, when we are told that we need to be coached, we often feel that we are failing and must improve or lose our jobs.

Therefore, as brilliant as a coach may be, initial discussion and investment from leadership are critical to effectiveness. Many well-meaning projects have gone awry because of poor strategic communication. Imagine if an organization sent the message that it was committed to the success of clinicians and their relationships with patients, and in this spirit, the organization was hiring coaches to invest in its clinicians. It may be a similar strategic approach but a vastly different message than "your scores are low and you need to report for remediation." (We will see more about the importance of institutional investment in Chapter 18.)

A Framework for Appreciative Coaching

Coaching techniques can reflect either a growth-oriented or a punitive approach. We advocate a method of appreciative coaching, first conceived by Dr. David Cooperrider, because it assumes the best in everyone and taps into internal motivation.[3] This three-stage approach marries the fundamental communication skills (see Chapters 3–5) with the approach to feedback (see Chapter 10):

- **Stage 1:** Pre-briefing—building rapport, discovering strengths, and dreaming of the ideal
- **Stage 2:** Setting up and managing live observation or skills practice
- **Stage 3:** Debriefing and next steps

The most effective coaches use these fundamental communication skills to demonstrate the strategies that they want to support. Let's say, for example, that you are in a Thai cooking class where you are assigned to cut carrots into a flower garnish. Even if you are a good cook, unless you have specific training in vegetable carving, you can destroy a lot of carrots before getting one that looks even semi-presentable. Effective coaches must make room for learners to make mistakes and go through all the awkwardness of learning a new skill before learners can achieve mastery.

STAGE 1: PRE-BRIEFING—BUILDING RAPPORT, DISCOVERING STRENGTHS, AND DREAMING OF THE IDEAL

An initial encounter with a coach is similar to the beginning of a clinical encounter. The coach must first build rapport and create an environment in which trust can grow. Coaches will accomplish these goals through greeting and introduction, small talk before big talk, and addressing communication barriers (see Chapter 3). In a coaching encounter, the coach will also need to discuss the agenda and its rationale, clarify time limits, and review how to manage introductions to patients during observations. These steps will take just a couple of minutes; in coaching as in clinical work, that small investment of time will pay big dividends later.

Imagine that you are a low-performing clinician who has been referred to a coach. You're being told that you're bad at what you do, which challenges a professional identity that you have worked hard for a long time to attain. At the very least, you will be wary of this coach. Imagine that this coach says to you, "I have a list here of all the things you need to do better. I'm here to make sure that you do them, or you're out of here." That coach might as well make you drop to the floor and do burpees to the quick rhythm of a whistle. Even for that small minority of you that loves burpees, the whistle and the punitive tone don't exactly make you feel inspired or motivated to take action.

Now imagine instead that the coach meets you with a warm handshake, a brief introduction of what is going to happen in the relationship, and a short period of small talk to get to know you better. You may still be somewhat suspicious, especially because you might recognize some of these tools from reading Chapter 3, but at least you're not doing burpees.

Then the coach asks you some questions:

1. When did you know you wanted to be a clinician? What led you to making that final decision?
2. What do you perceive to be your greatest strengths as a clinician?
3. If your patients are having a meal with friends and family, what do you hope they are saying about you and the kind of care you provided them? If members of your interprofessional team are talking among themselves about you, what do you hope they are saying about the kind of care and collaboration you provide?
4. If you have been coached in the past, what worked in helping you change behaviors?

This initial investment in the relationship is critical to building the first tendrils of trust that can develop into successful practice. Take a bit of time to answer one of these questions for yourself. What feelings come up for you? It's likely that other clinicians who are being coached will also have emotions come up as they answer. A coach's empathy can create a connection that will facilitate change.

The answers to these strength-finding questions lead into a phase of dreaming of the ideal. Essentially, we can make progress toward reaching our own dreams when we imagine that they have already come true. After a coach asks learners how they wish to be known, he or she can say, "If that were true today, what exactly would you look like, sound like, and be doing? What would make you stand out as exceptional?" This gives clinicians the chance to envision themselves as already successful. It might sound like a hokey exercise, but it is remarkable how this visioning process can enable us to pursue our goals with renewed inspiration.

Here is a tangible example of how this process might go. I (MKW) was coaching Dr. Harris, a hospitalist and the first woman physician in her family's four generations of clinicians. She identified several areas as strengths: noticing when patients appear worried and taking time to explore why, asking about barriers to following therapeutic plans and problem-solving, and advocating with specialists on behalf of patients. After I asked these questions, I noticed an easing of her initial suspicion and a shift in her guarded tone of voice. Her answers to question three were telling: she teared up a little when she said she hoped that patients and colleagues viewed her as compassionate, caring, competent, and respectful of autonomy. I told her that I noticed how fervently she wanted to connect with her patients, and that it must feel quite disappointing to get scores that didn't reflect that dream. She looked at me with a mixed expression of sadness and anger. I said to her, "I'm going to do everything I can to get you where you want to be." She reached out, grasped my hand firmly, and quietly said, "Thank you."

STAGE 2: SETTING UP AND MANAGING LIVE OBSERVATION OR SKILLS PRACTICE

With a firm understanding of the clinicians' strengths and an inspirational ideal of what they could potentially achieve, coaches can design a plan for achieving the dream. As first mentioned in Chapter 1, we know that better communication skills lead to better patient outcomes, increased clinician job satisfaction, decreased burnout, and benefits to the institution in which they work. It follows that focusing on developing those communication skills can lead to rewards for the clinician and the institution, now and in the future. To set up for success, one can't try to improve all the skills all at once. In the same way that baseball players don't do batting practice simultaneously with fielding practice, coaches are more likely to succeed if they work on one skill set at a time.

Coaches must have data to help them choose the relevant skill to start with. Data may include the clinician's reflections about learning goals, his or her observations prior to the design plan, patient experience scores and narratives, and anonymous focus group surveys of patients, among other possibilities. We know that some of this information is more easily accessible, so it may be attractive for coaches to use the most expedient approach. At the same time, the approach must feel relevant to the learner in order to instill a sense of motivation. The coach should strengthen the fundamental skills of the clinician that are consistent with his or her vision or dream. The scores will follow.

I shadowed Dr. Harris on her usual inpatient rounds during a typical hospitalist shift. After observing her interact with three hospitalized patients, it was clear to me that she intended to be, and indeed thought that she was, listening and showing empathy. Unfortunately, she didn't often express that empathy with reflection or PEARLS statements (see Chapter 4). I noticed that she frequently downloaded a lot of information without checking with the patient.

During this stage of coaching, the coach needs to balance the clinician's own reflections on performance with discussion and specific behavioral feedback (see Chapter 10). Coaches generally start by asking clinicians to reflect on what they did effectively and how close the actual behaviors were to their dreams. The coach then reports what was observed, attending to the learner's emotional cues, followed by specific behavioral feedback. The coach and learner can then work together to strategize on how to help the clinician get closer to the ideal self.

Dr. Harris thought that she had validated one patient's frustration, which was accurate. I reinforced that she had used one clear partnership statement and that the patient appeared to respond positively. I then asked what she did to accomplish her dream of being seen as compassionate. Dr. Harris said that she expressed her compassion by giving patients lots of information. As we talked, she realized that patients might not view this information download as compassionate. As a result, she resolved to talk less and listen more, and to look for and respond to emotional cues from patients. I agreed that she could increase her receptivity to emotion. We reviewed PEARLS together, and she took the initiative to try to use statements of emotion and legitimization during the next encounter.

My second observation with Dr. Harris was like rounding with a different clinician. She paused to hear the patient tell the whole story, and rather than immediately telling the patient what was going to happen for the day, she said, "It's completely natural to worry that you're never going to improve. I'm here to give you the best treatments we have to make your shortness of breath better." When we debriefed, she was very happy about the way the encounter went, and even more inspired when I shared with her the exact words she'd said to the patient, and reminded her of the patient's expression of gratitude.

STAGE 3: DEBRIEFING AND NEXT STEPS

When coaches conclude their observations, it can be very helpful when they recap the entire experience. Using the ART (Ask, Respond, Tell) technique (see Chapter 5), we ask learners to reflect on which behaviors demonstrated their strengths and which skills need more work. We then summarize our own perspective and identify a few specific things that we believe the learner can do to improve the patient or family experience. Finally, we ask the learner to commit to working on one or two specific skills.

We generally follow up coaching visits with a phone call or e-mail including a written summary of our observations. We attach relevant literature discussing the behaviors the learner committed to practice, and reinforce use of a skills card that outlines all the behaviors we were looking for during our observations.

Conclusion

Experienced clinicians are going to view fundamental skills as routine. When someone tells us we need to improve, it is natural to feel defensive and resistant. When we don't understand or believe in the coaching process, it is even harder to be emotionally on board with the process. We have outlined three coaching domains that will maximize success: strong empathy and emotion modulation skills, familiarity with organizational change management, and a robust and appreciative approach to the actual coaching process. We have also shown how the process itself is a series of applications of the fundamental communication skills (see Chapters 3–5) and requires facility with giving effective feedback (see Chapter 10). We have found coaching to be one of our most fulfilling tasks, as the benefits accrue to improved patient-clinician relationships as well as clinician well-being.

CHAPTER 12

Communicating Effectively on Healthcare Teams

As healthcare systems change, one area that is becoming more and more critical is teamwork. Nowadays, even a solo clinician in practice typically depends on a whole team of individuals, including nurses and support assistants, to get the work done. Emergency departments and surgical practices need more staff than ever before, including roles in trauma rooms and operating theaters. Inpatient settings have also seen a vast increase in necessary staff: in the 1970s, there were approximately 2.5 employees for every hospitalized patient—in the 1990s that number had increased to 15.[1]

Nearly every healthcare worker has had mixed experiences with working as part of a team. Similar to having multiple people in an exam room (see Chapter 3), an increase in the number of team members often results in exponentially more complex interactions and communication. Team training modules such as TeamSTEPPS, a teamwork system developed by The Agency for Healthcare Research and Quality (AHRQ) and the Department of Defense (DoD), invoke the importance of communication and have formats for information transfer, such as ISBAR.[2] However, there still remains a need to identify specific processes to enhance interactions and facilitate effective communication. This chapter identifies how communication can be used in teams to increase efficiency and improve quality of care.

Characteristics of Highly Functioning Teams

From sports to academics, we have all been on countless teams throughout our lives. When we reflect on the most remarkable teams we have been a part of, we can easily see how those teams stood out from the rest.

Take a moment to think about what made your most remarkable teams so special. Maybe they were just great fun to be on. Maybe you shared a competitive drive with other teammates or a desire to make beautiful music together.

When you think about what made your favorite teams special, you will most likely name one of the four characteristics of highly functioning teams:

1. **Cohesion:** the extent to which people feel valued on the team (With good cohesion, team members find their experiences meaningful.)
2. **Communication:** how the team processes information and how it handles diversity, feedback, and conflict
3. **Role Clarity:** whether the roles and responsibilities of team members are understood by all on the team
4. **Goals and Means Clarity:** the team's overall goal is clear and shared by all, and the means of getting there is also clear

There are many similar lists that describe what makes a great team. This framework has been validated in healthcare settings with a measure that can be relatively easily administered.[3] We will focus on cohesion and communication, as these unsurprisingly encompass most of the communication tools that lead to highly functioning teams.

COHESION

The first and most important step toward creating a highly functioning team is developing trust and cohesion among team members. Without trust, the other three characteristics of highly functioning teams cannot occur.[4]

Most of us have been a part of healthcare teams that have failed to meet their goals. Why do teams fail? Often, unanticipated dynamics or circumstances within the team can get in the way of meeting a shared objective. The operating room (OR) is characterized by teamwork, expertise, high stress, and at times unmet expectations. The following is an example of a common experience in the OR:

It was the end of a busy day. Most surgeries were completed, with the exception of a trauma case, which was taking much longer than anticipated. The surgeon was operating on the patient's fractured tibia. A second patient came in needing immediate surgery. Typically, the patient and the medical team would have to wait for the routine cleaning to take place before a room would be available. Because a previous case had finished early, a second room was already prepped for the new patient. The surgeon, pleased at the possibility of finishing his work for the day, asked others to finish his current case so that he could start the next one. He left a junior resident in charge of the patient with the fractured tibia and called in a physician assistant to close the case. The surgeon and his chief resident left to start the final case. The surgical technician stayed overtime and a new circulating nurse came in to help.

During changes like this, medical staff performs a "count" to make sure that all needles and sponges are accounted for before closing the incisions. The count concluded that a large sponge was missing. But the incisions in the leg were far too small to harbor a large sponge. The resident in the room said, "The count must be wrong. There's no way a sponge is in there. Please recount." The surgical technician agreed. The incoming circulating nurse reluctantly acquiesced, knowing that the whole operation would be stalled until the recount was completed. The physician assistant commented sotto voce that the sponge was "probably in the garbage." When the second count confirmed a missing sponge, emotions started to run high. The resident wanted to observe the other case that was just starting, and the physician assistant who was called in to help close had been leaving for the day. The surgical technician was offended at the comment about a sponge being in the garbage because it was her job to keep track of the sponges. The circulating nurse felt pressured by the other medical staff to "get things moving." The incident was extending the surgical time by more than 30 minutes.

Tempers flared, and the charge nurse was summoned to gain control of the situation. She entered the room and facilitated introductions from all team members. She carefully prompted each person to be concise and listened intently to the different perspectives, acknowledging each person's emotions. Having created quick rapport with everyone, she asked for ideas from the group. As the physician assistant had suggested, the sponge was found in the garbage, thrown there, as it turned out, by the surgeon prior to his departure from the room.

This story demonstrates how a team that was thrown together as part of a good idea had no cohesion. They didn't share common goals. When the charge nurse came onto the scene, she developed quick rapport with all team members and added cohesion to the team.

Too often, healthcare teams do not adequately get to know each other, not only in terms of their roles on a team but also personally. Turnover on teams, inability (or unwillingness) of team members to attend regular meetings or huddles, and diverse perspectives also can contribute to the lack of cohesion.

There are some reasonably simple but highly effective tools that can develop cohesion in a team. These tools mirror the skills of the fundamental skill sets (see Chapters 3–5):

- **Greeting:** Every meeting should begin with check-ins. These should be brief, one-sentence statements of how someone is doing and whether someone has to leave early. That way, there are no team meetings that begin with factual information, only to be interrupted by a key team member who has to duck out prematurely. Check-ins allow team members to remove themselves from the trance of usual work to be fully present and honest about their needs. Check-ins can further be enhanced by some small icebreaker questions, such as, "What's keeping you going today?" It may sound trite, but as human beings, particularly in healthcare, we all desire connection.

When we introduce check-ins, we should set ground rules to make sure check-ins don't take over the meeting. Cohesion efforts are important, but they shouldn't drag out to the point where they replace work.

- **Introductions:** Getting to know new team members, especially in high turnover situations, is key. If we haven't worked to integrate new people into a team, we cannot assume that they will just get up to speed automatically. It is admittedly a "speed bump" when someone new enters a position, but the speed bump can transform into a series of deep potholes and unintended poor communication in the absence of simple introductions.
- **Team Meeting Agenda-Setting:** Ideally, agendas for meetings are set ahead of time with input from team members. With adequate attention to process, meetings can then predictably start and end on time. If there is no agenda, participants should be asked concisely for a list of items they would like to cover, and then an agenda can be set. Otherwise, the meeting will achieve the ignominious, all-too-common categorization of "a waste of everyone's time."
- **Relationship-Centered Skills:** When emotions arise in a meeting, as they often do, using reflective listening and PEARLS (see Chapter 4) is necessary to further the cohesiveness of the team. Unless the group is particularly high functioning, hurt feelings on a team typically do not heal themselves. Instead, hurt feelings arise at inopportune moments, either underground in a way that undermines the work of the team, or openly and disruptively.
- **Next Steps:** Defining clear next steps at the end of a meeting, ideally using skills delineated in Chapter 5, not only will make the work of a team move forward but also will set accountability for work to be done. (This practice also supports another team characteristic, goals and means clarity.)

Even though the operating room story doesn't technically fall into the category of a "team meeting," team members had not introduced themselves, and were further hampered nonverbally by wearing surgical caps and masks. A quick set of greetings, a check-in, and agenda-setting about goals for the task at hand could have saved precious time. With relationship-centered skills, perhaps the quickly assembled team could have achieved closure without waiting for the charge nurse. Assiduously introducing these fundamental communication principles to healthcare team meetings can strongly enhance cohesion and trust development.

Cohesion creates an environment of inclusion that encourages creativity. One method to facilitate this is appreciative inquiry (AI). Appreciative inquiry is a way of asking questions of the team that encourages emphasis on the strengths and positive experiences rather than looking for problems and obstacles to success. The idea of AI is to note when something is working well and then ask, "What factors helped make this a good experience?" A follow-up question could be, "How can we use this strength in other circumstances to create another good experience the next time?" By asking appreciative questions, we recognize team member contributions, thereby reinforcing those behaviors and improving morale.

The Physician Assistant graduate program at Daemen College in Amherst, New York, where I (Jim Bell) am faculty, is an example of the benefit of AI and diversity. The full-time faculty is a mix of academics and practicing clinicians. The program director actively sought diversity when adding to the faculty over recent years, hoping to build from varied strengths. The team has equal gender representation and includes an MD pathologist who teaches anatomy; a psychologist who teaches writing, research, and statistics; an English professor who teaches research methods, writing, and interviewing skills; and practicing physician assistants in pediatric psychiatry, orthopedic surgery, emergency medicine, urology, cardiology, family practice, and asthma/immunology. The mix of perspectives has resulted in some very creative ideas on how to teach medicine to students, as well as significant respect for the expertise of all faculty members. Faculty members even ask each other occasionally for personal consultations for themselves and their families. The expertise of each member is more important than title or seniority and allows for more inclusive discussions and increased cohesion. There is a high level of trust among team members.

Relationships in teams take time to build—one check-in will help in the moment but will not suffice for the long term. In the current era of fragmentation of care and the necessity of handoffs, relationship development has never been more important. Some tools to use to foster relationships in the team are regular structured feedback (see Chapter 10), team huddles, and supported inclusive interactions outside the workplace. Suggested activities include retreats, local job fairs, community outreach activities, or social activities such as sporting events. Even just having lunch together as a team can enhance relationships among team members.

COMMUNICATION

As cohesion develops, using the fundamental communication skills listed in the previous section, the team can begin to move into advanced applications of these fundamental skills, two examples of which are feedback and huddles. Another important example is when conflict develops between team members (see Chapter 13).

Feedback on Teams

Many of us dread giving and receiving feedback. Yet productive feedback is critical for relationship building, personal improvement, and professional development. Why is feedback so uncomfortable for so many of us? It's the way feedback is usually delivered that makes us cringe. If our supervisors give feedback intermittently, without warning, and focus solely on problem areas, it's no wonder we develop negative feelings about the process. Feedback doesn't have to be something we dread. Feedback is productive and often welcomed when it is part of a regular, structured process that involves an honest dialogue about both strengths and opportunities for improvement. Regular, structured feedback can encourage deeper connection, provide opportunities to voice emotions that may be under the surface, and increase the productivity and satisfaction of team members.

Two research scientists were working in a lab studying the properties of inhalant medications. Anna worked early in

131

the morning, and Brian worked in the evening. They were friends and set periodic meetings to check in about the project. Brian had trained Anna on the equipment and procedures. As the project "lead," Anna was responsible for productivity. At one point in the project, Anna encountered a problem. Each morning she came to begin work, she discovered that the lab was set up differently from how she had left it. For three days, she spent 30 minutes reorganizing the lab before she could begin work. Finally, she asked for 15 minutes to meet with Brian to give feedback about lab procedures.

At their meeting, the two scientists began with a check-in. Anna told Brian that the project was on schedule and under budget. She also mentioned that she had discovered an alteration in the setup for each of the past three nights. Brian smiled and proudly indicated that he had developed a newer and more efficient way to do the tests (which was why they were under budget) and was pleased. Anna said, "It's great that this project is going well and that you are being creative. I really appreciate that." Anna paused to allow the initial feedback to settle in. Then she added, "Would you be open to something I've noticed?" Brian said, "Of course." Anna continued, "I find that due to your changes, I'm having to catch up each day, which puts me behind in the morning. Can you think of a way that we could keep being creative and efficient where I don't have to spend time catching up?" Brian expressed surprise that his ideas had caused mild chaos in the morning. In the future, he promised to call her if he changed something. They also agreed to have conversations on Fridays over beer to summarize changes during the week.

There was real potential for conflict in this situation. Brian was unintentionally making things harder for Anna. But they checked in with each other; agreed on an agenda so that no one felt ambushed; engaged in dialogic feedback, expresseing understanding about what the other was experiencing; and sought clarity of intent. They also

COMMUNICATING EFFECTIVELY ON HEALTHCARE TEAMS

established a regular opportunity to exchange feedback in the future. Had they handled the potential conflict differently, they could have ended up feeling resentful while making assumptions about the other person's intent (see Chapter 13). Instead, because they communicated so effectively, the potential conflict actually enriched their relationship.

Obviously, feedback among members of larger teams can become quite complicated. As a result, fundamental feedback skills for large teams are even more critical. Often, corrective feedback for an individual team member should be done in private. But clever workarounds are possible.

> On an inpatient internal medicine team of a nurse practitioner and physician assistant, the supervising physician notes that Ms. Evans, the physician assistant, thinks through the biomedical details of the case carefully, sometimes at the exclusion of understanding patients' biopsychosocial details. Mr. Phillips, the nurse practitioner, comes up with excellent discharge plans because of his deep understanding of patients' home situations, but the biomedical summaries are less crisp. On rounds, the physician says, "Ms. Evans, I love the way you so thoroughly go through each patient's differential diagnoses. Mr. Phillips, your social histories really make discharge planning a breeze. Thanks to you both."

On rounds the next day, guess how Ms. Evans changed her social histories, and how Mr. Phillips went through his differential diagnoses?

Team Huddles

Team huddles help to build spaces for both communication and relationship enhancement. As in football, huddles in healthcare settings are brief team meetings to discuss the current factors affecting the work of the day. These are not meant to be sit-down meetings with agendas and do not take the place of regularly scheduled meetings. Huddles vary in their goals and content but typically begin with initial check-ins, followed by updates of anything that is immediately relevant. Teams leading training and educational sessions will routinely huddle in the beginning of the day and at periodic breaks for as short as 30 seconds.[5] During one of these huddles, a team member indicated that a medical emergency had arisen with his son. Team members expressed their concern, assured him that he should leave to take care of his family, and then swiftly divided up his portion of the day's activities. A potentially disruptive event was efficiently addressed in a very short time because huddles were a regular part of the team and because team members had established relationships.

Putting It Together

At a large tertiary referral center, inpatient cardiology services were provided by teams of residents led by attending cardiologists. There were enough residents to build three teams (Cardiology 1, 2, and 3). The outcomes of this system were very good in terms of number of adverse events, length of stay, overhead cost, and patient experience.

Eventually the number of patients needing inpatient cardiology services grew to be too large for three teams. Rather than create a new system for providing cardiology care, the institution decided to create Cardiology 4, a team of nurse practitioners and physician assistants instead of resident doctors. Six months after the creation of Cardiology 4, it came as a surprise to everyone that every metric used to determine effectiveness of the team (overhead cost, duration of stay, adverse events, patient experience) was significantly better in the patients treated by Cardiology 4 than for all of the other teams.

Now that we know some of the characteristics of highly functioning teams, it should be no surprise why Cardiology 4 succeeded. There was a high amount of cohesion due to the permanent nature of the team members in Cardiology 4. This facilitated much richer relationships around care both within the team and with the other services. The team met in huddles frequently. This fact, combined with the team members' familiarity with each other, made more lengthy meetings unnecessary. Each team member's opinion was sought and the diversity of experience and profession was embraced. The hierarchy was much flatter on Cardiology 4, which promoted dialogue and an openness for creativity that did not exist in the much more traditional hierarchy of the resident teams. Individual clinicians consulted with each other nearly constantly. Feedback was common and frequent among members of the team. Although feedback was present on the resident teams as well, the frequency of the feedback in Cardiology 4 was higher and the content generally much more supportive.

Conclusion

Enhanced team communication and collaboration leads to improved patient experiences, better clinical outcomes, and reduced patient complaints. High-performing teams also experience heightened morale among team members and increased staff retention. Cohesion, communication, role clarity, and goals and means clarity are necessary to create high-performing teams. Teams can be created and enhanced using basic communication skills such as expressing empathy, managing conflict, giving effective feedback, supporting team member inclusion, and enumerating clear next steps. As team members learn to attend to the needs, strengths, and diverse backgrounds of colleagues, they enhance collaborative team performance.

CHAPTER 13

Challenging Conversations with Colleagues: Engaging with Conflict

magine yourself in the following scenario:

> Your job as nurse manager on the inpatient unit feels totally out of control. Nurse Smith, one of your best staff nurses, storms into your office and asks, "What am I supposed to make of the yelling coming out of room 104?" Nurse Smith tells you that Dr. Stein, the pulmonary doctor, berated the patient, Ms. Reuben, and made her cry. Dr. Stein had complained earlier that the patient had rolled her eyes while he was trying to tell her about the disease in her lungs.
>
> Just yesterday, Nurse Smith complained to you that Dr. Stein wasn't returning her pages, which made her furious. How can she provide care if she can't even get the orders clarified? You weren't trained on how to have these tough conversations in nursing school and are afraid of sitting down with clinicians who treat you dismissively. But you've got to do something. This conflict already feels like it's spiraled out of control!

The Problem

It's hard to imagine medical settings without conflict or challenging conversations. Our work environment is fast-paced and chaotic. Healthcare providers have undergone different kinds of training in diverse areas and as a result all belong to different communities whose different work cultures aren't always compatible, making conflict inevitable. Have you ever had a day at work when there was no conflict? The Joint Commission reported in 2009 that more than two-thirds of sentinel events can be traced to a conflict or breakdown in communication.[1] Conflicts often stem from differences in opinions about patient treatment, concerns over status and reputation, limited resources, workloads, and schedules. In this chapter, we will demonstrate how to apply some fundamental communication tools, many of which you have already read about, that greatly help in challenging conversations with colleagues.

Relational conflict refers to conflict due to personality clashes or interactions that result in negative emotions. This kind of conflict is what we unwittingly bring home with us and can keep us up at night. When conflicts are poorly managed, they can escalate to disruptive behaviors and failure to cooperate. Disruptive behaviors, in turn, may take the form of subtle insults or subverting another person's efforts by ignoring pages or withholding information. Behaviors can also escalate to yelling, abusive language, condescension, and berating others in front of peers or patients. Inappropriate conduct can lead to medical errors and reduced quality of care because we lose focus when our emotions run high.[2] If work environments are this toxic, it goes without saying that patients will have lower satisfaction with the care provided, and more turnover can result.[3]

Simply stated, conflict compromises our ability to do our jobs. When we are stressed or frustrated, our brain's emotional center, or amygdala, gets hijacked. Our response is to freeze, fight back, or flee. Our prefrontal cortex (or "higher brain") shuts down, and we revert to primitive brain functioning, which makes us react as though we are being attacked by a lion on the Serengeti. There is a better way.

Principled Negotiation Provides a Framework

Having a framework greatly helps us to move away from emotionally charged responses so we can effectively resolve our communication challenges. This means gaining the necessary conflict management skills so we can engage in constructive dialogue, use active listening, avoid making assumptions, separate the person from the problem, distinguish interests from positions, and prepare for challenging conversations. Let's look more closely at each of these six principles.

1. ENGAGE IN CONSTRUCTIVE DIALOGUE

A good working relationship depends on open two-way communication so that team members can understand each other's perspectives and work through differences. Typically, though, we go down a one-way street, advocating for our own point of view before learning about the other person's perspective. Think of the last time you encountered a car going the wrong way down a one-way street. You may have felt surprised, angry, confused, frightened . . . or all of the above. Similarly, in a conflict, when we're confronted with a differing view, we often stop listening and default to making generalizations (e.g., "Why don't you ever listen?") and judgments (e.g., "You *never* think about how this is affecting the rest of the team!"). These responses cause our colleagues to dig in their heels, and the conversation either shuts down or escalates. Neither outcome is positive or leads to solutions.

Let's instead open up the incoming direction on the two-way road. We can make an open-ended statement that displays curiosity: "Tell me more about where you're coming from" or "Help me understand your perspective better." These nonjudgmental statements will do a lot to de-escalate the conflict. If they are delivered authentically, the other person can sense our desire to understand where he or she is coming from. After we elicit a fuller understanding of the other person's viewpoint, we can then offer our own perspective. And once the relevant perspectives are on the table, we can successfully begin to move toward negotiation of a mutually agreeable solution.

2. USE ACTIVE LISTENING

As discussed in Chapter 4, active listening means we are listening deeply, not just using our ears but also our heart. We need to understand the words (or "text") that our colleague is sharing as well as the subtext and the context. "Subtext" refers to nonverbal messages your colleague sends via tone, pace, and body language; "context" refers to the backstory (e.g., background information, our colleague's personality, and our previous history with him or her). Active listening means that we are open to fully hearing the other perspective(s) and are even willing to change our minds about where we stand.

If what we hear raises defenses or emotions, we are at risk for the emotional hijack mentioned previously, and we may lose our ability to effectively listen. At those times, consider pausing to manage your emotional reaction before responding. This may require postponing a difficult conversation by a few hours or a day until it is possible to think clearly. How many times have you thought of exactly the right thing to say, or regretted something you said, well after a difficult conversation has ended? This happens in part because our emotions can get in the way of our thinking.

In communication involving emotions, it is important to realize that almost 90 percent of the message is conveyed via the tone and other nonverbal messages we send, rather than the words we choose.[4] When our tone contradicts the words, the tone usually supersedes the verbal message. It is important to express our emotions carefully, without sarcasm and with a calm tone of voice. Check in with your own feelings before speaking. If you are in touch with your own emotions, you will be able to control the nonverbal messages you are sending.

We can say something like, "I think we're both pretty worked up now. Let's plan to talk again in the morning." Once we have regained our emotional balance, we can more effectively participate in principled, rather than emotion-based, negotiation.

3. AVOID MAKING ASSUMPTIONS

In our complex, fast-paced world, we naturally need to process information quickly and automatically by making assumptions about what others are doing and thinking. And generally, this works OK. But when we become polarized, we need to step back and review how we arrived at the conclusions we did. The "ladder of inference," popularized by Chris Argyris and Peter Senge, dates back to Plato.[5] This useful construct illustrates how our assumptions may be flawed and can contribute to a conflict.

Examine the ladder in Figure 13.1, and start climbing from the bottom, as one does with most ladders. We start with an immense pool of observable data. Since we can't possibly take in everything going on around us, we unconsciously and automatically climb one rung on the ladder by selecting data, and assume that our perspective represents the truth. We confuse our perceptions with reality and, without recognizing it, we instantaneously add meaning to the data we select, climbing another rung. We often make assumptions about another's intent, which we can't possibly know. Up another rung. Our brain then automatically draws conclusions, and we're ready to take action before checking our assumptions. Then, most dangerous of all, the next time we interact with that person, the reflexive loop leads our brain to seek out data that confirm our prior beliefs. We have climbed the ladder of inference, typically in a matter of milliseconds.

FIGURE 13.1 Ladder of Inference

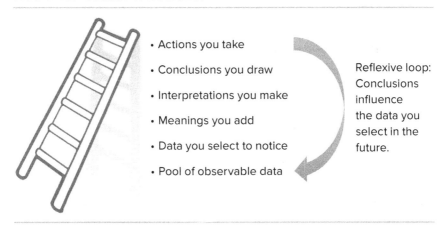

- Actions you take
- Conclusions you draw
- Interpretations you make
- Meanings you add
- Data you select to notice
- Pool of observable data

Reflexive loop: Conclusions influence the data you select in the future.

In the following example, you can see how this can lead to trouble. You are trying to finish up a QI project at the hospital, working with your colleague, Nurse Lopez. If we slow down the process using the construct of the ladder of inference, this is what is happening:

- **Data you select to notice**: Nurse Lopez has not responded to your e-mails in which you have repeatedly asked her to share the data she has gathered. You then leave a voicemail and then a second. You receive no response.
- **Meanings you add**: You decide Nurse Lopez is purposely ignoring you.
- **Interpretation:** Now that you think of it, the last time you presented at a national meeting together, you disagreed about who would go first and ended up getting most of the credit. She was annoyed with the outcome, and now you are convinced she is getting back at you by ignoring you.
- **Conclusion**: Nurse Lopez is ignoring you so that your presentation will fail.
- **Action**: At the next team meeting, you ignore her, and others notice. You decide you are not going to share any more data with her.
- **Reflexive loop**: You start looking for other examples of ways Nurse Lopez is trying to undermine you.

Climbing the ladder of inference is an example of what Dr. Daniel Kahneman calls "System 1" thinking—fast, automatic, instinctive, and emotional.[6] System 1 thinking involves associating new information with existing patterns or thoughts. When we recognize that our brains have led us to jump to conclusions that polarize us from teammates, we need to move to System 2 thinking, which is slower, more logical, deliberative, and conscious.

In this example, we need to question our assumptions and ask, "What story am I telling myself? Could there be a different interpretation of Nurse Lopez's behavior?"

In reality, it turns out that Nurse Lopez's mother was critically ill, so Nurse Lopez left town for 10 days to be with her mom and depended on a colleague to tell you (it slipped the colleague's mind). The family crisis prevented her from responding in a timely way to e-mail or phone messages. As a result, she fell behind on her work and assumed that you would understand. Her lack of response was based on an entirely different story from the one your brain had imagined.

So the next time you notice that you are assuming a teammate has negative intentions, ask yourself, "Why might a reasonable, well-intentioned person behave this way?"

4. SEPARATE THE PERSON FROM THE PROBLEM[7]

We've discussed how tough it is to solve problems calmly without creating misunderstandings, hurt feelings, and frustration. When we have challenging relationships with our team members, the tension, in turn, can get in the way of resolving problems. Even when our prior relationships are good, if we feel frustrated or angry about a problem, we may unwittingly direct that anger toward a colleague, who can then feel like the target. Blaming leads to defensiveness, and people are likely to shut down, stop listening, or even retaliate. What began as a small conflict then escalates, sometimes to major proportions. Let's say you work with a physician who frequently comes to afternoon clinic 15 minutes late, which throws off the schedule for all subsequent patients. As the team nurse, you are very frustrated by this since the patients usually express their complaints to you. You appreciate his energy, clinical knowledge, and work ethic, but you don't think he understands the impact of his tardiness on his teammates or patients.

When you imagine approaching the physician to voice your concern, try and disentangle the person from the problem in order to avoid stimulating a defensive response. It's natural to vilify others and portray ourselves in the best light. But when working on teams, we need to reach agreement on the facts *and* maintain good working relationships. What does this look like? Earlier, we said that good working relationships depend on mutually understood perspectives and open two-way communication. In this example, rather than fuming in private, begin the conversation with curiosity. Consider why he may be arriving late, and whether there is a way to solve this problem. This approach applies the skills of ART (Ask, Respond, Tell) from Chapter 5. Rather than jumping down his throat, find a way to calmly ask something like: "It looks like it's tough for you to get to your Tuesday afternoon clinic by 1 p.m. Unfortunately, it's caused some patient complaints. Is there anything I can do to help with this?"

You learn that he has a Tuesday management meeting that he has to attend. The meeting begins at noon and usually runs late, making it

143

impossible to get to afternoon clinic on time. This is where the Respond step of ART is crucial, and where PEARLS (see Chapter 4) are extremely effective tools. Remember that understanding and validating someone's perspective does not mean that you agree with it.

Respond with empathy: "It sounds frustrating when your meeting tends to run over, and by the time you get to clinic, it already feels out of control."

"Yeah, you have that right—Tuesdays are really stressful!"

As you use active listening, your colleague can feel calmer after expressing his views and emotions and will be more open to listening. And now that you have a good understanding of his perspective, you can tell your own perspective, carefully avoiding triggering his emotions. You could say, "Some of your patients and I share that frustration," spoken with a slow pace and calm tone.

Until both parties' emotions are expressed, it is generally premature to try and identify potential solutions. We often jump to solutions too quickly, before emotions are aired, and that tendency is important to resist. With minimal effort, you both realize that if the physician starts and ends his afternoon clinic 15 minutes later, then patients will be seen in a timely way. You will hear fewer complaints, he will be less stressed, and his patient experience scores might even improve.

Before ending the conversation, it is useful to explicitly recognize that you have differing perceptions and verbally summarize what you have heard to ensure agreement. For example, "Thanks for sharing what is going on. I was looking at it from the team and patient perspective. I'm confident we can fix this now that I understand your challenges."

Advanced applications with issues of diversity, culture, and hierarchy on teams are explained in Chapters 14–15.

5. DISTINGUISH INTERESTS FROM POSITIONS[8]

Interests and positions both come up when tension rises—understanding the difference between them can help us sort through conflict. Positions are the concrete things or outcomes that we want, which often form the basis for debate. Interests are deeper, often intangible, and not initially expressed. Interests reflect the motivations for our positions; our interests may involve our own internal desires, fears, or concerns.

Let's look at another example of how to distinguish between interests and positions.

Hospital production pressure has resulted in cost-reduction efforts across all departments. Currently about one-third of patients undergoing total hip replacement do not leave the operating room until late afternoon, but the physical therapy department shuts down at five. Dr. Lee, head of orthopedics, and Mr. Taylor, head of physical therapy, tackle this:

> DR. LEE: Our post-op patients need to get out of bed the day of surgery, so we need your physical therapists to stay late to see them. (Her position)
>
> MR. TAYLOR: Sorry. We can't do that. (His position)

Rather than getting entrenched in their conflicting positions, the two colleagues need to explore the other's position and ask *why*—not looking for a justification but rather an understanding of the other's perspective. This process requires an advanced application of ART. It's advanced because it requires deft handling of strong emotions that often arise in conflict situations like this. Only then will a potential solution emerge. Let's see the ART model in action:

> DR. LEE: Help me understand what the problem is. (Ask)
>
> MR. TAYLOR: Our PT budget prevents us from paying overtime—it is just cost prohibitive. (His interest: keeping under budget)
>
> DR. LEE: Yes, keeping costs down is something we all share as department heads, isn't it? (Respond) From our standpoint, we have to reduce our length of stay to reduce costs for our hip replacement patients. The best way to do that is to get them out of bed and home a day sooner. (Tell) Can we work together to see if there is any way we can do this? (Her interest: reducing costs)
>
> MR. TAYLOR: Well, I do have a couple of PTs who have been asking to do four 10-hour shifts a week—I wonder if that would help. (His interest: satisfying staff desire for modified schedule)

Exploring the other side's interests is the basis for dialogue. By gently probing with "I'm curious about the reasons you think/feel . . ." or "Help me understand why that won't work for you," it is possible to uncover the other side's interests, leading to effective resolution of the stalemate. When we explore the underlying interests of both parties, we usually identify shared interests, which can form the foundation for a stronger relationship. The goal is to discover and build on shared interests (what is known in the vernacular as "common ground") before tackling the incompatible ones. It's also helpful if we work to identify tradeoffs, since what matters most to one person may not matter as much to another, and we can often create value and each have our interests met. Finally, when we discover our colleagues' interests that are incompatible with our own, acknowledging the importance of those interests can go a long way to demonstrate that, even though we may not agree, we can respect what matters to them.

Prepare for Challenging Conversations[9]

Although we can never script a difficult conversation, preparation is tremendously helpful. We often skip this step at our peril. Remember our goal is not to win but to come up with a joint solution that will provide the best care possible and encourage a collaborative work environment.

There are multiple aspects to preparation. First, it is useful to reflect on our goals for the relationship and the conversation. We should brainstorm what timing, tone, and words to use to enable the other party to hear our perspectives. In addition, we need to identify our own interests as well as those of the other party. When our brains have caused us to leap up the ladder of inference, it requires humility to climb down and question the assumptions we made that may have contributed to the conflict. Discussing our contribution to the problem is disarming and serves as a useful way to encourage others to share their contributions as well. When we emotionally prepare for challenging conversations, we are better able to maintain our equanimity, which allows us to actively listen to our colleagues and help them manage their emotional reactions.

Conclusion

Healthcare environments are highly interdependent. In order to prevent adverse events and errors, and to improve the quality of care we provide, we need to learn to work together more effectively. Challenging conversations with colleagues arise on a daily basis. With practice and this simple framework, we can gain the skills to navigate challenging conversations, move beyond fight-or-flight reactions, and transform conflict into an opportunity to develop effective collaboration.

CHAPTER 14

Culture and Diversity

M r. Jackson is an African-American man in his 50s, known to the staff in the clinic as a difficult patient, not because he is angry or disrespectful but because his health only worsens and never improves. The clinicians and nurses in the office try to treat him with kindness but never seem to be able to get past what they perceive as his "disengagement." Dr. Barrett, Mr. Jackson's primary care clinician, feels resigned and sometimes hopeless. Though Dr. Barrett would never openly criticize him, she privately wonders whether Mr. Jackson just doesn't care about his diabetes, hypertension, and chronic kidney disease. Whenever Dr. Barrett asks her patient, "Do you have any questions about your health?," the answer is almost always, "No."

In my travels as an educator, I (Denise Davis) often survey healthcare professionals about whether they have had training in communicating across racial, ethnic, language, and other differences. During one session at a regional academic conference, the only hand that went up belonged to a medical student from my home institution! When I initiate these conversations, people tell me that when these sensitive topics come up in healthcare, they simply don't know what to say.

The major risk is that if we don't address these issues, we miss critical opportunities for building trust and improving quality of care for minority patients. When we make a point to tackle the sensitive issues of race and ethnicity in healthcare, we learn how to improve care for minority patients and provide better care for everyone across another critical cultural divide—healthcare professionals and their patients.

Though I've never met a clinician or nurse who voiced an intention to discriminate against patients, reliable research indicates that unconscious bias is both real and very common among physicians and nurses. For example, observational studies show that African-American patients' visits with clinicians are shorter than white patients' visits, and they experience less positive emotional connection and less sharing of decision-making with white clinicians than with African-American clinicians.[1]

We know from a variety of studies that minority patients (African-American, Latino, Native American, LGBT, and some Asian-American groups) have poorer health outcomes than their majority counterparts.[2] For example, end-stage kidney disease is twice as common for black patients as compared to white patients; Latino patients develop end-stage kidney disease at approximately three times the rate of white patients.[3] Many of these patients require dialysis, a treatment that is often lifesaving but results in severe disruptions in the patient's physical, social, and economic life, not to mention the lives of the patient's loved ones. Other examples include women identifying as lesbian who are less likely to undergo recommended screening for breast cancer or cervical cancer,[4] and Asian-American groups with significantly lower cancer screening rates and high cancer mortality.[5]

What can we do to ensure that all our patients receive equal treatment? By addressing these disparities, we seek to reduce inequity, improve patient experience for minorities, and simultaneously improve the experience of healthcare professionals. Mr. Jackson, the patient mentioned at the beginning of this chapter, triggers negative emotions in his healthcare team because team members feel frustrated and hopeless when they interact with him. Dedicated clinicians want to change a patient's poor health. When we are unable to do so, it can feel like a personal failing and can impact the level of support we offer. Learning more about how to communicate effectively with minority patients can help clinicians enjoy these relationships and find ways for patients to achieve better health.

Dr. Barrett is having challenges in communicating with Mr. Jackson in part because she is making assumptions and inferences about Mr. Jackson without explicitly bringing up her concerns. This is a common trap that clinicians often fall into. Most clinicians I meet tell me that they treat everyone the same and don't see color, and many may feel anxious about coming across as anything but supportive. Dr. Barrett does not want to be seen as discriminatory, or worse, a racist. But she is avoiding addressing an elephant in the room: race and its effect on health, healthcare, and the patient-clinician relationship.

I know of a patient with a very different story. Mr. Young is an African-American man in his 50s who has learned to care for his chronic illnesses over time, in partnership with his physician and the healthcare team. He feels comfortable talking about his relationship with his clinician, including the difficulty he feels in discussing sexual concerns with a female clinician. His clinician has also invited conversations about what it was like for him to live in the American South as a young black man, and how his life has changed and has not changed since he moved to a politically liberal, urban, coastal city. How can we achieve this alternative to the typical guilt-ridden interactions that commonly affect clinicians?

Good Communication Takes Practice

Comparing Mr. Jackson and Mr. Young, it's easy to think that some clinicians naturally have the comfort, confidence, and skills to discuss sensitive topics. But it's important to recognize that good communicators about sensitive topics are made, not born. I look back on my early years as a physician, and I feel embarrassed about how often I lacked the courage to open a conversation about differences. I thought that being a "good doctor" was enough.

It turns out that the fundamental skills presented earlier (see Chapters 3–5) are powerful resources for improving communication across many differences. In the United States, racial differences, especially differences between white and black patients, have been extensively researched. But these communication techniques can go beyond bridging racial and ethnic divides. Committing ourselves to adopting the fundamental communication skills will help, or even resolve, many of the challenges we face when treating patients across a variety of differences. The following recommendations are evidence-based, in part on medical literature[6] and in part on a series of focus groups I conducted of African-American patients in the San Francisco Bay Area. I learned to enhance my practice from these groups of men and women who became my teachers, and I have found these principles to be very effective for many, if not most, of my encounters with patients, families, and learners who present differences, obvious or subtle.

THE BEGINNING OF THE ENCOUNTER

Human beings have evolved to judge others as friend or foe very quickly. Our species has survived in part because of our ability to make snap judgments about whether another person will harm us or help us. These judgments are unconscious, and they happen in milliseconds. Therefore, the way we initiate a patient encounter is critical (see Chapter 3). To more effectively begin encounters where difference is present, we must prioritize building trust with patients, many of whom may harbor mistrust from personal or vicarious experiences of bias and discrimination. One need only think of the infamous Tuskegee experiments on black men to remember how the healthcare system defied moral standards of practice and undermined trust.[7] For minority patients who may have low trust, we can win or lose the ballgame in the first few minutes. And the risk is real. Low-income whites, highly educated blacks, and people who experience economic barriers in obtaining healthcare are more likely to perceive discrimination in their clinicians.[8]

Research shows that race-concordant patient-clinician visits (where the race of the patient and clinician are the same) show improved patient experience. Instead of attributing this improvement to some amorphous halo effect in which black patients always magically feel more comfortable with black physicians, careful observations of interactions were revealing: smiles and laughter were prominent.[9] Trust underlies this level of comfort. We can create a strong foundation of trust at the beginning of an interview with a warm greeting, a well-paced and generous introduction to the patient and everyone else in the room, and a clear explanation of our role.

> **DR. MEREDITH:** Mr. Thomas, I'm Dr. Meredith. It's a pleasure to meet you, though I'm sorry I'm meeting you on a day that you don't feel well. I'm a family practitioner, which means

I take care of adults and children, men and women of all ages for their general health. I've worked here at the Wright Clinic for ten years and I love what I do. May I get you a cup of water and hang up your coat?

If this does not ring true to the reader, I agree. It's not typical. Yet, when I have used exactly these skills with patients billed as "difficult," their responses have usually been very warm and positive. After an elaborate introduction, similar to the one just described, that included years in practice with an explanation of my specialty, one patient said, with a smile on his face, "No one has ever done that before." These may seem like trivial interventions, but they are not easy changes to make when we are rushed, burdened by productivity metrics, and annoyed by the electronic health record. In addition, data suggest that only 40 percent of interns at a major East Coast research hospital actually introduced themselves to patients in the hospital. Only 37 percent of interns explained their role, and, sadly, a mere 9 percent sat down and looked the patient in the eye.[10]

Beginning encounters in this way is certainly different than many of the rushed introductions I've witnessed during my observations of clinicians and nurses. An effective opening like this may require an additional 15 to 20 seconds, but the return on investment is almost always well worth the additional time up front. Higher levels of trust are associated with improved health outcomes, including diabetes management, hypertension,[11] and improvement in cardiovascular disease risk factors (see Chapter 1), conditions that disproportionately affect African Americans, Latinos, and Native Americans.

ADDRESSING BARRIERS

The hierarchy that separates physicians and patients is exaggerated for patients from the black community. How better to address this social phenomenon than to practice relationship-centered skills at the beginning of an encounter? The story of one of my family members illustrates this.

Dr. Fannie Fiddmont went to see a new primary care clinician near her home in Littleton, Colorado. Into the exam room walked a friendly, young white male physician. "Hi, Fannie," he said. That was Dr.

Fiddmont's first and last visit to see that physician. My beloved Aunt Fannie is an African-American educator who experienced the injustice of segregation while growing up in Texas before the US Supreme Court's *Brown v. Board of Education* decision. Using titles shows respect and is an important part of setting the stage for a successful visit.

One additional important barrier is language. Many researchers have found that patients with limited English proficiency report more problems with clinical interactions than patients proficient in English. Even when translation services are high quality and readily available, clinicians may intentionally choose not to use the services because of time constraints.[12] Patients with language barriers have lower patient satisfaction, longer hospital stays, and an increased risk of misdiagnosis.[13]

From a workshop in St. Paul, Minnesota, I learned, from a group of very caring surgeons who treat many Somali patients, to say to the patient via the translator: "I wish that I spoke your language."

WHEN IN DOUBT, LISTEN TO THE PATIENT: THE PATIENT'S PERSPECTIVE

Think about the hierarchy in our lives as healthcare professionals. With equals, we share important details about our work, our qualifications, and our lives. We don't think of our patients the same way we think about our colleagues, but it is critical that we treat them as equals. A framing statement, related to the ideas and expectations questions discussed in Chapter 4, can help mitigate the social stratification that interferes with partnership: "You know your body. I am interested in what you know to be good for your health and what you have found to be negative."

Another potential way to deepen understanding of the patient's perspective is to acknowledge the past and present in order to make the future better. The 1999 Institute of Medicine report *Unequal Treatment* analyzed health disparities in the United States, revealing that minority patients often receive lower quality medical treatment.[14] Complex reasons cause these disparities. The document takes aim at how social factors, including unconscious bias and stereotyping, influence the patient-clinician encounter. We must also remember the effects of trauma, internalized oppression (internalized negative stereotypes and beliefs that become part of the self-image of individuals belonging to marginalized groups), and learned helplessness on the thoughts, feelings, and behaviors of minority patients.

One of the most challenging communication tools required of healthcare clinicians is acknowledging the realities of injustice and unequal treatment. Sometimes you must name the elephant in the room. One example follows:

> "Historically, African Americans, patients without insurance, and other minority groups have received treatment that was not equal to the care given other, more privileged groups. I wish I didn't have to ask, but I will because I'm an advocate for you. Do you ever feel you have been treated differently?"

I have found this question to be extraordinarily powerful.

EMPATHY AND RESPECT

The PEARLS statements introduced in Chapter 4 work with almost any person. In particular, addressing emotional cues and respect are probably the two highest-yield items. Empathy may well be the universal solvent for bias and disparities in healthcare and could be lifesaving in preventive health: "For Latino women, perceptions of higher professional empathy and less negative emotions were associated with better continuity of cancer screening."[15] Because every human, regardless of demographic differences, experiences emotion, the impact of empathic statements that recognize emotional cues cannot be overemphasized.

Respect is "fundamental to understanding and thinking about how patients should be treated."[16] Respect is more than just thinking that we are being respectful—it requires specific words, accompanied by authentic nonverbals. We can demonstrate respect in the way we talk with our patients, deepening their trust and strengthening our relationships with them.

For example, a clinician seeing a patient with diabetes might use brief statements to demonstrate respect, such as:

"I have a great deal of respect for you, Ms. Minaya. You have put together a detailed account of your blood sugars since our last visit. You have done a lot to try to keep up with your medicines."

MORE ABOUT TRUST

In the 1970s the financial services firm Smith Barney featured the phrase, "They make money the old-fashioned way . . . they *earn* it." The same can be said about trust in relationships with patients. Simply stating, "*I want to earn your trust*" can be extremely effective.

Rarely is there a good time to address racial, ethnic, or other differences on a first visit, when building a foundation of rapport is paramount. But as we get to know our patients, we may find that inviting conversations about differences is beneficial. Going back to the example of Mr. Jackson, we may recall that Dr. Barrett has been repeating the same conversations without success, spending a great deal of time spinning his wheels and going nowhere. If Dr. Barrett summons the courage to broach a conversation about their differences, she may learn about the experiences that have caused Mr. Jackson to mistrust healthcare professionals. In reality, Mr. Jackson grew up in circumstances in which racial segregation and poverty ruled. As clinicians, we may fear that starting conversations about race and ethnicity is like opening Pandora's box. Instead, these conversations often help us to connect more deeply with our patients so we can get off the hamster wheel of repeating the same defeating conversations over and over again. To gain a better understanding of Mr. Jackson's life and perspective, Dr. Barrett could start out by saying, "I would like to get to know you better as a person, including good and bad experiences you've had with clinicians."

Several years ago, one of the trainees I supervised was seeing an African-American man with a serious health problem who had lost faith in his previous healthcare team. He sought out a second opinion at a Veterans Administration hospital associated with a prestigious academic institution. The trainee practiced some of the skills offered in this chapter. Despite the patient's mistrust, after the trainee said, "*I know trust takes time, and I want to earn your trust,*" the patient left the visit saying to her, "I want you to be my clinician forever." Coincidence? I think not.

DELIVERING DIAGNOSES AND TREATMENT PLANS

Focus group participants identified educational disparities as a source of difficulty in relationships with healthcare professionals. Historically, African Americans and Latinos have been forced into segregated low-resource public schools, resulting in generations of black and brown people having less opportunity to receive a high-quality education, the foundation of health literacy.[17] One female focus group participant said, "Some people may not know enough to ask the right questions." This is one of the causes for a condition called "white coat silence."[18] When a well-meaning clinician or nurse asks a patient with low health literacy, "Do you have any questions?," the answer is often, "No."

This same patient may have health concerns that need to be addressed. So what can we do to get a different response? ARTful (Ask, Respond, Tell) communication (see Chapter 5) is an effective alternative that will draw patients out and give clinicians information to better support them. A simple way to start an ARTful conversation is to change the closed-ended "Do you have any questions?" to "What questions or concerns do you have about the diabetes medication?" The answer is almost universally, "Actually, I have some."

Patients often ask about the following concerns:

- Side effects of medicines
- Cost of medicines
- Duration of treatment: do you have to take it forever?
- Alternatives to medicine: e.g., what could I do naturally to reduce my blood sugar?

Finally, African-American clinicians are more likely to share medical decision-making with their black patients.[19] This finding can be generalized to help all clinicians succeed in connecting with patients. Some clinicians I have coached become anxious about giving a patient with little training and experience in medicine power to prescribe their own treatment. Hearing and even reflecting back patients' ideas does not mean that what they request is what we ultimately recommend or prescribe. Partnership with patients is not just a catchphrase; it's essential in order to decrease disparities at the level of the patient-clinician relationship and to provide safe, high-quality care that promotes adherence.

Conclusion

Intentional and effective practice of the evidence-based fundamental communication skills outlined in previous chapters will also improve communication across racial, ethnic, language, and other differences. Additional higher order skills that identify and address the elephant in the room require courage, practice, compassion, and wisdom.

CHAPTER 15

Communicating Across Hierarchy

Take a look at the following true stories, described in brief:

A male surgeon swears at a female clinician over the phone. When he later apologizes, he says, "I never would have spoken to you that way if I had known you were a physician."

A physician remarks one day, "We're now being dictated to by administrators, the people who weren't smart enough to get into medical school."

When a nurse disagrees with a doctor's plan of care, he offers to give her $50 to pay for her application to medical school so that she can gain decision-making authority.

A nurse manager reports that a senior physician who rounds with residents and fellows on her floor fails to acknowledge or make eye contact with the bedside nurses caring for mutual patients.

These true stories from our work in healthcare reflect mismanaged hierarchies. Managing hierarchies effectively is essential because hierarchy represents a necessary but potentially toxic aspect of healthcare culture. This chapter presents various hierarchy challenges and offers tools for building a more effective workplace using relationship-centered communication skills.

It is easy to defend the importance of hierarchy. If every member of an orchestra tries to be the conductor, the entire performance will be botched. Musicians need to know to whom to turn for instructions. In healthcare, if clinicians are resuscitating a patient, each person needs a clear understanding of who does what and who is in charge to maintain order and ensure that the most qualified person will ultimately make the decisions. No one would advocate eliminating all hierarchy in healthcare settings. However, it is essential to consider the potential harms of hierarchy and ways to mitigate these harms without eliminating the benefits.

Hierarchy is defined as a system in which people are ranked above or below each other with regard to status and/or power. Hierarchy can signal who is more important, who is more valued, and who has more control and authority. Many types of hierarchy exist in healthcare. Any of the following may find themselves elevated or depressed in hierarchies: doctors, nurses, physical therapists, pharmacists, men, women, people from different racial and ethnic groups, executives, case managers, technologists, administrators, and secretaries. The list goes on. Hierarchies also exist with regard to how much different people are paid. What message do we send about how we value our colleagues when we pay cardiologists more than infectious disease specialists or men more than women?

Hierarchies can be stressful. Research on primates and humans has consistently shown relationships between social hierarchy, biological measures of stress, and health.[1] People need to feel valued and respected, with control over their environments and activities. When team communication norms convey a different message—one of devaluing, disrespect, and control by others—team health and function will likely suffer. The questions "Who is in control?," "Who is most important?," and "Who has power over whom?" have great psychological impact for most people. There is a reason children protest to their parents, "You're not the boss of me."

We can manage hierarchies in healthcare better by applying relationship-centered communication skills. Listening, power sharing, curiosity, reciprocity, expressions of empathy, and transparency regarding our motivations, goals, and feelings can all help establish and sustain effective relationships in settings of hierarchy.

Hierarchy in Healthcare Teams and Organizations

Unnecessary and inappropriate hierarchies can result in diminished team performance and unsafe care. When one of us was a student, a patient suffered a stroke after receiving 10 times the appropriate dose of a medication that raises blood pressure. The nurse had warned the physician that the dose seemed too high but was told not to question his orders. Power differences blocked communication and resulted in a significant patient injury. Cases like these in healthcare and aviation have led to changes in both industries that give key participants an active voice regardless of their rank.[2]

Hierarchy can be communicated both explicitly and implicitly and is often emphasized in the education of healthcare professionals. In the "hidden curriculum" of our training, we learn our first lessons about those who are expected to speak up and who are expected to keep quiet, who are to be treated with respect and who are to do as they are told.[3] Hierarchy is reinforced both inside and outside the clinical setting. In many institutions, exclusive dining spaces and preferential parking provide physicians with enhanced access. Unspoken understandings among team members and patients often result in physicians being addressed with the title "Dr.," while other team members are addressed by their first names or not at all. When senior physicians enter an interprofessional team meeting and all seats are occupied, other team members may feel compelled (or expected) to vacate their seats. As discussed in Chapter 3, introductions and nonverbal cues matter: they are the ways in which we, effectively or ineffectively, establish rapport and set the stage for subsequent communication.

Some hierarchical distinctions serve functional purposes. A physician taking a call from home may rely on preferred parking to provide prompt care in urgent clinical situations. However, other hierarchical distinctions impede communication with potential detriment to patient care. While the tradition of a "doctor's lounge" may, in part, be intended to facilitate discussions of patient care and foster a sense of collegiality among physicians, other team members may feel excluded and devalued, and an opportunity for interprofessional communication is lost.

Adding to the complexity of formal hierarchy in healthcare is its intersection with other identifiers, including gender and race. These identity differences affect communication with patients (see Chapter 14), and also among team members (see Chapter 12). For example, women working in healthcare are often assumed to be nurses, and many black physicians share stories of being identified by patients and other healthcare professionals as custodial staff. When others make assumptions about roles based on gender or race, anyone may feel a need to be more adamant about asserting their own position of authority, with the unintentional effect of undermining team relationships. Our organizations are threatened both by the hierarchy that demeans nursing and custodial roles and by the sexism and racism that create associations between categories of people and professional roles.

Traditionally, hospitals have drawn a distinction between medical staff and all other staff. The delineation was relatively simple because there were fewer roles, and formal designation of power was fairly straightforward: those who wrote the orders held the power and were entitled to make governing decisions. With increasing diversity of professional roles, the "in" and "out" groups have messier borders. Where do nurse practitioners, physician assistants, optometrists, and psychologists belong? They may write orders to be implemented by nurses, but should they hold the same governing power as physicians? A range of answers exists, and varied structural solutions have been employed. In some institutions, only physicians are eligible to be members of the medical staff and thus to vote on bylaws decisions, and yet these bylaws may affect physician assistants, nurse practitioners, and others. Similarly, the dominant position of physicians is reflected by physician assistants, nurse practitioners, and others being referred to as "nonphysicians," "physician extenders," or "mid-level providers." The implication is that a nurse is a "low-level provider" and a physician is a "high-level provider," with relative value apportioned on the same sliding scale.

One challenge when attempting to flatten hierarchies is that groups accustomed to being elevated within hierarchies may fear they will lose their special designation. In one of our hospitals, all team members who provide direct patient care were asked to wear a badge identifying them as a "caregiver." Some physicians protested the change, expressing concern that the uniqueness of their role was diminished by what seemed to be an excessively inclusive and vaguely worded category. "I completed medical school and residency, and I am a physician, not a caregiver," one said. If we blur role differences, we risk creating confusion and stripping people of a part of their identities; if we accentuate role differences in the wrong way, we risk making some groups feel unimportant and devalued. Yet the question of whether a scrub nurse has a different and distinct role compared to an anesthesiologist is not the same question as how a scrub nurse ranks in importance compared to an anesthesiologist. When applied to hierarchy, the goal of relationship-centered communication is for people to feel valued without having to feel superior.

Best Practices

How does adopting a relationship-centered framework guide us in communicating effectively across hierarchy? Table 15.1 shows a summary of the ways in which core team attributes relate to hierarchy.

TABLE 15.1 **Key Issues to Attend to in Managing Hierarchy**

	Poorly Managed Hierarchy	Well-Managed Hierarchy
Roles	Different roles are clearly ranked, with some more important than others.	Roles are clearly distinguished without unnecessary ranking.
Respect	Some team members feel disrespected and that they are perceived to be unimportant.	All team members are actively recognized as important members of the team and are treated with respect.
Voice	Team members feel that their voices are not welcome or heard.	Team members experience that their voices are expected and responded to.
Power and Control	Team members' predominant experience is being told what to do and how to do it. They are handed decisions from above that are not informed by their experience and local environment.	All team members are given some freedom in determining how to accomplish work goals. They understand the decision-making process, and decisions take their experience and local environment into account.

Of course, real life rarely presents a dichotomous choice between "poorly managed" and "well-managed." There is no one-size-fits-all solution, and the complexities of dysfunctional hierarchy do not lend themselves to rapid resolution. Our effectiveness depends on multifaceted and sustained efforts.

In the following sections are some best practices toward fulfilling this vision of a well-managed hierarchy.

1. BE THOUGHTFUL ABOUT HOW AND WHEN TEAM MEMBERS ARE ADDRESSED

Consider this example. Rounds take place on ward 9V. The attending physician, Dr. Livingston, goes from room to room with two interns and a medical resident. The nurses call him Dr. Livingston. He calls them by first name. He and the nurses refer to the interns simply as "Dr.," and it's unclear if they know their names.

How often have we been on medical teams where the leader does not know everyone's name? When we watch our children's sports teams practice or visit their classrooms, we've noticed that the coaches and teachers know all the kids' names. They see it as part of their professional responsibility. Chapter 3 highlighted the importance of introductions and names during patient interactions. Proper introductions are also important to effective team interactions. While some may roll their eyes at the perceived redundancy of introductions, it is important to recognize that assumptions about being known by one's name and role (or the irrelevance of knowing another's name and role) are very much tied to the power of hierarchy.

As coaches and teachers know, we can work together more effectively when we make it a priority to know who everyone is. Investing a minute or two at the beginning of a team discussion can have an equalizing effect and foster more balanced participation. Consistency in addressing fellow team members may also help to counteract hierarchy. If physicians are addressed as Dr. X, then consider addressing other team members by last name as well (Ms. or Mr. X, Nurse X, for example). Alternatively, all team members might choose to refer to one another by their first names.

2. IMPLEMENT PROCESSES THAT SUPPORT PARTICIPATION AND DECISION-MAKING BY ALL TEAM MEMBERS

Here's another illustrative example. Dr. Diaz is medical director of a primary care clinic. In the past year the clinic has transitioned to a team-based model of care. After much effort, the logistics of this major change have been implemented, including daily huddles. Aware of the need for efficiency, Dr. Diaz typically begins the huddle by providing updates and listing priorities for the day. She is always careful to ask if anyone has questions or comments. Most days she remembers to end the huddle by thanking the team members for their hard work. While all team members are present and on time for the huddle (no small feat), Dr. Diaz notices that a medical assistant, Ms. Lewis, and a social worker, Mr. Gonzalez, rarely speak. The huddles are shorter as a result, but clinic flow is often delayed later in the day when these same team members raise important concerns to colleagues (and, indirectly, to Dr. Diaz).

Dr. Diaz is a well-intentioned leader who recognizes the importance of creating formal opportunities for interprofessional team communication. However, her experience demonstrates that bringing all team members together and asking for their input is often not enough to counteract the silencing effect of hierarchy. In the same way that asking a patient, "Do you have any questions?" as we walk out the door is likely to have low yield, both the timing and the wording of Dr. Diaz's invitation undermine her intention of fostering balanced participation. By running the huddle and initiating it with her agenda and perspective, Dr. Diaz risks sending an implicit message to the team about the relative (and lesser) value of their agendas and perspectives, a message that is most likely reinforced throughout the healthcare system. What might she do differently to achieve her desired results?

Dr. Diaz decides to make team huddles the subject of the next staff meeting. She invites each team member to share his or her perspective about what is working and what could be more effective in the huddles. After everyone else has spoken, she shares her perspective and explicitly names the importance of all voices being heard during the huddle. She asks the team to generate "team huddle ground rules" that incorporate staff feedback, including the need to promote balanced participation and efficiency. Based on team discussion following a suggestion by Mr. Gonzalez, a plan is made to rotate the responsibility of facilitating the huddle. The ground rules are posted in the huddle workspace and referenced at the beginning of each huddle. During the next month, Dr. Diaz notices increased participation by Ms. Lewis and Mr. Gonzalez. In the few instances when they don't speak, Dr. Diaz calls for a "ground rules" check-in and asks what the team might do to ensure all voices have been heard. Others begin to emulate this behavior, and Dr. Diaz observes the team accepting greater responsibility for the effectiveness of the huddles.

In Chapter 13, respect for autonomy and collaborative decision-making were named as important components of effective conflict engagement. While Dr. Diaz could try to develop a solution for this problem on her own, doing so might only reinforce the problematic dynamic she seeks to change. By engaging the team in problem solving, she not only yields a more effective solution but also conveys that she values all perspectives.

Dr. Diaz is intentional in her decision to share her perspective last. When those who are lower on the hierarchy are given opportunities to contribute early in the discussion, they may perceive less risk of contradicting others. Formulating ground rules makes expectations explicit and promotes shared accountability for upholding functional team norms. By relinquishing her role as "leader" of the huddle, Dr. Diaz helps to build all team members' skill and comfort in participating actively. These skills are directly applicable to other team interactions, including those that involve speaking up about safety concerns.

3. CREATE A JUST CULTURE[4]

A risk in hierarchical cultures is that people lower in the hierarchy may feel unsafe if there is a culture of blame rather than a culture of problem solving. A "just culture" is one in which teams adopt a problem-solving approach so as to prevent future problems rather than an approach that focuses on blaming people. This does not mean that individuals are not accountable for their behavior. Rather, it recognizes that problems often occur because systems are flawed and make it too easy for things to go wrong. When an intern discharges a patient with the incorrect dose of her diabetes medication, a just culture supports focused feedback for the intern in the context of a broader team discussion of the system by which orders are reviewed and implemented. The intern learns that naming and investigating errors as a team is a process of improvement, not one of shaming.

4. DELEGATE SO THAT TEAM MEMBERS HAVE SOME CONTROL OVER THEIR LOCAL ENVIRONMENT

While it is frequently necessary to communicate organizational goals that need to be accomplished, look for opportunities to give team members freedom to choose how to accomplish those goals. While employees expect to be told what needs to be done, it can feel demeaning to be told how to do it. We accept it when our spouses tell us to take out the trash; we are offended if they tell us *how* to take out the trash. Furthermore, the results are likely to be better when informed by varied perspectives. On Dr. Diaz's team, for example, Mr. Gonzalez proposes an effective modification to the facilitation of team huddles. Similarly, if a hospital ward is tasked with reducing the readmission rate or average length of stay for patient falls, it can be beneficial to allow the people working on the ward to develop solutions so that the solutions are informed by the specific conditions on the ward.

5. APPLY PRINCIPLES OF RECIPROCITY AND MUTUALITY TO TEAM INTERACTIONS, INCLUDING FEEDBACK

Reciprocity can be a powerful way to flatten hierarchy. For instance, when a leader has a feedback conversation with someone he or she supervises, it is an opportunity to receive feedback on his or her leadership as well as to give feedback on the other's performance. Chapter 10 framed effective feedback as a relational process in which inquiry, empathy, and specific observations are used to foster shared agenda setting for continued professional development. While hierarchical relationships offer both explicit and implicit permission for unidirectional feedback (from the top to the bottom of the hierarchy), this approach may limit receptivity to feedback and the accompanying growth opportunities that exist for all team members, regardless of their position. So, in addition to the team-based interventions Dr. Diaz used to improve huddles, she might also have one-on-one conversations with each team member. She could start by offering a self-assessment of her own leadership skills and then openly invite feedback, a process that can foster balanced team participation.

6. HOLD TEAM MEMBERS ACROSS THE HIERARCHY TO THE SAME STANDARDS

When an institution sets policies and standards and then selectively enforces them, with only some groups held accountable, resentment grows and leaders may be perceived as hypocritical. If nurses are expected to arrive to clinic on time but doctors are allowed to show up late, nurse morale and team cohesion suffer. An organization that allows its surgeons to verbally abuse residents or nurses in the operating room cannot reasonably proclaim to value treating people with respect and compassion. Effectively detoxifying hierarchy in healthcare requires all team members to uphold professional standards and communicate respectfully regardless of role.

7. FOSTER TRANSPARENCY BY ACKNOWLEDGING HIERARCHY AND ITS EFFECTS

One of the more effective ways to detoxify hierarchies is to acknowledge them. This can make it safe to talk openly about tensions and make team members feel better understood and supported. If one group (doctors, men, respiratory therapists, for example) is doing most or all of the talking, naming the dynamic (preferably by a member of the group) can make it easier to address the issue. It may be as simple as saying, "I notice that we've heard from several of the physicians, and I'm wondering what the nurses and administrators in the room think about the issue." If processes or procedures are put into place to improve the work environment by managing hierarchies more effectively, it helps to be transparent about the goal. We can imagine Dr. Diaz saying, "It's important to me that everyone on our team feels respected and has a voice in our meetings. I want to change the way we run our huddles in order to achieve those goals." The effectiveness of transparency depends on implementation of the previously discussed best practices. Team members are most likely to communicate openly as members of a just culture in which leadership has demonstrated its capacity to both give and receive productive feedback.

Conclusion

Modern healthcare is highly structured and hierarchical. There are many rules about who is allowed to do what. Many of these distinctions are critical for patient care and safety. However, these distinctions have also been used to create "in" groups and "out" groups. Who gets to eat in the special dining room? Who gets the best parking spots? Who are called by their first names, and who are called by their titles? Who finds that people don't even bother to remember their names? Who is expected to speak, and who is expected to listen? Who gets away with bad behavior, and who gets reprimanded? Who is treated with respect, and who is disrespected or ignored?

By answering these questions *and* taking the necessary steps to promote an environment in which everyone feels valued, respected, and empowered, we create more effective teams and a stronger and more engaged workplace culture. The effectiveness of relationship-centered communication is best realized when its fundamental principles are applied in all relationships, including those across hierarchy.

PART IV

INSTITUTING COMMUNICATION INITIATIVES

CHAPTER 16

Teaching the Skill Sets

Ponder, for a moment, the last time you had to learn a new skill as an adult. What circumstances made learning effective? What circumstances made learning more challenging?

Now imagine that you are 30 years into practice and are told that you have to change the way you conduct your initial interview of a patient. How do you feel? How easy or hard will it be to change? What would make it easier?

Every time I (Ellen Pearlman) start a train-the-trainer workshop, I find myself in a room with 12 experienced physicians who are faced with this challenge. There are days when I think to myself, "Who do I think I am, that I can teach under these impossible circumstances?" and wonder if it is going to be worth it. Yet workshop after workshop, I emerge with the satisfaction of witnessing physicians have new light bulbs go off in their heads for the first time in many years of practicing medicine.

In this chapter, I will describe the best methods to teach communication skills and make them stick. A published review article named these the best strategies: role-play, feedback, and small group discussion.[1]

The Power of Role-Play

I was recently running a train-the-trainer session and had just finished giving a brief presentation on Skill Set Three, the use of ART (Ask,

Respond, Tell) in educating and counseling (see Chapter 5). The trainers I was working with were highly engaged and clearly perceptive, and they prided themselves on their communication skills. As we broke up into small groups, one remarked, "This seems pretty straightforward!" After a couple rounds of practicing with patient-clinician scenarios, the group wanted to exercise their muscles at a scenario involving colleagues. One of the nurse managers exclaimed, "Oh, I have one! I recently had to bring in one of our night nurses for falling asleep on the job." "Great!" I replied. "Would you be willing to play her or him?"

What followed was anything but ART. The physician assigned to play the nurse manager, after starting with "Do you know why you are here?" ripped into the unsuspecting night nurse for her unacceptable behavior of falling asleep on the job.

During the debrief of the role-play, everyone nodded in agreement that this approach is exactly what would happen on the job. When I asked if ART was used, they tentatively nodded their heads. Then one participant offered, "Well, the opening question wasn't exactly open-ended." And the physician playing the nurse manager added, "I guess I didn't really respond with empathy." When I asked if this was a dialogue or a monologue, they clearly recognized that the manager had "downloaded" on the nurse.

"Let's try it again, this time starting with an open-ended question, responding with empathy, and using more than one ART cycle," I suggested. What followed was a magical "aha" moment.

> **NURSE MANAGER:** Can you tell me all about what happened the other night? (Ask)
>
> **NURSE:** I am so sorry—I fell asleep on the job. I promise it will never happen again!
>
> **NURSE MANAGER:** I can see that you are upset about it. (Respond)
>
> **NURSE:** My mother was hospitalized two days ago and both of my kids were home sick with a stomach virus. I didn't get my usual sleep during the day. I knew we were short-staffed and didn't want to call in sick, but I guess maybe I should have.
>
> **NURSE MANAGER:** It sounds like you had your hands full! I appreciate your desire to help. (Respond) I also agree

with you that if you don't feel like you can give 100 percent, it is safer for patients if you call in sick. Sounds like you know it is unacceptable to fall asleep on the job—important things can be missed. (Tell)

NURSE: Oh, definitely! I was horrified when I woke up. I felt really lucky that nothing serious had gone wrong.

The group was profoundly affected by this version. Some of the group members were concerned that "the message," i.e., falling asleep was unacceptable, wasn't made clear enough. Yet the participant playing the nurse reassured them, "It was all the more powerful because he took the time to hear me out, *and* I was already feeling ashamed." "But what if you hadn't been feeling bad? What if you were an employee who didn't care?" the others exclaimed. Once again, she rebuffed them, "Then that would have been part of your Tell. Not only does this approach prevent you from making assumptions, it helps you diagnose the problem by assessing the nurse's perception of the problem!" The entire group walked away from the experience convinced that ART could be a powerful tool.

This example demonstrates the power of role-play. Role-play allows adult learners to:

- Practice new skills—skills that may seem easy on paper but harder in practice
- Experience what it is like to be a difficult patient or colleague, and thus gain insight into and empathy for that person
- Compare and contrast new and old approaches with patients or colleagues.

It is for these reasons that we strongly endorse the use of role-play when learning new communication skills. Like learning to master a tennis or golf stroke, communication skills require deliberate practice.

Making Role-Play Successful

When I first ran workshops on running role-play, I said, "Whatever you do, don't call it a role-play." I initially advocated this approach because of the typical moans and eye-rolling I'd get after announcing that we would do a role-play. Others have similarly tried to diminish this effect by calling it "real play." Over time, I have come to accept the response and to use it to elicit group members' experiences about role-play—to address the elephant in the room. It can help in three ways: (1) to acknowledge its artificial nature, (2) to explain its purpose ("We wouldn't be doing this if everyone could do it right the first time") and (3) to advocate for the opportunity to try something new and potentially make mistakes without any adverse consequences. In my experience, it is a tiny minority of people who truly can't participate in a role-play and get something out of it. And as luck would have it, often participants will volunteer positive prior experiences with role-play, so that you won't need to do all of the convincing.

Facilitating role-play is a skill in itself that also requires practice. Let's start by reviewing a scenario where the role-play unfolds poorly. In this scenario, Dr. Thompson is a cardiologist who has graciously volunteered to practice Skill Set One (see Chapter 3). She proceeds to elicit the patient's chief complaint and dives immediately into the history of the present illness when one of the observers calls a "time-out":

> OBSERVER: You didn't elicit all of the concerns.
>
> ANOTHER OBSERVER (JUMPING IN): But she is just the consultant. It isn't really her job to elicit concerns that aren't connected to the visit.
>
> FACILITATOR (REDIRECTING): Maybe the patient can tell us how she felt. (Turning to the person playing the patient)
>
> PATIENT: Well, I was really most concerned that I had a heart attack, but she didn't even get to that.

At this point, Dr. Thompson's eyes begin to well up with tears. She had been nervous conducting an interview in front of her peers to begin with and clearly had failed at the task given to her. She feels ashamed.

Unfortunately, I have seen many examples like this one where role-plays are poorly managed, resulting in either undermined learning or unintentional humiliation of a participant who has been brave enough to practice in front of others. I have even seen facilitators curse when someone doesn't follow a communication skills process exactly as prescribed.

For these reasons, I recommend always adhering to two guiding principles. All other basic rules will follow.

GUIDING PRINCIPLE #1

It is your job as the facilitator to prevent the participant practicing the new skill from being humiliated in public.

Always remember that the participant practicing the new skill is in a vulnerable position, no matter how senior the participant is or how confident he or she seems. The participant is practicing something new in front of other people for the first time and is prone to being easily shamed. A few simple steps can ensure the role-play is not humiliating.

Rule #1

Move your chair to sit next to the participant practicing the new skill and let him or her know you will be nearby as a "coach," as shown in Figure 16.1.

FIGURE 16.1 **Supportive Seating Arrangement**

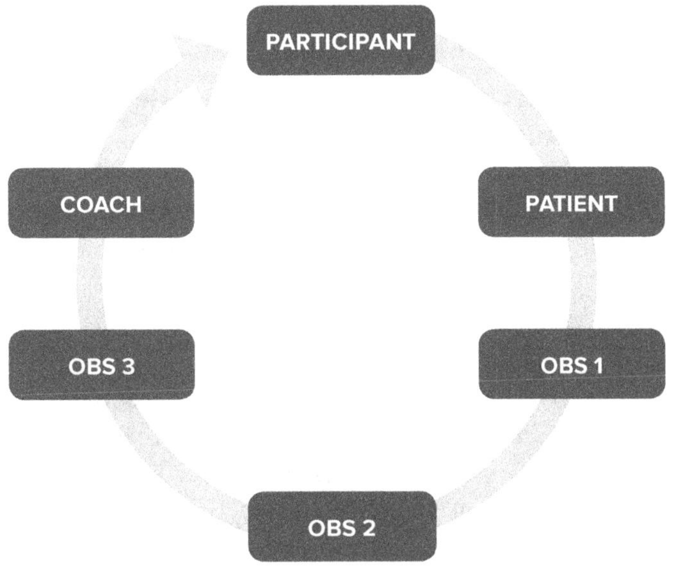

That way, if the learner in the "hot seat" has any trouble, you are right there to offer support. You may even coach him or her by giving suggestions under your breath.

Note: The benefit of this setup is that you are nicely arranged to debrief in order: participant practicing the new skill, then participant playing the patient, then the observers, and then you have the final say.

Rule #2

Review the skills that the participant is going to practice, ideally with the help of a "cheat sheet" such as a handheld card, poster, flip chart, or blackboard with the skills written down.

This review helps the participant focus on the task at hand and the cheat sheet helps the participant figure out where he or she is in the process at any given point.

Rule #3

Only you or the participant can call a "time-out."

Let him or her know that if you call a time-out, it doesn't mean he or she has done something wrong. This rule gives the power to the participant and to you, the skilled facilitator. Now the role-play cannot be derailed by an observer.

Rule #4

Once a time-out has been called, check in with the participant practicing the new skill first.

This rule gives you the opportunity to assess the participant's vulnerability. A simple "How is it going?" can let you know how critical the person is being of him or herself or how nervous he or she is feeling.

Rule #5

Reinforce effectiveness before giving corrective feedback.

As we saw in Chapter 10, studies have shown that people are more likely to incorporate constructive criticism if it is given in a ratio of four reinforcing observations to one corrective observation. The idea is that if you shore up someone's confidence, he or she will be more receptive to criticism. I also believe that when practicing a new skill, it is just as important for "muscle memory" to highlight the effective aspects as it is to critique what was less effective.

Note that it is human nature—especially in medical culture—to go directly to criticism. As a facilitator, you will need to redirect both the participant practicing the new skill and the observers to start with reinforcing feedback. It can help to set this as a ground rule and to remind people that you will "get to that, but let's first start with what was effective."

When you do get to corrective feedback, remember to have the participant practicing the new skill self-reflect first. If he or she offers self-criticism, ask the participant playing the patient to respond from his or her perspective before moving to the observers for comment. Keeping in mind the ratio of four reinforcing to one corrective observation, try to focus on only one piece of criticism and get feedback from the others on that one piece, rather than soliciting additional corrective observations.

Rule #6
Give the participant the opportunity to re-practice.

As with all new skills, it takes time to learn. After he or she has been given both reinforcing and corrective feedback, it can be helpful to have the participant give it one more try to experience success. Finally, soliciting "takeaways" from the participant is an ideal way to conclude the role-play, e.g., "What are you taking away from this experience that you can use in your practice?" This, by the way, illustrates the ART technique (Chapter 5) yet again.

GUIDING PRINCIPLE #2
For learning to occur, the scenario must be relevant.

In revisiting the role-play involving Dr. Thompson, let's imagine a second version of the same scenario:

> Dr. Thompson is a cardiologist who has graciously volunteered to practice Skill Set One (eliciting all concerns and negotiating the agenda). She proceeds to elicit the patient's chief complaint and dives immediately into the history of the present illness and then times herself out. The facilitator

asks her, "How is it going?" She responds that even though she is feeling a little nervous, it went OK. When asked what she felt she did effectively, she responds that she felt she elicited the chief complaint and listened attentively. The participant playing the patient confirms.

When asked what she could have done more effectively, she responds, "Well, I didn't really elicit ALL the concerns. I guess I don't really think that is appropriate in my role as a consultant. I can see a primary care doc doing that, but I don't want to give her the false impression that I can help her with things I can't really do anything about."

It is clear from this scenario that, first and foremost, Dr. Thompson doesn't buy into this skill set—it doesn't seem relevant to her day-to-day practice. As a consequence, she has not practiced the actual skill set, and is thus unlikely to employ it in real life. When the facilitator checks in with Dr. Thompson first, a key barrier to her learning experience is revealed, setting up a teaching opportunity.

Making the skills and scenarios relevant to the participants is critical for buy-in, practice, and retention. There are a number of ways to accomplish buy-in. Rather than telling the participants how you think the skills are relevant, it can be more powerful for them to discover relevance themselves. For example, it can be helpful to simply query, "What is your version of a doorknob question?," "Can you imagine a time when eliciting all concerns would be helpful?," or, "Is there a way to frame the 'what else' that makes it clear you are asking for concerns related to the heart?"

Other Forums for Practice

In addition to role-playing in small groups, three other forums are especially helpful for practicing communication skills: (1) standardized patient encounters, (2) videotape review, and (3) coaching by an observer.

Standardized patient encounters are essentially role-plays but with actors playing patients. They can be done in a clinical skills lab with feedback given by the standardized patients. Alternatively, the actors can participate in small group role-play as just described. If actors are not readily available or affordable, I have had success training staff and faculty members to play patients. One notable disadvantage of this model is that the participants themselves don't get the experience of being a patient and feeling the direct impact of the skills being practiced.

Videotape review of role-plays, standardized patient encounters, or real patients is particularly helpful for self-reflection. Participants are able to watch by themselves, just with a facilitator, or with a small group. They are able to reflect on their effectiveness in real time. If equipment or logistics are a barrier, a simple audio recording using "Voice Memo" on a smartphone is a handy alternative.

Finally, direct observation by a coach is a great option for continued practice that allows feedback on real patient interactions, tailored to the individual (see Chapter 11). Observation can be time limited and focused on a single skill or expanded to longer time periods and encompassing more skill sets. Feedback can be based on predetermined skills checklists or notes taken by the observer.

Table 16.1 summarizes the relative advantages and disadvantages of these three practice methods.

TABLE 16.1 Comparing Other Forums of Practice

	Requires	Advantages	Disadvantages	Low-Cost Versions
Standardized Patient Encounters	Actors, training time, setup logistics	Less artificial/ more "real"	Less opportunity to gain insight from role reversal	Faculty or staff play patients
Videotape Review	Equipment, setup logistics, consent from patients	Allows for self-reflection, playback	Less opportunity to re-practice	Audiotape on smartphone
Direct Observation by Coach	Trained coach, coordinated time	In-the-moment feedback on "real" encounters	Less opportunity to re-practice	Use of checklist for observation by less trained observer

Conclusion

Teaching communication skills is both challenging and gratifying. It requires providing opportunities for learners to practice skills in situations that are relevant and realistic. Role-play is perhaps the cheapest and logistically easiest form of practice, yet requires a skilled facilitator to (1) ensure the participant practicing new skills is not humiliated in public, and (2) ensure the scenario in which the skill is being practiced is relevant and realistic. The use of standardized patients, videotape review, and direct observation by a coach are useful adjuncts for practicing communication skills. While this overview can get you started with facilitating teaching through role-play, Chapter 17 explains how useful a train-the-trainer model can be for developing and deepening facilitation skills.

CHAPTER 17

Train-the-Trainer Programs: Establishing Local Influence

I f you are reading this chapter, we're guessing that you are committed to improving patient experience scores for your institution. But how? Many clinicians may seem either uninterested in or threatened by this work. And although many patients are very satisfied with their clinicians' communication and care, other patients have complaints that need to be addressed. You may have found it confusing that some of the same practitioners receive both high praise and problematic feedback from different patients.

Across the country, healthcare leaders like you are struggling to find ways to improve communication experiences for patients, clinicians, and teams. "Train-the-trainer" (TTT) programs in communication skills can offer sustainable solutions to support internal change efforts.

What are the advantages of hosting a TTT program in your own institution? First, rather than hiring outside experts to teach communication skills to all clinicians, you can reduce costs in the long run by having your internal staff learn these skill sets. Second, internal trainers often develop a sense of community and enhanced learning by engaging with each other.[1, 2] Finally, through their communication skills expertise, internally developed trainers may realize new opportunities for career advancement and potential for leadership roles. These trainers can support your clinicians and educators to help create a culture change to promote the entire patient experience effort.[3]

In this chapter, we describe the format of TTT programs to prepare future communication skills trainers, explain why these programs work, and provide examples to show how these programs have affected the institutions that have adopted them.[4]

Format of TTT Programs

The TTT program for communication skills has five distinct phases, shown in Table 17.1.

TABLE 17.1 Overview of Train-the-Trainer Programs

PHASE I	Preparing by Obtaining Institutional Buy-In, Selecting Future Trainers
PHASE II	Experiencing Fundamental Communication Skills Workshops
PHASE III	Mastering Small-Group Facilitation Skills and Workshop Flow • Iterative practice of communication and small-group facilitation skills • Managing challenging participation
PHASE IV	Going Live • Increasing level of authenticity: co-facilitation of live workshops with the senior faculty member who is leading the project, then finally solo facilitation of live workshops with close observation and minimal intervention by the senior faculty leader.
PHASE V	Ensuring Viability and Long-Term Maintenance of Program

PHASE I: PREPARING BY GAINING INSTITUTIONAL BUY-IN AND SELECTING FUTURE TRAINERS

Ms. Gray is in charge of patient experience at a health system. Leadership positions are in flux, creating an atmosphere of uncertainty and instability. Ms. Gray is committed to improving patient experience and doesn't want to wait for leadership to stabilize before taking action. She chooses to hire highly experienced TTT program consultants from a reputable organization known for its effective communication curriculum.

Ms. Gray carefully identifies a small group of local clinicians to become communication skills trainers. These "future trainers," mainly junior staff who believe in creating better relationships with patients, volunteer to spend extra time and energy for this effort. They find ways to cover their clinical duties and promise to work nights and weekends to make up for time spent learning to become trainers and teaching others. Ms. Gray provides training space but lacks authorization to hire an assistant to take care of logistical details. Even with these barriers, the TTT program consultants successfully train the future trainers to deliver effective communication skills workshops. Unfortunately, the senior executive leadership for the health system is unwilling to provide protected time for either her internal future trainers or for participants who would need to cancel clinical time to attend these workshops.

Ultimately, clinicians are hesitant to sign up for the training, since it would add to their already busy schedules. The new trainers, despite their commitment and willingness to help, are unable to sway their colleagues without higher-level support. So while Ms. Gray's initial efforts hold promise, the program does not accomplish its goal of heightening patient experience.

This cautionary tale emphasizes an important fact: institutional buy-in for establishing a TTT program and supporting its efforts is essential. With institutional backing, initiatives from your patient experience officers and interested staff members thrive. In order for your TTT programs to be successful, you must provide the following support: space to conduct training, financial backing, strong administrative staff, protected time for future trainers, and other resources required to maintain the program. (Chapter 18 will elaborate on institutional factors to maximize success.)

While preparing to begin the TTT process, you will also need the proper personnel and a realistic timeline to carry out the requisite tasks.

1. Having a skilled and organized project coordinator is important for a successful launch and program rollout.

2. TTT program consultants tasked with preparing and coaching future trainers should have extensive prior experience in teaching communication skills, program/curriculum development, and organizational development. Many consultant faculty at ACH, for example, have worked for a decade or more in these areas. When consultants have this level of experience, your clinicians can gain confidence in the entire training process.

3. When choosing internal future trainers, you should look for individuals with emotional intelligence, keen observational skills, and a willingness and capacity to learn and adopt learner-centered facilitation skills. Department chairs, supervisors, or other institutional leaders can sponsor future trainers to reach as many clinicians as possible. Future trainers must also have sufficient standing in the organization to be viewed as credible. For example, the program can include less experienced members of your organization, but it should not be run solely by students, visiting interns, and junior staff members. Future trainers can have varying levels of preexisting experience in communication skills; all, however, must be willing to undergo the training and be interested in the process.

4. The timeline should map Phases II and III of the certification process for future trainers (see Table 17.1), as well as Phase IV, rollout of the full program. The project coordinator must choreograph the intricate dance of calendars between the visiting TTT program consultants and the entire group of identified future trainers. This level of scheduling detail is not for the faint-hearted or overcommitted.

PHASE II: PARTICIPATING IN A FUNDAMENTAL COMMUNICATION SKILLS TRAINING WORKSHOP

For future trainers to become experts in fundamental communication skills, they need a standardized approach and common syntax. They can accomplish this by participating in a standard communication skills workshop, run by TTT program consultants, before preparing to teach the program to colleagues. Instead of utilizing didactic presentations,[5] effective workshops use facilitated skills practice, where small group leaders closely observe and conduct structured debriefs using effective feedback principles (see Chapters 10 and 16). TTT program consultants give brief presentations and demonstrations, but only to contextualize the skills that will be the basis of future trainers' efforts.

As they undergo the standard communication skills training, future trainers learn on three different levels. First and primarily, they are learners who are practicing these fundamentals. Second, as they participate in the skills practice, they may develop insights into what future learners may experience. Third, they are training to become trainers and observe TTT program consultants as role models who demonstrate the facilitation skills that the future trainers will eventually become certified in.

PHASE III: MASTERING SMALL GROUP FACILITATION SKILLS AND WORKSHOP FLOW

> Q: How do you get to Carnegie Hall?
>
> A: Practice, practice, practice.

The point of this old joke is that mastery of anything requires practice. If you sit down to practice for hours and hours at the piano, you may not necessarily improve in mastery. In fact, all those hours of practice in some cases might cement mistakes that you are consistently making.

Literature suggests that we need more than mere practice to develop mastery. Instead, mastering a process includes not only deliberate practice (i.e., practice toward a specific goal) but also feedback.[6] For example, a piano teacher or tennis coach can point out areas of effective performance and mistakes being made. In the case of TTT programs, consultants create practice exercises to help future trainers master fundamental communication skills and learn how to train others to acquire these skills.

> Before becoming a physician, Dr. Sanchez was a gifted teacher who had received accolades from an exclusive boarding school. After six years as a hospitalist, Dr. Sanchez was selected to be a future trainer. He was an enthusiastic

learner in small groups and a dynamic speaker. However, when it came to small-group communication skills work, he tended to lecture, from which it was not easy to learn skills. Through diligent work and some uncomfortable adoption of constructive feedback from TTT program consultants, he eventually became successful at facilitating learning from his participants instead of giving them information downloads, however entertaining.

As future trainers improve their fundamental communication and facilitation skills, they need more advanced practice in challenging scenarios. Future trainers can thereby practice a range of tools that they can use in various scenarios: with a silent participant, a silent group, a talkative participant, and a resistant learner, among others. Throughout this phase of training, future trainers become skilled in observation, learn how to discern between merely allowable versus exemplary communication skills, and become adept at conducting supportive and honest feedback conversations.

PHASE IV: GOING LIVE

When cast members from "Saturday Night Live" scream, "Live from New York—It's Saturday Night!" they do so with authentic excitement. Even with significant iterative practice, there is no more energetic moment than when the whole thing "goes live." A successful training process creates future trainers who can do their jobs independently of TTT program consultants. This is different from the traditional "see one, do one, teach one" approach. Instead, this method actively coaches future trainers toward success.

Future trainers undergo rigorous simulated practice in Phase III above, achieving familiarity with the basic skills and logistics of leading the workshop. Concurrent with these practice sessions, it is most helpful for future trainers and program leaders to create buzz for the upcoming program, recruit participants, and send invitations to targeted individuals and department leaders. Project coordinator staff can assist with registration and reminders for recruitment. After completion of these practice sessions, it's time to go live by welcoming actual participants to the course. Future trainers cofacilitate these classes with a TTT program consultant. The consultant ensures that participants, students, and/or trainees are engaged in the learning process. The TTT program consultant also provides guidance, intervenes when necessary, and helps with logistics.

After consultants give future trainers the green light to move to the next and final training stage, future trainers begin independently facilitating workshops. In this phase, the TTT program consultant is physically present but largely silent. By staying in an observation role, the consultant is able to see what the future trainers' strengths and weaknesses are. The consultant intervenes minimally and mostly provides feedback during breaks.

The final observation and feedback from the TTT program consultant marks the conclusion of the program certification process. Certification typically includes a list of competencies and activities that the future trainers must demonstrate to move forward independently. The full program rollout launches in Phase V.

PHASE V: ENSURING VIABILITY AND LONG-TERM MAINTENANCE OF THE PROGRAM

After putting so much work into a program, you will want to do everything you can to make sure it will be effective—not just in the short term but well into the future. Although we list Phase V after Phase IV, efforts to ensure viability really should happen before Phase IV or at least simultaneously with Phase IV.

As seen in the earlier example with Ms. Gray, future trainers can undergo training, but if the institutional milieu is not conducive to adopting a viable program, the program will never meet its goals. Reviewing methods to create culture change is critical to the ultimate success of both the future trainers and the entire change effort itself. (We explore a detailed process for successfully creating institutional change in Chapter 18.)

An organized structure for the full program rollout is integral to program success. One way you can achieve this is by establishing a registration and reminder system for program participants. The project coordinator can implement a registration system with options ranging from e-mail RSVPs to a formal scheduling system/link, and should work with clinic scheduling personnel to make sure the workshop is appropriately scheduled so that clinical time of class participants is blocked. A reminder system to update registered participants with the details regarding their session supports attendance. Due to late cancellations and no-show attendees, the project coordinator may consider overbooking registration space (e.g., allowing eight participants to register for a session that allows only six). The project coordinator may also explore options for a convenient meeting space to extract attendees from the normal routine of clinical practice with a quiet, comfortable environment that optimizes engaged learning. Providing food and refreshments to maximize comfort and to avoid the distraction of doing work during breaks enhances the uptake of similar workshops.[7]

Ultimately, avoid regarding the TTT program as a quick, one-time fix—rather, it should metamorphose into an ongoing resource that benefits not only patients but also the health system as a whole. Sustaining the TTT program includes ongoing observation of trainers, further development of more advanced communication skills training, and possible use of some of the applications outlined in Part III of this book. Essentially, the TTT process establishes a community of interested and engaged trainers who can learn from each other to grow their skills. Attending regional and national conferences on teaching communication skills can also contribute to this growth. Finally, sharing experiences with other TTT learning communities across the country can provide additional powerful and inspirational ways to accomplish individual, group, and institutional goals.

Examples of TTT Programs

Due to the increased interest in and commitment to this work at institutions across the United States, ACH has partnered with several powerful healthcare institutions. This section will highlight some programs that have transformed the institutions that have adopted them.[8] One common hallmark across all programs is the high satisfaction with which participants rate their experience with the communication skills course: nearly 90 percent of attendees agree or strongly agree that they learned relevant communication skills that they can readily apply to their clinical practices.

MAYO CLINIC IN PHOENIX

Mayo Clinic in Phoenix (MCP), AZ, is ranked nationally in 10 adult specialties and is a 268-bed general medical and surgical facility with more than 13,000 admissions in the most recent year reported.[9] As an early adopter of communication skills training in 2004, MCP identified local physician leaders to collaborate with faculty members of the ACH to develop a peer-facilitated course, known locally as the Communication in Healthcare (CIH) course. Improvements in patient experience data include:

- statistically significant improvements in patients' perceptions of excellence in survey domains directly related to clinician communication and completely under the clinician's control
- an 18 percent decrease in patient complaints for clinicians who participated in the communication course, when compared to those who did not[10]

In an effort to continue the internal development, two MCP trainers advanced to the ACH Faculty-in-Training (FIT) program, culminating in their faculty status with ACH. These local faculty were then able to assume full responsibility for the local MCP course and for the training of additional course trainers. The program has expanded beyond the fundamental course to address broader educational needs within the system. For example, trainers offer customized training for residents and fellows, assist with the simulation center, and guide implementation of the new interpersonal skills curriculum for the new Mayo Medical School.

CLEVELAND CLINIC

Cleveland Clinic (CC) is a large, nonprofit, integrated health system that is ranked as one of the nation's top hospitals. Its national and international footprint has expanded year after year, and CC is well known for its drive toward innovation and quality. In the past, CC was less known for its patient experience.

In 2006, CC began a cultural shift toward empathy and teamwork. This shift is outlined in former CC Chief Experience Officer Jim Merlino's book, *Service Fanatics*.[11] In 2009, CC doctor communication was at the 24th percentile of all U.S. hospitals, and multiple efforts were started to tackle this metric. Since physician communication training

191

needed to be added to these efforts, a collaboration with ACH faculty began in 2011. In total, 17 individuals were trained to facilitate the Four Habits Model[12] during this collaboration. From 2011 to early 2013, these trainers helped teach communication skills to 900 CC physicians and scores improved to the 59th national percentile.[CMS data]

CC transitioned to the R.E.D.E. Model[SM] of Communication[13] in June 2013. It shares several well-known evidence-based best practices in communication[14] and further builds upon the foundational concepts of relationship-centered care as highlighted by Beach and Inui.[15] The R.E.D.E. communication program, known as Foundations of Healthcare Communication (FHC), explicitly and concretely aligns relationship-centered values and mission with the communication skills themselves.[16]

The R.E.D.E. FHC training debuted in June 2013 and became a CEO mandate for all CC physicians, necessitating the training of more than 3,000 physicians in seven months. A 2016 study[17] found that full day R.E.D.E. FHC training led to:

- higher adjusted overall doctor communication Clinician & Group Consumer Assessment of Healthcare Providers and Systems (CGCAHPS) scores compared to controls (p<.03)
- higher improvement in Hospital Consumer Assessment of Healthcare Providers and Systems (HCAHPS) Respect domain score compared to controls (p=.015)
- increased levels of empathy as rated by the Jefferson Scale of Empathy (p<.001)
- decreased levels of burnout, as assessed with the Maslach Burnout Inventory for emotional exhaustion (p<.001), depersonalization (p<.003), and personal accomplishment (p<.04)
- overall high satisfaction with the course itself, in many domains

These results were especially interesting in that physicians' communication ability improved regardless of baseline CGCAHPS, specialty, and years in practice. Doctor communication ratings continued to improve and are at the 67th percentile nationally in reports for 2016.[18]

The Center for Excellence in Healthcare Communication (CEHC) continues the communication work initiated in 2009 and has currently trained more than 7,000 individuals, both internally and externally.

While the cultural focus was originally on training physicians, CEHC embraces advanced care providers (ACPs) in this work. The FHC course is a part of the onboarding process. An additional 58 Cleveland Clinic trainers, both physicians and ACPs, have been trained by CEHC faculty. As part of sustainability efforts, trainers receive quarterly faculty enrichment days and new trainers are recruited and trained every 18 months.

With the R.E.D.E. Model as a foundation, CEHC has created nine additional R.E.D.E. half-day courses. To keep the learning engaging and experiential, CEHC has deepened its expertise in unique teaching methods, such as warm-ups, sociodrama, and improv. Online communication training has been developed to further enhance sustainment efforts. Additionally, CEHC provides individualized peer communication coaching, 10- to 15-minute learning bursts, and workshops created with departments around specific communication needs. Based on the experience of launching training for experienced clinicians, CC published a book in 2016 on key strategies and practical tips for designing and implementing a successful program.[19]

UNIVERSITY OF MARYLAND

With 43 academic units, a faculty of more than 3,000 physicians and research scientists, and more than $400 million in extramural funding, the University of Maryland School of Medicine (UMSOM) is regarded as a prominent biomedical research institution in the United States.[20] In March 2016, UMSOM launched an initiative that customized the standard ACH evidence-based curriculum within their Program for Excellence in Patient-Centered Communication (PEP).[21]

Despite concerns regarding the early mandatory nature of enrollment in this full-day program, even reluctant participants usually reported positive experiences. For example, initial participant feedback evaluations (n=115) reflect a strong positive response across participants:

- 87 percent of participants rated the course as good or very good
- 85 percent of participants would recommend the course to a colleague
- 81 percent of participants agreed that they plan to make changes in their professional work as a result of this training.

Even more important, CGCAHPS® results for the group of faculty physicians who participated in a PEP workshop (the coached group) indicate a promising trend. Prior to program launch, the coached group ranked in the 18th percentile nationally in the physician communication quality domain. By March 2017, the coached group improved to the 60th percentile and outperformed the group of faculty physicians who had not been coached by nearly 30 percentage points.

Of the six individual survey items that comprise the physician communication quality domain of CGCAHPS, the coached group made the most significant strides in the areas of listening carefully and explaining clearly. More specifically, performance on the survey item "provider gave easy-to-understand instructions" improved from the 20th percentile nationally in 2015 to the 79th percentile nationally by March 2017. Performance on the survey item "provider explained things in a way that was easy to understand" reached the 71st percentile nationally by March 2017, up from the 21st percentile in 2015. Finally, the survey item "provider listened carefully to patient" increased from the 13th percentile in 2015 to the 63rd percentile in March 2017. These early outcomes have encouraged the institution to reinvest in the program by recruiting a new cohort for the TTT process and exploring ways to expand the program to other members of their healthcare teams.[22]

SAN MATEO MEDICAL CENTER

San Mateo Medical Center (SMMC) is a public general medical and surgical hospital in San Mateo, CA, with 137 beds. Survey data for the latest year available shows that the hospital had more than 3,500 admissions.[23] SMMC started their TTT program in June 2016. Trainers were strategically selected across specialties and departments, and to include various leadership roles. Program efforts have shown excellent success. By May 2017, trainers trained more than 80 percent of their primary care providers. The program is currently focused on specialists and emergency department clinicians.

SMMC reports a steady improvement in their CGCAHPS scores in the provider communication section, leading to a steady improvement in "likely to recommend" scores for the ambulatory department.

Engagement scores for providers have also steadily improved since the communication program launched. For example, the net promoter score for the question, "How likely are you to recommend SMMC as a place to work?" has increased by 11 points, and the score for the question, "How likely are you to recommend SMMC as a place to come for care?" has increased by 16 points.

WAKE FOREST BAPTIST HEALTH SYSTEM

Wake Forest Baptist is an integrated system in Winston-Salem, NC, that operates 1,000 acute care, rehabilitation and psychiatric care beds, outpatient services, and community health and information centers.[24] With enthusiastic support and solid financial backing from senior health system leadership, the Program to Enhance Relationship-Centered Care (PERCC) began in January 2016 and went "live" in March 2016, facilitated by a cadre of nine physician trainers representing internal medicine, hospital medicine, surgery, pediatrics, and critical care/anesthesiology. As of May 2017, more than 300 physicians, 125 advanced practice providers (APPs), and more than 70 nurses, healthcare educators, and senior residents have attended workshops. Although there was some initial concern about blending audiences, PERCC workshops engage a mix of providers (e.g., nurses, APPs, and physicians), which has promoted understanding and mutual respect.

Positive reviews by respected senior clinicians earned credibility for PERCC, and attendees consistently rate PERCC the "best faculty development program we've ever had at Wake Forest." While enrollment is intentionally voluntary, several departments count PERCC attendance toward the "quality component" of their compensation plans. Testimonials that "PERCC works" were confirmed by patient experience surveys for the initial 70 ambulatory physician attendees. In the first six months after attending a workshop, physicians saw a significant improvement in their CGCAHPS scores on "Provider Communication Quality" when compared with a control group of non-attendees (p=0.026).

With the aim of establishing a common communication language across every facet of the health system, PERCC was incorporated into the communication skills curriculum for Wake Forest medical students (2016) and the Physician Assistant Program (2017). PERCC workshops have been tailored to fit the needs of two major residency programs (internal medicine and emergency medicine), with more programs starting each year. Trainees, nurses, and faculty working together in clinical settings are applying communication approaches learned in PERCC to the care of their patients.

TEXAS CHILDREN'S HOSPITAL

Texas Children's Hospital (TCH) in Houston, TX, is consistently ranked among the top children's hospitals in the nation.[25] In late 2015, TCH launched an initiative called Breakthrough Communication. Anticipating future public reporting of CAHPS Child Hospital Survey results, the program's goal is to reinforce the practice of relationship-centered care to improve and ensure consistency of care coordination systemwide.

After conducting focus groups with patients and families, TCH created a curriculum that incorporated the stakeholders' expressed needs and expectations. This customized relationship-centered communication training includes addressing the different ages and stages of pediatric and obstetric patients. The program also emphasizes a triadic method of communication (patient-family member-provider) as opposed to a dyadic method (patient-provider) seen more commonly in predominantly adult populations.

The hospital selected 13 providers to participate in the ACH-sponsored TTT program in order to teach Breakthrough Communication to the rest of its physician staff. Trainings began in July 2016, and in the first nine months, they trained more than a third of the medical staff. Feedback from providers has been extremely positive and enthusiastic, as the training provides tools to benefit patients as well as providers' daily encounters.

Early results show:

- over 90 percent of participants said the skills were relevant to their practice and have implemented them in their activities
- a statistically significant reduction in physician burnout, as measured by the Maslach burnout inventory three months postsurvey

UNIVERSITY OF CALIFORNIA, SAN FRANCISCO

The University of California, San Francisco (UCSF) Health System, associated with an academic center that is ranked annually among the top 10 hospitals in the nation, is an integrated healthcare network serving multiple inpatient and outpatient sites across the San Francisco Bay Area. In late 2015, UCSF launched a TTT program and has now trained hundreds of providers across mixed specialty areas. Participants attend on a voluntary basis and are encouraged to do so based on professional development goals, rather than on patient experience data incentives.

Similar to the feedback reports we collect from participants attending ACH courses at various institutions across the United States, feedback samples were provided by participants after attending the one-day UCSF course.[26]

Multiple participants note the impact on the quality and effectiveness of their care of using the communication tools. For example, by asking a patient for a list of topics to cover, an otolaryngology physician assistant elicited the patient's concern for a skin lesion that wasn't the original reason for the visit—and made a new diagnosis of an intranasal melanoma. Another noted a conversation with parents about placing tubes in the ears of their child, a procedure that was recommended but had not been acceptable to the parents after several visits with other colleagues. Using empathy and eliciting the parents' perspective, the provider found that the parents' position on the procedure changed easily, allowing them to move forward with the indicated procedure.

The TTT program also enables local trainers to continue advancing communication skill improvement, beyond simply offering the one-day course. At UCSF's Center for Enhancement of Communication in Healthcare, 90-minute sessions allow participants to build on their learning from the foundational one-day course. These courses help learners to delve deeper into specific challenges in communication and follow the same structure of brief didactic material introduced in small group settings with emphasis on skills practice. Four "microskills" courses are now available: Anger, Conflict, Breaking Bad News, and Feedback.

UNIVERSITY OF ARKANSAS FOR MEDICAL SCIENCES

The University of Arkansas for Medical Sciences (UAMS) is the state's only health sciences university; it is composed of five colleges (Medicine, Nursing, Pharmacy, Health Professions, and Public Health), a graduate school, and the UAMS Medical Center (hospital and associated ambulatory practices). Following an ACH-led TTT program and certification in late 2016, 12 carefully recruited UAMS "Communication Champions" began delivery of the program, known as MASTER Classes (**M**astering **A**dvanced **S**kills **T**o **E**nhance **R**elationships). In February 2017, faculty physicians and advanced practice staff began attending the class. House staff started participating in the program in June 2017.

Outcomes from the first quarter of MASTER Class training have been very encouraging, as seen in the feedback responses from a sample of 175 participants[27]:

- 93 percent assessed the education material as "helpful"
- 90 percent of those participants rated the course as "excellent" or "good"
- 88 percent strongly agreed or agreed that what they learned in the MASTER class will allow them to make helpful changes in the way they interact with patients, staff, and trainees

Anecdotally, the Champions have observed that a significant number of participants start the day skeptical about the value of the class and are reluctant to give up a full day of clinical practice. Almost invariably, attendees leave intrigued by the utility of the new communication framework and skills they have practiced to do their most fundamental work: connect with patients in a way that enhances clinical outcomes, patient satisfaction, and provider satisfaction. Comments on the course evaluations frequently credit the skills of the Communication Champions, who make the learning immediately credible and relevant to clinical practice. Educational leaders in the College of Medicine are incorporating the ACH model into the medical students' communication skills curriculum. There are conversations about adapting the model for use with teams from clinical units across the hospital and ambulatory practices.

ZUCKERBERG SAN FRANCISCO GENERAL

Zuckerberg San Francisco General Hospital and Trauma Center (ZSFG) is a Level I trauma center and safety net hospital staffed by University of California, San Francisco faculty and trainees in collaboration with the San Francisco Department of Public Health. The hospital's ACH train-the-trainer program launched in 2014, and the relationship-centered communication (RCC) program has seen steady growth since.

A distinguishing focus of the ZSFG RCC program is its application to interprofessional teams (see Chapter 12). All members of the healthcare team are welcome to ZSFG's RCC workshops, and customized workshops are offered for intact teams, including coordination of RCC retreats for as many as 75 participants from primary care clinics. Preparatory needs assessments coordinated by team leadership enable trainers to focus workshop content and skills practice effectively. Pre-work identifies a team's strengths (e.g., appropriate collaboration to address lengthy patient agendas), as well as opportunities for intentional improvement and practice (e.g., direct team communication when perspectives differ).

Zuckerberg San Francisco General Hospital and Trauma Center has made three revisions to the core RCC workshop: (1) didactic presentations using language inclusive of all participating team members; (2) trainer demonstrations of fundamental skills using team-based scenarios; and (3) small-group skills practice structured to balance participation across roles. Examples of team-based scenarios used for demonstrations include following a patient from registration with a clerk, to screening by a medical assistant, to the exam room with a physician, and, finally, to discharge teaching with a nurse. Alternatively, application of RCC to challenging team encounters may be demonstrated: a typical instance could be a charge nurse using open-ended questions and empathy (see Chapter 4) to explore a resident physician's concerns about clinic workflow. Small-group assignments are designed to optimize a collaborative, interprofessional learning environment and, in the case of intact teams, allow for facilitated skills practice of cases faced jointly by team members on a day-to-day basis. This learning environment provides teams with opportunities to strengthen not only communication skills but also relationships.

Qualitative feedback from participants supports the utility of these sessions. One nurse manager related, "Now all members of our team, from clerks to nurses to physicians, have a shared vocabulary to help us create a more welcoming environment for patients and staff alike." More specifically, participants recognize that effectively eliciting perspective with open-ended questions and listening in response are skills relevant to both patient and team interactions: "I will be more intentional in my interactions with colleagues and also more proactive in reaching out to staff to elicit feedback." From another participant, "The RCC skills help me to step back and slow down in order to really listen to my patients and coworkers. What I learn makes me a better educator and nurse." Empathy for fellow team members may also be enhanced: "[I will] be more conscientious of the complexities of coworkers' jobs."

Creating a learning environment in which these insights are possible requires skillful facilitation, including attention to the impact of hierarchy and interventions designed to support engagement of all team members. Zuckerberg San Francisco General Hospital and Trauma Center continues to refine its efforts, which include professional diversification of the facilitation team itself. By fostering compassion and respect in all relationships, ZSFG seeks to enhance and accelerate the impact of its RCC program beyond provider change to culture change, which ultimately includes all team members.

Conclusion

A wealth of evidence across institutions and geographic locations supports the train-the-trainer program model. We now know that clinicians' communication skills are teachable to clinicians across institutions and geography, that their increased skill levels lead to enhanced patient outcomes, and that customized solutions for institutions can succeed. When we train future trainers, allowing them to practice and receive feedback with increasing levels of autonomy, we arm ourselves with internal experts who can teach our clinicians and ultimately support the overall patient experience. The process of developing effective trainers is only one step in a complex journey toward improving overall experiences and outcomes. The successes of these program exemplars reflect the necessary strong commitment by organizational leaders and the trainers who deliver these programs.

CHAPTER 18

Implementation and Planning: Supporting Organizational Change

ffective communication is critical to positive patient experience. We are becoming more aware of the power of effective communication as a pathway for creating more meaningful connections, expressing empathy, and improving experiences, safety, and quality outcomes. However, believing in the value of communication is only the beginning. Healthcare leaders must develop and implement a thoughtful strategic plan when instituting a communication skills program that will effect change across an organization.

Chapter 17 explained the train-the-trainer process for developing internal trainers, a valuable tool to successfully implement communication skills programs. If you want to change the culture of an institution, there are additional processes that can help make your initiative a success. You can use this general framework as a guide:

1. Identify the problem or question.
2. Gather data.
3. Generate provisional solutions.
4. Plan, act, and adapt.

Notably, this framework is meant to be a social process characterized by coalition building and consultation. In this chapter, we explore the choices and processes at "Sample Hospital," a fictional example drawn from our years of experience across the country.

Identify the Problem or Question

> Ms. Conner serves as the Director of Patient Experience at Sample Hospital. As she examines patient experience survey reports, she notices that clinician communication remains consistently low, despite a recent push to create awareness of the importance of patient-centered care. Over the past year, patient experience score reports have been administered to each clinician; those with lower scores have been told that they must improve. While some claim to recognize the importance of patient experience, no one seems motivated to change. Some individuals have disputed the findings with statements like "the surveys are invalid," "my patients really like me," "we don't have time," and "it's not my job to make patients happy."

Ms. Conner needs to take action to raise patient experience. For the remainder of this case study, we are going to follow two possible pathways. As we notice the similarities and differences between the paths, we can consider how they might reflect or guide us in our own organizational change efforts.

Pathway A

Eager to see improvement, Ms. Conner decides to develop a communication skills program for clinicians. She believes that patients at Sample Hospital deserve to feel respected, understood, and cared for. She wonders: How can we develop a program that makes a real impact? How can we engage clinicians and inspire them to express more empathy? What will it take to truly inspire change at Sample Hospital? Armed with her spreadsheets of patient experience scores and patient complaints, she gathers information about leading communication skills programs to present to her management team.

Pathway B

Ms. Conner understands that there is a connection between patient experience and the communication skills of clinicians. She also knows that clinicians have a deep sense of pride in their work and that being told they need communication skills training carries the implication that they are doing it "wrong"—a message known to generate great resistance. She also believes that best practices and evidence is only one-half of the equation—truly engaging with clinicians to understand their experiences and concerns is key. Over the next month, she speaks with formal and informal leaders in her institution, hoping to be able to form a small task group to explore the following question: "What support or skills do clinicians need to make patient encounters as efficient and effective as possible?"

As we explore both pathways, you may recognize that Pathway A represents a more traditional attempt to instigate change. One risk of this option is that Ms. Conner will seize on a solution too quickly and miss critical opportunities to engage key stakeholders. In fact, this approach was one that Ms. Gray took in Chapter 17, resulting in a lost opportunity. As discussed in previous chapters, we encourage leaders to engage others through "dialogue" rather than "monologue." Parallel to using the ART (Ask, Respond, Tell) cycle when communicating with patients (see Chapter 5), when leaders invest in assessing and sharing understanding (as seen in Pathway B), they increase the likelihood that the plan will be accepted and that changes may occur.

As you identify the problem or question related to changing the communication skills environment, you may want to consider the five classic W questions: *who, what, when, where,* and *why.* For example: Who is most impacted by the problem? What are you trying to change? When do you need to address this problem? Where is the issue more concerning (e.g., department, specialty, clinic, etc.)? Why should you address this problem? Exploring questions like these may also be helpful across the phases of any major management effort.

Gather Data—Including Numbers, Experiences, Stories, and Observations

Pathway A

Ms. Conner has very high-quality data about both her institution and how it compares to other health systems across the country. She makes a very strong case for the link between clinicians' interpersonal skills and outcomes such as patient experience, safety, malpractice risk, readmission rates, and quality of care indicators (e.g., adherence to treatments and chronic disease management). She has projected the costs of a systemwide training program against expected savings over 10 years.

Pathway B

Ms. Conner starts her task group meetings with a report comparing local patient experience and outcomes to national trends. "These numbers bring our awareness to something we need to pay attention to. They also suggest great potential for us to improve. What do we need to understand further about the experience of our clinicians and our particular health system so we can do our best to communicate our desire for this project to be in partnership with our clinicians? If we can't understand where they are coming from, we can't offer something of value to them."

The group proposes a series of "Taking the Pulse" lunches in all the clinical and service areas. The 45-minute format includes a 2-minute speech from the Chief of Service, a story of outstanding service by a clinician in that unit, and a focused discussion answering the question, "What is the most challenging aspect of your clinical communication with patients, and how can we support your work to meet that challenge more effectively?"

While the idea of gathering data will certainly involve patient experience survey reports, we recommend delving more deeply into a diverse range of "data." These data may include personal stories and experiences from patients, families, *and* clinicians. Observations of interactions across multiple contexts provide valuable insight. Data should also include other metrics such as quality and safety reports, staff engagement scores, malpractice claims, patient complaints, and more.

In Pathway A, Ms. Conner's data set is limited to quantitative or fact-based data, used in support of a course of action that she already feels committed to. Her case is reasonable and rational. But it rests on a foundation that has not been created to include other voices or per-spectives—most notably, those who will be most affected by a proposed training. She also misses the chance to find the links between what she cares most about and what her clinicians are experiencing.

The team in Pathway B offers another approach to data collection as they conduct the lunches over a two- to three-month period. They discover that clinicians are anxious about increasing expectations for patient contact (i.e., through secure electronic messaging) and about conversations with patients seeking opioids. The sessions also highlight a sense of change fatigue among the group following the adoption of a new electronic health record system, a safety campaign emphasizing the importance of handwashing, the implementation of nurse-physician bedside rounding, and the hiring of a new hospital president and CEO. The quantitative data collected in Pathway A are crucially informa-tive. The ideas shared in Pathway B are proposed as added resources for developing a more robust understanding of the problem. Addi-tionally, collecting stories and gathering ideas will engage a broader constituency of stakeholders. People are much more likely to accept and support change when they feel that their voices were heard in the early stages of that change.

Generate Provisional Solutions

Pathway A

Ms. Conner's commitment to her patient experience role creates a sense of urgency to drive change, and she plans to launch a communication skills program as soon as possible. She develops a catchy title and description for the program and creates a PowerPoint presentation using fundamentals she learned while attending a recent conference. She decides to offer a 90-minute workshop session for clinicians, who can sign up to attend during lunch breaks (this is all the time she hopes for from busy clinicians).

Ms. Conner creates a flyer and starts visiting department meetings to build awareness about the importance of communication and the impact on patient experience, while announcing the upcoming opportunity. She sends e-mail blasts to all clinicians with dates and registration information. The first two workshops are well attended, mostly by younger clinicians and those who are known as top performers. The next several workshops have very low attendance, and Ms. Conner is discouraged. She wonders: Why don't these clinicians care about patient experience? Can't they take just 90 minutes of their day to learn about communication? What can I do to engage them?

Pathway B
Ms. Conner's task force reviews all the numbers and experiences shared during the lunches and decides that a tailored communication skills course using a facilitator training program model is the best approach. Aware of the degree of change fatigue, the task force approaches the leadership team with their findings and with several critical requests. One is for support in acknowledging and thanking staff for their efforts to date. The other is for a strong mandate and the financial support for the proposed communication skills initiative. The task force requests that several delegates of the leadership team be supported to do a site visit at a comparable institution that completed a communication skills training program the year before. There is general agreement as to the direction everyone wants to take, but there is also a desire to feel as fully informed and prepared as possible before the project is widely announced.

Now might be a good time to reflect on similar changes that might be occurring in your own organization's culture. We all know that the landscape of healthcare is rapidly changing, and healthcare clinicians are increasingly given no choice but to adapt. These changes are often disruptive, frustrating, and stressful. As in the case of Sample Hospital, there may be multiple initiatives under way. A communication skills program can feel like yet another time-consuming task, with the risk of being perceived as one more "flavor of the month." When launching a successful program, you must first assess the local culture. What are the past or current program initiatives? What was the impact of the programs? What is the current level of morale among clinicians and staff?

In her eagerness to implement a program, Pathway A Ms. Conner inadvertently overlooked several factors within the local culture that might impact the level of interest and engagement among her target participants. Again we see the risks that Ms. Conner takes, singlehandedly owning such a huge amount of the responsibility and drive for the project. But support from C-suite leaders is critical. While these leaders need not engage in the intricate details or logistics of the program delivery, it is critical that they buy in to the concept. This will likely make—or break—the program.

Invested leaders will reflect on and respond to the local culture, especially within the context of a targeted population (e.g., physicians, nurses). Like Ms. Conner did in Pathway B, you can consider strategies for most effectively addressing the current needs of the organization by forming a group of leaders to contribute thoughtfully to the process.

This book outlines a set of useful and meaningful skills to help change the ways that clinicians communicate with patients, families, and their teams. Sometimes, you will need to generate temporary solutions that are customized both to the needs of your organization and to the individuals who co-create a local culture. As you decide on options and next steps, you may again want to consider the five W questions: Who should be involved in a change effort? What would a program or solution look like (e.g., workshops, coaching, videos)? When would the effort begin and end? Where should the effort start (e.g., inpatient versus outpatient; nurses versus physicians versus entire team; specialty versus department)? Why are you committed to the proposed effort?

Plan, Act, and Adapt

Pathway A

Following her disappointment with the initial response to her enthusiastic plan for a hospital-wide communication skills course, Ms. Conner takes a different tack. She recognizes the need to adapt after the failed launch of the 90-minute lunch sessions. In an effort to respond, Ms. Conner further explores how healthcare systems have successfully implemented communication skills programs. She invites a guest facilitator to lead a pilot session and recruits allies who represent the population of targeted learners to attend the pilot version of a revised program. These allies make a point of actively recruiting several people who were doubters. The pilot participants are given time to reflect on how the proposed program will translate to their larger setting.

Three months after the pilot program, Ms. Conner takes a delegation including her CEO and Chief of Staff to another large hospital within the Sample system where participants share the story of the process, including the rewards and setbacks. The new hospital is invited to consider its readiness to embark on its own communication skills enhancement program.

Encouraged by the experience of their peers, Ms. Conner moves things more quickly this time. A train-the-trainer program, modeled after the revised pilot program, is up and running at the new hospital location within three months. The process of bringing the enhanced communication skills training to all five of the system's hospitals takes two and a half years. Although this is longer than the executive team's goal of 18 months, the adaptation is ultimately considered successful. Patient experience scores significantly increase and, unexpectedly, absenteeism decreases slightly for the first time in years. Several of the original pilot groups contact Ms. Conner's office about training in advanced communication skills around end of life care.

Pathway B

The leadership team is comfortable and highly committed to a train-the-trainer program. A launch is planned in six months. As part of the launch, the leadership conducts a "thanks for your commitment to excellence" campaign to appreciate all staff for their participation in the change initiative over the preceding two years. The thank you includes a message to clinicians that foreshadows a "clinician-led" professional development initiative to improve clinician effectiveness during the clinical encounter and to support compassionate care during difficult conversations.

There is also a smaller project developed to help educate patients about "how to talk with your team," including pathways and processes to divert all but the most relevant electronic messages away from the clinicians. 80 percent of the local site leaders who formed part of the original task group have signed up to be trainers.

The framework outlined in this chapter can help guide your thinking as you contemplate and prepare for action. As described in the case of Sample Hospital, Pathway B represents a smoother approach. However, we often embark on a change effort with too little preparation, as seen in Pathway A. The key lesson here is not that Ms. Conner failed in Pathway A. Instead, we can reflect on how Ms. Conner successfully adapted and redirected along the way. The next section provides practical considerations to guide you in your planning. Your actions, and the subsequent success or failure of your plans, will be directly influenced by the level of thoughtful and strategic preparation.

Practical Considerations

The next section includes some final practical details to consider as you drive your initiative. We intend these suggestions to be contingent upon continuous assessment and adaptation as you embark on any change effort.

- **Engage Leaders:** Successful change efforts are highly dependent on the extent to which key leaders embrace the program. Executive leaders (e.g., CEO, CNO, and CMO) must approve funding and time allocations. We recommend that leaders enroll as participants in one of the initial workshop offerings to provide feedback and authentically endorse the effort.
- **Identify a Project Management Team:** An effective project management team will likely involve both executive/senior leaders and operational project managers. The roles and responsibilities of each team member should be identified clearly. Senior leaders will likely serve as thought leaders or steering committee members. Project managers will oversee the operational tasks of program development and delivery such as messaging about the program, recruiting participants, scheduling, registration, preparing materials, and more.
- **Seek Wise Counsel:** Planning a successful program requires support from a variety of sources. As we plan the content and delivery method, we will need to enlist individuals who have the knowledge and skills necessary to guide the curriculum and to engage learners. Although a train-the-trainer program is a highly effective way to develop a cadre of internal expertise (see Chapter 17), that approach is not for everyone. We might instead identify one or two champions who can develop or offer the necessary expertise. Many systems invite visiting communication experts to provide a more immediate solution.
- **Tailor the Message:** Consider approaches to best reach and motivate the target audience (the clinicians who will engage in the new program). Your organization may have internal marketing or communication staff members who can lend support as you craft announcements and prepare materials. Promotional assets may include e-mail invitations, short in-person presentations at department meetings, print materials, a webpage, and more. Make sure to get formal endorsements from key leadership and respected colleagues. Creating a campaign to announce and promote the initiative is an often overlooked, yet crucial, part of planning.

Conclusion

In this chapter we offered four elements to consider as we embark on organizational change processes: (1) identify the problem or question, (2) gather data, (3) generate provisional solutions, and (4) plan, act, and adapt. Our case examples were meant to highlight the importance of taking an actively social and inclusive approach whenever possible.

There is a saying in science: "All models are bad, but some are more useful than others." The most important mindset for change is to pay close attention to what arises in us, our colleagues, and our organization as we experience the work of supporting communication skills training. From our experience will emerge the guidance for what to continue doing, what to consider changing, and what to stop.

It is important to acknowledge that nothing is ever as neat and tidy as a change-management model might have one believe. Having this process proceed with many bumps and missteps isn't necessarily a failure of planning or strategy—it's the very nature of the business.

NOTES

Preface

1. Stewart, J. *Bridges Not Walls. A Book About Interpersonal Communication*, 11th ed. New York: McGraw-Hill, 2012. (Not the Jon Stewart formerly of *The Daily Show.*)
2. Lipkin Jr., M., S. M. Putnam, and A. Lazare, eds. *The Medical Interview: Clinical Care, Education, and Research*. New York: Springer-Verlag, 1995.
3. Fortin, A. H. VI, R. C. Smith, F. C. Dwamena, and R. M. Frankel. *Smith's Patient-Centered Interviewing: An Evidence-Based Method*, 3rd ed. New York: McGraw-Hill Professional, 2012.
4. Details of the training can be found at http://www.ACHonline.org/Programs/Faculty-in-Training-Program. For a description of the effect of the training on 25 years of program graduates, see Chou, C. L., K. Hirschmann, A. H. Fortin VI, and P. R. Lichstein. "The Impact of a Faculty Learning Community on Professional and Personal Development: the Facilitator Training Program of the American Academy on Communication in Healthcare," *Academic Medicine* 89(2014): 1051–1056.

Chapter 1

1. Lipkin Jr., M., S. M. Putnam, and A. Lazare. "The Medical Interview: Clinical Care, Education, and Research," *New York: Springer* (1995): ix.
2. Tresolini, C. P., and the Pew–Fetzer Task Force. "Health Professions Education and Relationship–Centered Care," *San Francisco: Pew Health Professions Commission* (1994).
3. Beach, M. C., T. Inui, and the Relationship–Centered Care Research Network. "Relationship–centered Care: A Constructive Reframing," *Journal of General Internal Medicine* 21 (2006): S3–8.
4. Lown, B. A. "A Social Neuroscience–Informed Model for Teaching and Practicing Compassion in Health Care," *Medical Education* 50 (2016): 332–342.

5. Shanafelt, T. D., L. N. Dyrbye, and C. P. West. "Addressing Physician Burn-out: The Way Forward," *The JAMA Network* 317 (2017): 901–902.

6. Among many others, the following is a list of representative references: Dwamena, F. et al. "Interventions for Providers to Promote a Patient–cen-tred Approach in Clinical Consultations," *Cochran Database System Review* (2012): CD003267; Gabay, G. "Perceive Control Over Health, Communi-cation and Patient–physician Trust," *Patient Education and Counseling* 98 (2015): 1550–1557; Haskard, K. B. et al. "Physician and Patient Communi-cation Training in Primary Care: Effects on Participation and Satisfaction," *Health Psychology* 27 (2008): 513–522; Pollak, K. et al. "Effect of Teaching Motivational Interviewing Via Communication Coaching on Clinician and Patient Satisfaction in Primary Care and Pediatric Obesity–focused Offices," *Patient Education and Counseling* 99 (2) (2016): 300–303; Rao, J. et al. "Communication Interventions Make a Difference in Conversations Between Physicians and Patients: A Systematic Review of the Evidence," *Medical Care* Apr 45 (4) (2007): 340–349; Rathert, C., M. D. Wyrwich, and S. A. Boren. "Patient–centered Care and Outcomes: A Systematic Review of the Literature," *Medical Care Research and Review* August 70(4) (2013): 351–379.

7. A representative sample of references includes: Lelorain, S. et al. "A System-atic Review of the Associations Between Empathy Measures and Patient Outcomes in Cancer Care," *Psycho–Oncology* 21 (2012): 1255–1264; Lux-ford, K. et al. "Improving Clinician–carer Communication for Safer Hospital Care: A Study of the 'TOP 5' Strategy in Patients with Demen-tia," *International Journal for Quality Health Care* June 27 (3) (2015): 175–182; Robinson, J. D. et al. "Consultations Between Patients with Breast Cancer and Surgeons: A Pathway from Patient–centered Commu-nication to Reduced Hopelessness," *Journal of Clinical Oncology* 31 (2013): 351–358; Trevino, K. M. et al. "The Lasting Impact of the Therapeutic Alli-ance: Patient–oncologist Alliance as a Predictor of Caregiver Bereavement Adjustment," *Cancer* October 1 (121; 19) (2015): 3534–3542; Verheul, W., A. Sanders, and J. Bensing. "The Effects of Physicians' Affect–oriented Com-munication Style and Raising Expectations on Analogue Patients' Anxiety, Affect and Expectancies," *Patient Education and Counseling* 80 (3)(2010): 300–306.

8. Benner, J. S. et al. "A Novel Programme to Evaluate and Communicate 10–year Risk of CHD Reduces Predicted Risk and Improves Patients' Mod-ifiable Risk Factor Profile," *International Journal of Clinical Practice* 62 (2008): 1484–1498.

9. Meterko, M. et al. "Mortality Among Patients with Acute Myocardial Infarction: The Influences of Patient–centered Care and Evidence–Based Medicine," *Health Services Research Journal* October 45 (5 Pt 1) (2010): 1188–1204.

10. Curry, L. A. et al. "What Distinguishes Top-Performing Hospitals in Acute Myocardial Infarction Mortality Rates? A Qualitative Study," *Annals of Internal Medicine* 154 (2011): 384–390.

11. Record, J. D. et al. "Reducing Heart Failure Readmissions by Teaching Patient-centered Care to Internal Medicine Residents," *Archives of Internal Medicine Journal* May 171(9) (2011): 858–859.

12. Hojat, M. et al. "Physicians' Empathy and Clinical Outcomes for Diabetic Patients," *Academic Medicine* 86 (2011): 359–364.

13. The following are representative references. For blood pressure: Schoenthaler, A. et al. "Provider Communication Effects Medication Adherence in Hypertensive African Americans," *Patient Education and Counseling* 75 (2) (2009): 185–191. For diabetes: Greenfield, S. et al. "Patients' Participation in Medical Care: Effects on Blood Sugar Control and Quality of Life in Diabetes," *Journal of General Internal Medicine* 3 (1988): 448–457. For HIV: Flickinger, T. E. et al. "Clinician Empathy Is Associated with Differences in Patient-clinician Communication Behaviors and Higher Medication Self-efficacy in HIV Care," *Patient Education and Counseling* 99(2) (2016): 220–226. For elderly patients with polypharmacy: Moral, R .R. et al. Collaborative Group ATEM-AP Study. "Effectiveness of Motivational Interviewing to Improve Therapeutic Adherence in Patients Over 65 Years Old with Chronic Diseases: A Cluster Randomized Clinical Trial in Primary Care," *Patient Education and Counseling* August 98(8) (2015): 977–983. Weitzman, S. et al. "Improving Combined Diabetes Outcomes by Adding a Simple Patient Intervention to Physician Feedback: A Cluster Randomized Trial," *Israel Medical Association Journal* 11 (2009): 719–724.

14. Di Palma, J. A., and J. L. Herrera. "The Role of Effective Clinician–Patient Communication in the Management of Irritable Bowel Syndrome and Chronic Constipation," *Journal of Clinical Gastroenterology* 46(9) (2012): 748–751.

15. A couple of randomized controlled trials in primary care headed by Bob Smith demonstrate benefits in patients with medically unexplained physical symptoms, sometimes called "somatization": Smith, R. C. et al. "Primary Care Clinicians Treat Patients with Medically Unexplained Symptoms: A Randomized Controlled Trial," *Journal of General Internal Medicine* 21 (2006): 671–677; Smith, R. C. et al. "Primary Care Physicians Treat Somatization," *Journal of General Internal Medicine* 24 (2009): 829–832.

16. Trummer, U. F. et al. "Does Physician–patient Communication that Aims at Empowering Patients Improve Clinical Outcome? A Case Study," *Patient Education and Counseling* 61 (2006): 299–306.

17. Lee, J. et al. "Perioperative Psycho-educational Intervention Can Reduce Postoperative Delirium in Patients After Cardiac Surgery: A Pilot Study," *International Journal of Psychiatry Medicine* 45(2) (2013): 143–158.

18. Steinhausen, S. et al. "Short– and Long–term Subjective Medical Treatment Outcome of Trauma Surgery Patients: The Importance of Physician Empathy," *Patient Prefer Adherence* September 18(8) (2014): 1239–1253.
19. Fox, S. A. et al. "Cancer Screening Adherence: Does Physician–patient Communication Matter?," *Patient Education and Counseling* 75(2) (2009): 178–184.
20. Two representative studies imply that adding psychosocial dimensions to physical and biomedical treatments improves cancer survival. One examined the interactions of palliative care clinicians who establish goals of care and assist with decision–making in addition to addressing physical symptoms (Temel, J. S. et al. "Early Palliative Care for Patients with Metastatic Non–small–cell Lung Cancer," *New England Journal of Medicine* August 363(8) (2010): 733–742). The second is a Cochrane review article that found that psychological interventions improved quality of life measures and 12–month cancer survival for women with metastatic breast cancer (Mustafa, M. et al. "Psychological Interventions for Women with Metastatic Breast Cancer," *Cochrane Database of Systematic Reviews* June 4(6) (2013): CD004253.)
21. Arora, N. K. et al. "Physicians' Decision–making Style and Psychosocial Outcomes Among Cancer Survivors," *Patient Education and Counseling* 77 (2009): 404–412; Bakitas, M. et al. "Effects of a Palliative Care Intervention on Clinical Outcomes in Patients with Advanced Cancer: The Project ENABLE II Randomized Controlled Trial," *The Journal of the American Medical Association* August 302(7) (2009): 741–749; Lelorain, S. et al. "A Systematic Review of the Associations Between Empathy Measures and Patient Outcomes in Cancer Care," *Psycho–Oncology* 21 (2012): 1255–1264; Robinson, J. D. et al. "Consultations Between Patients with Breast Cancer and Surgeons: A Pathway from Patient–centered Communication to Reduced Hopelessness," *Journal of Clinical Oncology* 31 (2013): 351–358; Tulsky, J. A. et al. "Enhancing Communication Between Oncologists and Patients With a Computer–Based Training Program: A Randomized Trial," *Annals of Internal Medicine* 155 (2011): 593–601; Venetis, M. K. et al. "An Evidence Base for Patient–centered Cancer Care: A Meta–analysis of Studies of Observed Communication Between Cancer Specialists and Their Patients," *Patient Education and Counseling* 77(3) (2009): 379–383.
22. Temel J. S. et al., op cit.
23. Oliveira, V. C. et al. "Effectiveness of Training Clinicians' Communication Skills on Patients' Clinical Outcomes: A Systematic Review," *Journal of Manipulative and Physiological Therapeutics* 38(8) (2015): 601–616; Kravitz, R. L. et al. "Influence of Patient Coaching on Analgesic Treatment Adjustment: Secondary Analysis of a Randomized Controlled Trial," *Journal of Pain Symptom Management* 43 (2012): 874–884; Sarinopoulos, I. et al. "Patient–centered Interviewing is Associated with Decreased Responses to

Painful Stimuli: An Initial fMRI Study," *Patient Education and Counseling* 90(2) (2013): 220–225.

24. Street Jr., R. L. et al. "Exploring Communication Pathways to Better Health: Clinician Communication of Expectations for Acupuncture Effectiveness," *Patient Education and Counseling* 89 (2012): 245–251.

25. Epstein, R. M. et al. "Patient–Centered Communication and Diagnostic Testing," *Annals of Family Medicine* September-October 3(5) (2005): 415-421; Stewart, M., B. L. Ryan, and C. Bodea. "Is Patient–centred Care Associated with Lower Diagnostic Costs?," *Health Policy* May 6(4) (2011): 27–31. Both studies are in the family medicine literature. The Epstein study found decreased costs but also increased visit length.

26. Wright, A. A. et al. "Associations Between End–of–Life Discussions, Patient Mental Health, Medical Care Near Death, and Caregiver Bereavement Adjustment," *Journal of the American Medical Association* 300(14) (2008): 1665–1673; Zhang, B. et al. "Health Care Costs in the Last Week of Life: Associations with End–of-life Conversations," *Archives of Internal Medicine Journal* March 169(5) (2009): 480–488.

27. Kelley, J. M. et al. "The Influence of the Patient–clinician Relationship on Healthcare Outcomes: A Systematic Review and Meta–analysis of Randomized Controlled Trials," *PLoS One* 9(4) (2014): e94207.

28. Baker, L., D. O'Connell, and F. Platt. "'What else?' Setting the Agenda for the Clinical Interview," *Annals of Internal Medicine* November 143(10) (2005): 766–770; White, J., W. Levinson, and D. Roter. "'Oh, by the way . . .' The Closing Moments of the Medical Visit," *Journal of General Internal Medicine* 9 (1994): 24–28.

29. Marvel, M. K. et al. "Soliciting the Patient's Agenda: Have We Improved?," *Journal of the American Medical Association* 281 (1999): 283–287.

30. Farrell, M. H., and S. A. Christopher. "Frequency of High–quality Communication Behaviors Used by Primary Care Providers of Heterozygous Infants After Newborn Screening," *Patient Education and Counseling* 90(2) (2013): 226–232; Levinson, W., P. Hudak, and A. Tricco. "Systematic Review of Surgeon–patient Communication. Strengths and Opportunities for Improvement," *Patient Education and Counseling* 93(1) (2013): 3–17; McInnes, I. B., B. Combe, and G. Burmester. "Understanding the Patient Perspective—Results of the Rheumatoid Arthritis: Insights, Strategies & Expectations (RAISE) Patient Needs Survey," *Clinical and Experimental Rheumatology* May-June 31(3) (2013): 350–357.

31. Haywood Jr., C. et al. "An Unequal Burden: Poor Patient–provider Communication and Sickle Cell Disease," *Patient Education and Counseling* 96 (2) (2014): 159–164; Smith, A. et al. "Sharing vs Caring: The Relative Impact of Sharing Decisions Versus Managing Emotions on Patient Outcomes," *Patient Education and Counseling* 82 (2001): 233–239; Weissman, J. S. et al. "Resident Physicians' Preparedness to Provide

Cross–cultural Care," *Journal of the American Medical Association* 294 (2005): 1058–1067.

32. Farrell, M. H., et al., op cit; Acher, A. et al. "Using Human Factors and Systems Engineering to Evaluate Readmission After Complex Surgery," *Journal of the American College of Surgeons* October 221(4) (2015): 810–820; Deuster, L. et al. "A Method to Quantify Residents' Jargon Use During Counseling of Standardized Patients About Cancer Screening," *Journal of General Internal Medicine* December 23(12) (2008): 1947–1952; Slatore, C. G. et al. "Distress and Patient–centered Communication Among Veterans with Incidental (not Screen–detected) Pulmonary Nodules. A Cohort Study," *Annals of the American Thoracic Society* 12(2) (2005): 184–192.

33. Coppola, K. M. et al. "Accuracy of Primary Care and Hospital–based Physicians' Predictions of Elderly Outpatients' Treatment Preferences with and Without Advance Directives," *Archives of Internal Medicine* 161 (2001): 431–440; Gulbrandsen, P. et al. "Confusion in and About Shared Decision Making in Hospital Outpatient Encounters," *Patient Education and Counseling* September 96(3) (2014): 287–294; Levinson, W. et al., 2013, op. cit; Mulley, A. G., C. Trimble, and G. Elwyn. "Stop the Silent Misdiagnosis: Patients' Preferences Matter," *British Medical Journal* 345 (2012): e6572; Smith, A. et al., op. cit; Zikmund–Fisher, B. J. et al. "The DECISIONS Study: A Nationwide Survey of United States Adults Regarding Common Medical Decisions," *Medical Decision Making* 30 (2010): 20S–34S.

34. Nagraj, S. et al. "Changing Practice as a Quality Indicator for Primary Care: Analysis of Data on Voluntary Disenrollment from the English GP Patient Survey," *BMC Family Practice* June 25 (14) (2013): 89.

35. Acher, A. et al. "Using Human Factors and Systems Engineering to Evaluate Readmission After Complex Surgery," *Journal of the American College of Surgeons* October 221(4) (2015): 810–820.

36. Ambady, N. et al. "Surgeons' Tone of Voice: A Clue to Malpractice History," *Surgery* 132 (2002): 132:5–9; Domino, J. et al. "Lack of Physician–patient Communication as a Key Factor Associated with Malpractice Litigation in Neonatal Brachial Plexus Palsy," *Journal of Neurosurgery Pediatrics* February 13(2) (2014): 238–242; Hickson, G. B., and S. S. Entman. "Physician Practice Behavior and Litigation Risk: Evidence and Opportunity," *Clinical Obstetrics and Gynecology* December 51(4) (2008): 688–699; Levinson, W. et al. "Clinician–patient Communication. The Relationship with Malpractice Claims Among Primary Care Clinicians and Surgeons," *Journal of the American Medical Association* 277 (1997): 553–559; Dmochowski, R. R. et al. "Medical Malpractice Claims Risk in Urology: An Empirical Analysis of Patient Complaint Data," *The Journal of Urology* May 183(5) (2010): 1971–1976; Vincent, C., M. Young, and A. Phillips. "Why Do People Sue Doctors? A Study of Patients and Relatives Taking Legal Action," *The Lancet* June 343(8913) (1994): 1609–1613.

37. Baker, L. et al., op. cit.
38. Pollak, K. et al., op cit.
39. Luxford, K. et al., op. cit.
40. Krasner, M. S. et al. "Association of an Education Program in Mindful Communication with Burnout, Empathy, and Attitudes Among Primary Care Physicians," *Journal of the American Medical Association* 302 (2009): 1284–1293.
41. Boissy, A. et al. "Communication Skills Training for Physicians Improves Patient Satisfaction," *Journal of General Internal Medicine* 1(7) (2016): 755–761.
42. Bonvicini, K. A. et al. "Impact of Communication Training on Physician Expression of Empathy," *Patient Education and Counseling* 75 (2009): 3–10; Brock, D. M. et al. "Effectiveness of Intensive Physician Training in Upfront Agenda Setting," *Journal of General Internal Medicine* November 26(1) (2011): 1317–1323; Kennedy, D. M., J. P. Fasolino, and D. J. Gullen. "Improving the Patient Experience Through Provider Communication Skills Building," *Patient Experience Journal* 1(1) (2014): 56–60; Record, J. D. et al., op cit.; Riess, H. et al. "Empathy Training for Resident Physicians: A Randomized Controlled Trial of a Neuroscience–informed Curriculum," *Journal of General Internal Medicine* 27 (2012): 1280–1286.
43. Pollak, K. et al., op cit.
44. Helitzer, D. L. et al. "A Randomized Controlled Trial of Communication Training with Primary Care Providers to Improve Patient–centeredness and Health Risk Communication," *Patient Education and Counseling* 82(1) (2011): 21–29; Yuen, J. K. et al. "A Brief Educational Intervention to Teach Residents Shared Decision Making in the Intensive Care Unit," *Journal of Palliative Medicine* May 16(5) (2013): 531–536.
45. Lee, A. L., E. M. Mader, and C. P. Morley. "Teaching Cross–cultural Communication Skills Online: A Multi–method Evaluation," *Family Medicine* April 47(4) (2015): 302–308.
46. Asuncion, A. et al. "A Curriculum to Improve Residents' End–of–Life Communication and Pain Management Skills During Pediatrics Intensive Care Rotation: Pilot Study," *Journal of Graduate Medical Education* September 5(3) (2013): 510–513; Markin, A. et al. "Impact of a Simulation–based Communication Workshop on Resident Preparedness for End–of–life Communication in the Intensive Care Unit," *Critical Care Research and Practice* (2015): 534879.
47. Ericsson, K. A. "Deliberate Practice and the Acquisition and Maintenance of Expert Performance in Medicine and Related Domains," *Academic Medicine* 79(10 Suppl) (2004): S70–81.
48. Berkhof, M. et al. "Effective Training Strategies for Teaching Communication Skills to Physicians: An Overview of Systematic Reviews," *Patient Education and Counseling* 84 (2011): 152–162.

Chapter 2

1. Lee, T. H. "The Word that Shall Not Be Spoken," *New England Journal of Medicine* 369 (November 7, 2013): 1777–1779.
2. Boissy, A. et al. "Communication Skills Training for Physicians Improves Patient Satisfaction," *Journal of General Internal Medicine* 7 (July 31, 2016): 755–761.
3. Centers for Medicare & Medicaid Services (CMS). "Hospital Consumer Assessment of Healthcare Providers and Systems (HCAHPS) Fact Sheet." Baltimore, MD: CMS, June 2015. http://www.hcahpsonline.org/Files/HCAHPS_Fact_Sheet_June_2015.pdf.
4. Centers for Medicare & Medicaid Services (CMS). "Hospital Value-Based Purchasing," last modified February 15, 2017, https://www.cms.gov/Medicare/Quality-Initiatives-Patient-Assessment-Instruments/hospital-value-based-purchasing/index.html?redirect=/hospital-value-based-purchasing/.
5. Wolf, J. A. et al. "Defining Patient Experience," *Patient Experience Journal* 1, no. 1 (2014): 7–19.
6. LaVela, S. L., and A. S. Gallan. "Evaluation and Measurement of Patient Experience," *Patient Experience Journal* 1, no. 1 (2014): 28–36.
7. Barry, M. J., and S. Edgman-Levitan. "Shared Decision Making—The Pinnacle of Patient-Centered Care," *New England Journal of Medicine* 366 (2012): 780–781.
8. Balogh, E. P., B. T. Miller, and J. R. Ball, eds. *Improving Diagnosis in Health Care: Consensus Studies Report*. Washington, DC: National Academies Press, 2015.
9. Oshima, E., and E. J. Emmanuel. "Shared Decision Making to Improve Care and Reduce Costs," *New England Journal of Medicine* 368 (2013): 6–8.
10. Marvel, M. K. et al. "Soliciting the Patient's Agenda: Have We Improved?," *JAMA* 281 (January 20, 1999): 283–287.
11. Dwamena, F. et al. "Interventions for Providers to Promote a Patient-Centred Approach in Clinical Consultations," *Cochrane Database of Systematic Reviews* 12 (2012): 1–160.
12. Weiss, R., E. Vittinghoff, and W. G. Anderson. "Hospitalist Empathy Is Associated with Decreased Patient Anxiety and Higher Ratings of Communication in Admission Encounters," *Society of Hospital Medicine Meeting Abstracts* 11 (2016).
13. Safran, D. G., W. Miller, and H. Beckman. "Organizational Dimensions of Relationship-Centered Care. Theory, Evidence, and Practice," *Journal of General Internal Medicine* 21 (2006): S9–15.
14. Lichstein, P. R. "Returning to the Bedside: Notes from a Clinical Educator," *North Carolina Institute of Medicine Journal* 76, no. 3 (2015): 174–179.
15. Kahn, M. W. "Etiquette-Based Medicine," *The New England Journal of Medicine* 358 (2008): 1988–1989.

16. Lehmann, L. S. et al. "The Effect of Bedside Case Presentations on Patients' Perceptions of Their Medical Care," *The New England Journal of Medicine* 336 (1997): 1150–1155.

17. Stein, J. et al. "A Remedy for Fragmented Hospital Care," *Harvard Business Review*. November 20, 2013, https://hbr.org/2013/11/a-remedy-for-fragmented-hospital-care.

18. Wofford, M. M. et al. "Patient Complaints about Physician Behaviors: A Qualitative Study," *Academic Medicine* 79, no. 2 (February 2004): 134–138.

Chapter 3

1. Hammerstein II, O., and R. Rodgers. "Do-Re-Mi." *The Sound of Music*. RCA Victor, 1965. CD recording.

2. Wallace, L. S. et al. "Setting the Stage: Surgery Patients' Expectations for Greetings During Routine Office Visits," *Journal of Surgical Research* 157 (2009): 91–95.

3. Swayden, K. J. et al. "Effect of Sitting vs. Standing on Perception of Clinician Time at Bedside: a Pilot Study," *Patient Education Counseling* 86, no. 2 (February 2012): 166–71.

4. Marvel, M. K. et al. "Soliciting the Patient's Agenda: Have We Improved?," *JAMA* 281, no. 3 (January 20, 1999): 283–287.

5. White, J., W. Levinson, and D. Roter. "'Oh, by the way . . . ': The Closing Moments of the Medical Visit," *Journal of General Internal Medicine* 9, no. 1 (1994): 24–28.

Chapter 4

1. Halpern, J. "From Idealized Clinical Empathy to Empathic Communication in Medical Care," *Medicine, Health Care, and Philosophy* 17, no. 2 (2014): 301–311.

2. Derksen, F., J. Bensing, and A. Lagro-Janssen. "Effectiveness of Empathy in General Practice: a Systematic Review," *British Journal of General Practice* 63, no. 606 (2013): e76–84.

3. Hojat, M. et al. "Patient Perceptions of Physician Empathy, Satisfaction with Physician, Interpersonal Trust, and Compliance." *International Journal of Medical Education* 1 (2010): 83–87.

4. Kelley, J. M. et al. "The Influence of the Patient-Clinician Relationship on Healthcare Outcomes: a Systematic Review and Meta-Analysis of Randomized Controlled Trials," *PLOS ONE* 9, no. 4 (2014): e94207. doi: 10.1371/journal.pone.0094207.

5. Gallese, V. "Mirror Neurons, Embodied Simulation, and the Neural Basis of Social Identification," *Psychoanalytic Dialogues* 19 (2009): 519–536.

6. Lown, B. "A Social Neuroscience-informed Model for Teaching and Practising Compassion in Health Care," *Medical Education*, 50 (2016): 332–342. doi: 10.1111/medu.12926.

7. Levinson, W., R. Gorawara-Bhat, and J. Lamb. "A Study of Patient Cues and Physician Responses in Primary Care and Surgical Settings," *JAMA* 284 (2000): 1021–1027.
8. Suchman, A. et al. "A Model of Empathic Communication in the Medical Interview," *JAMA* 277 (1997): 678–682.

Chapter 5

1. Whyte, W. H. "Is Anybody Listening?," *Fortune* 14, no. 3 (September 1950): 174. This quotation is often misattributed to George Bernard Shaw.
2. Kalet, A., and C. Chou, eds. *Remediation in Medical Education: A Mid-Course Correction.* New York: Springer, 2014.
3. Moral, R. R. et al. "Effectiveness of Motivational Interviewing to Improve Therapeutic Adherence in Patients over Sixty-Five Years Old with Chronic Diseases: A Cluster Randomized Clinical Trial in Primary Care," *Patient Education and Counseling* 98, no. 8 (August 2015): 977–983; Kelley, J. M. et al. "The Influence of the Patient-Clinician Relationship on Healthcare Outcomes: A Systematic Review and Meta-Analysis of Randomized Controlled Trials," *PLOS ONE* 9, no. 4 (2014): e9420; Rocco, N. et al. "Patient-Centered Plan-of-Care Tool for Improving Clinical Outcomes," *Quality Management in Health Care* 20, no. 2 (April–June 2011): 89–97.
4. Yin, H. S. et al. "Liquid Medication Dosing Errors in Children: Role of Provider Counseling Strategies," *Academic Pediatrics* 14, no. 3 (May–June 2014): 262–270.
5. Pollak, K. et al. "Effect of Teaching Motivational Interviewing via Communication Coaching on Clinician and Patient Satisfaction in Primary Care and Pediatric Obesity-Focused Offices," *Patient Education and Counseling* 99, no. 2 (February 2016): 300–303.

Chapter 6

1. Murthy, V. H. "Ending the Opioid Epidemic: A Call to Action," *New England Journal of Medicine* 375 (December 22, 2016): 2413–2415.
2. Saha, S., J. J. Arbelaez, and L. A. Cooper. "Patient-Physician Relationships and Racial Disparities in the Quality of Health Care," *American Journal of Public Health* 93, no. 10 (2003): 1713–1719.

Chapter 7

1. Pearce, C. et al. "Doctor, Patient, and Computer—A Framework for the New Consultation," *Journal of the American Medical Informatics Association* 78 (2009): 32–38.
2. Blumenthal, D., and M. Tavenner. "The 'Meaningful Use' Regulation for Electronic Health Records," *The New England Journal of Medicine* 363 (2010): 501–504. PubMed, http://dx.doi.org/10.1056/NEJMp1006114.

3. Toll, E. "A Piece of My Mind. The Cost of Technology," *The Journal of the American Medical Association* 307, no. 23 (2012): 2497–2498.

4. Margalit, R. S. et al. "Electronic Medical Record Use and Physician-Patient Communication: an Observational Study of Israeli Primary Care Encounters," *Patient Education and Counseling* 61, no. 1 (April 2006): 134–141.

5. Ferkeitich, A. K., and D. J. Frid. "Depression and Coronary Heart Disease: a Review of the Literature," *Clinics in Geriatric Medicine* 9 (2001): 50–56.

6. Harman, J. S. et al. "Electronic Medical Record Availability and Primary Care Depression Treatment," *Journal of General Internal Medicine* 27, no. 8 (August 2012): 962–967.

7. Ratanawongsa, N. et al. "Association Between Clinician Computer Use and Communication with Patients in Safety-Net Clinics," *The Journal of the American Medical Association Internal Medicine* 176, no. 1 (2016): 125–128.

8. Verghese, A. "Culture Shock—Patient as Icon, Icon as Patient," *The New England Journal of Medicine* 359, no. 26 (2008): 2748–2751.

9. Sinsky, C. et al. "Allocation of Physician Time in Ambulatory Practice: a Time and Motion Study in Four Specialties," *Annals of Internal Medicine* 165 (2016): 753–760.

10. Shanafelt, T. D. et al. "Relationship between Clerical Burden and Characteristics of the Electronic Environment with Physician Burnout and Professional Satisfaction," *Mayo Clinic Proceedings* 91, no. 7 (July 2016): 836–848.

11. Sinsky, C. "Texting While Doctoring a Patient Safety Hazard," *Annals of Internal Medicine* 159, no. 11 (2013): 782–783.

12. Frankel, R. M., and J. J. Saleem. "Attention on the Flight Deck: What Ambulatory Care Clinicians Can Learn from Pilots about Complex Coordinated Actions," *Patient Education and Counseling* 93, no. 3 (December 2013): 367–372.

13. Graber, M. L. et al. "Electronic Health Record-Related Events in Medical Malpractice Claims," *Journal of Patient Safety* (November 6, 2015): doi: 10.1097/PTS.0000000000000240.

14. Duke, P., R. M. Frankel, and S. Reis. "How to Integrate the Electronic Health Record and Patient-Centered Communication Into the Medical Visit: A Skills-Based Approach," *Teaching and Learning in Medicine* 25, no. 4 (2013): 358–365.

15. Woodcock, E. W. *Mastering Patient Flow to Increase Efficiency and Earnings.* Englewood, CO: Medical Group Management Association, 2000.

16. Cuddy, A. *Presence: Bringing Your Boldest Self to Your Biggest Challenges.* Boston, MA: Little, Brown and Company, 2015.

17. Toll, E. "A Piece of My Mind. The Cost of Technology," *The Journal of the American Medical Association* 307, no. 23 (2012): 2497–2498.

Chapter 8

1. Senge, P. M. *The Fifth Discipline: The Art and Practice of the Learning Organization.* New York: Doubleday, 1990.
2. Miller, W. R., and S. Rollnick. *Motivational Interviewing: Helping People Change.* New York: The Guilford Press, 2013.
3. Ibid.
4. As the originators of motivational interviewing, Miller and Rollnick continue to be the definitive source on MI. They have updated the theory and model over the years, but both the spirit and the techniques described here draw heavily on their pioneering work and remain a cornerstone of MI. For a more in-depth read, see their book (2013), particularly Chapters 2, 6, 8, and 13.

Chapter 9

1. Mulley, A., C. Trimble, and G. Elwyn. "Stop the Preference Misdiagnosis: Patients' Preferences Matter," *British Medical Journal* 345 (2012): e6572; Hoffman, R. M. et al. "Prostate Cancer Screening Decisions: Results from the National Survey of Medical Decisions (DECISIONS Study)," *Archives of Internal Medicine* 169, no. 17 (2009): 1611–1618, doi: 10.1001/archinternmed.2009.26; Ling, B. S. et al. "Informed Decision-making and Colorectal Cancer Screening. Is it Occurring in Primary Care?," *Medical Care* 46 (2008): S23–29; Coppola, K. M. et al. "Accuracy of Primary Care and Hospital-Based Physicians' Predictions of Elderly Outpatients' Treatment Preferences with and without Advance Directives," *Archives of Internal Medicine* 161 (2001): 431–440; Zikmund-Fisher, B. J. et al. "The Decisions Study: a Nationwide Survey of United States Adults Regarding Common Medical Decisions," *Medical Decision-making* 30 (2010): 20S–34S.
2. Ling, B. S. et al. "Informed Decision-making and Colorectal Cancer Screening. Is it Occurring in Primary Care?," *Medical Care* 46 (2008): S23–29.
3. Ling, B. S. et al. "Informed Decision-making and Colorectal Cancer Screening. Is it Occurring in Primary Care?," *Medical Care* 46 (2008): S23–29; Coppola, K. M. et al. "Accuracy of Primary Care and Hospital-Based Physicians' Predictions of Elderly Outpatients' Treatment Preferences with and without Advance Directives," *Archives of Internal Medicine* 161 (2001): 431–440; Zikmund-Fisher, B. J. et al. "The Decisions Study: a Nationwide Survey of United States Adults Regarding Common Medical Decisions," *Medical Decision-making* 30 (2010): 20S–34S.
4. Hoffman, R. M. et al. "Prostate cancer screening decisions: results from the National Survey of Medical Decisions (DECISIONS study)," *Archives of Internal Medicine* 169 (2009): 1611-1618.
5. Institute of Medicine (US) Committee on Quality of Health Care in America. *Crossing the Quality Chasm: A New Health System for the 21st Century.* Washington (DC): National Academies Press (US) (2001).

6. Hibbard, J. H., and Greene, J. "What the evidence shows about patient activation: better health outcomes and care experiences; fewer data on costs," *Health Affairs* 32, no. 2 (2013): 207-214.

7. Elwyn, G., A. Edwards, and R. Thompson, eds. *Shared Decision Making in Health Care: Achieving Evidence-based Patient Choice.* 3rd ed. Oxford: Oxford University Press, 2016. Oxford Scholarship Online, 2016. doi: 10.1093/acprof:oso/9780198723448.001.0001.

8. Fisher, B. et al. "Twenty-Year Follow-Up of a Randomized Trial Comparing Total Mastectomy, Lumpectomy, and Lumpectomy Plus Irradiation for the Treatment of Invasive Breast Cancer," *The New England Journal of Medicine* 347 (2002): 1233–1241; Veronesi, U. et al. "Twenty-Year Follow-Up of a Randomized Study Comparing Breast-Conserving Surgery with Radical Mastectomy for Early Breast Cancer," *The New England Journal of Medicine* 347 (2002): 1227–1232; Collins, E. D. et al. "Can Women with Early-Stage Breast Cancer Make an Informed Decision for Mastectomy?," *Journal of Clinical Oncology* 27 (2008): 519–525.

9. Mulley, A., C. Trimble, and G. Elwyn. "Stop the Preference Misdiagnosis: Patients' Preferences Matter," *British Medical Journal* 345 (2012): e6572.

10. Greene, J. et al. "When Patient Activation Levels Change, Health Outcomes and Costs Change, Too," *Health Affairs* 34, no. 3 (2015): 431–437.

11. Paling, J. "Strategies to Help Patients Understand Risks," *British Medical Journal* 327 (2003): 745–748; Gigerenzer, G. et al. "Helping Doctors and Patients Make Sense of Health Statistics," *Association of Psychological Science* 8, no. 2 (2008): 53–96.

12. Collins, E. D. et al. "Can Women with Early-Stage Breast Cancer Make an Informed Decision for Mastectomy?," *Journal of Clinical Oncology* 27 (2008): 519–525.

13. Houts, P. S. et al. "Using Pictographs to Enhance Recall of Spoken Medical Instructions," *Patient Education and Counseling* 35 (1998): 83–88.

14. Stacey, D. et al. "Decision Aids for People Facing Health Treatment or Screening Decisions," *Cochrane Database of Systematic Reviews* (January 28 2014): doi: 10.1002/14651858.CD001431.pub4.

15. "Osteoporosis Decision Aid," Mayo Clinic Shared Decision-making National Resource Center, version 3.4.4, accessed January 4, 2017. https://osteoporosisdecisionaid.mayoclinic.org/index.php/osteo.

Chapter 10

1. Van de Ridder, J. M. et al. "What Is Feedback in Clinical Education?," *Medical Education* 42, no. 2 (2008): 189–197.

2. Gottman, J., and R. W. Levenson. "What Predicts Change in Marital Interaction over Time? A Study in Alternative Methods," *Family Processes Journal* 38.2 (1999): 143–158.

Chapter 11

1. Gawande, A. "Personal Best," *The New Yorker* October 3, 2011, http://www .newyorker.com/magazine/2011/10/03/personal-best.
2. The Associated Press. "Joe Maddon Keeps His Cubs Moving, and Guessing," *The New York Times* July 9, 2016, https://www.nytimes.com/2016/07/10/sports /baseball/joe-maddon-keeps-his-cubs-moving-and-guessing.html?_r=0.
3. Cooperrider, D., and D. Whitney. *Appreciative Inquiry: A Positive Revolution in Change.* San Francisco: Berrett-Koehler Publishers, Inc., 2005.

Chapter 12

1. Gawande, A. "Cowboys and Pit Crews." *The New Yorker* May 26, 2011, http: //www.newyorker.com/news/news-desk/cowboys-and-pit-crews.
2. "TeamSTEPPS 2.0," Agency for Healthcare Research and Quality, Rockville, MD. Last modified September 2016, accessed March 17, 2017. https:// www.ahrq.gov/teamstepps/instructor/index.html.
3. Stock, R. et al. "Measuring Team Development in Clinical Care Settings," *Family Medicine* 45 (2013): 691–700.
4. Lencioni, P. *The Five Dysfunctions of a Team: A Leadership Fable.* San Francisco: Jossey-Bass, 2002.
5. Shunk, R. et al. "Huddle-Coaching: a Dynamic Intervention for Trainees and Staff to Support Team-Based Care," *Academic Medicine* 89 (2014): 244–250.

Chapter 13

1. The Joint Commission. "Behaviors that Undermine a Culture of Safety," *Sentinel Event Alert*, no. 40. July 9, 2008, http://www.jointcommission.org /sentinel_event_alert_issue_40_behaviors_that_undermine_a_culture_ of_safety/.
2. Riskin, A. et al. "The Impact of Rudeness on Medical Team Performance: A Randomized Trial," *Pediatrics* 136 (August 2015): 487–495.
3. Haraway, D. L., and W. M. Haraway. "Analysis of the Effect of Conflict-Management and Resolution Training on Employee Stress at a Healthcare Organization," *Hospital Topics* 83, no. 4 (February 2005): 11–17.
4. "Mehrabian's Communication Research: Professor Albert Mehrabian's Communications Model," Businessballs, accessed March 19, 2017. http:// www.businessballs.com/mehrabiancommunications.htm.
5. Senge, P. M. et al. *The Fifth Discipline Fieldbook: Strategies and Tools for Building a Learning Organization.* New York: Crown Business, 1994.
6. Kahneman, D. *Thinking, Fast and Slow.* New York: Farrar, Straus and Giroux, 2011.
7. Fisher, R., W. L. Ury, and B. Patton. *Getting to Yes*, 3rd ed. New York: Penguin Books, 2011.
8. Ibid.

9. Stone, D., B. Patton, and S. Heen. *Difficult Conversations: How to Discuss What Matters Most.* New York: Penguin Books, 2010.

Chapter 14

1. Cooper-Patrick, L. et al. "Race, Gender, and Partnership in the Patient-Physician Relationship," *JAMA* 282 (August 11, 1999): 583–589.
2. Betancourt, J. R., and R. K. King. "Unequal Treatment: The Institute of Medicine Report and its Public Health Implications," *Public Health Reports* 118, no. 4 (July–Aug 2003): 287–292.
3. National Institute of Diabetes and Digestive and Kidney Diseases. "A Summary Report. National Kidney Disease Education Program: Reducing Disparities, Improving Care." Washington DC: NIH Publication 14-7381.2014. Accessed from https://www.niddk.nih.gov/health-information/health-communication-programs/nkdep/about-nkdep/summary/Documents/nkdep-summary-report-508.pdf on March 18, 2017.
4. Buchmueller, T., and C. S. Carpenter. "Disparities in Health Insurance Coverage, Access, and Outcomes for Individuals in Same-Sex Versus Different-Sex Relationships, 2000–2007," *American Journal of Public Health* 100, no. 3 (March 2010): 489–495.
5. Kandula, N. R. et al. "Low Rates of Colorectal, Cervical, and Breast Cancer Screening in Asian Americans Compared With Non-Hispanic Whites," *Cancer* 107, no. 1 (2006): 184–192.
6. Cooper-Patrick, L. et al. "Race, Gender, and Partnership in the Patient-Physician Relationship," *JAMA* 282 (August 11, 1999): 583–589.
7. Mays, V. M. "Research Challenges and Bioethics Responsibilities in the Aftermath of the Presidential Apology to the Survivors of the U. S. Public Health Services Syphilis Study at Tuskegee," *Ethics & Behavior* 22, no. 6 (2012): 419–430.
8. Stepanikova, I., and G. R. Oates. "Perceived Discrimination and Privilege in Healthcare: The Role of Socioeconomic Status and Race," *American Journal of Preventive Medicine* 52 (2017): S86–S94.
9. Cooper-Patrick, L. et al. "Race, Gender, and Partnership in the Patient-Physician Relationship," *JAMA* 282 (August 11, 1999): 583–589.
10. Hutzler, L. et al. "Do Internal Medicine Interns Practice Etiquette-Based Communication? A Critical Look at the Inpatient Encounter," *Journal of Hospital Medicine* 11 (2013): 631–634.
11. Schoenthaler, A. et al. "Provider Communication Effects Medication Adherence in Hypertensive African Americans," *Patient Education and Counseling* 75, no. 2 (2009): 185–191.
12. Diamond, L. et al. "Getting By: Underuse of Interpreters by Resident Physicians," *Journal of General Internal Medicine* 24 (2009): 256–262.

13. Chen, P. W. "When the Patient Gets Lost in Translation," *The New York Times* (April 23, 2009) http://www.nytimes.com/2009/04/23/health/23chen.html. Accessed March 19, 2017.

14. Betancourt, J. R., and R. K. King. "Unequal Treatment: The Institute of Medicine Report and its Public Health Implications," *Public Health Reports* 118, no. 4 (July–Aug 2003): 287–292.

15. Amador, J., P. Flynn, and H. Betancourt. "Cultural Beliefs about Health Professionals and Perceived Empathy Influence Continuity of Cancer Screening Following a Negative Encounter," *Journal of Behavioral Medicine* 38 (2015): 798–808.

16. Beach, M. C. et al. "Are Physicians' Attitudes of Respect Accurately Perceived by Patients and Associated with More Positive Communication Behaviors?," *Patient Education and Counseling* 62 (2006): 347–354.

17. Kutner, M. et al. *The Health Literacy of America's Adults: Results from the 2003 National Assessment of Adult Literacy* (NCES 2006–483). U.S. Department of Education. Washington, DC: National Center for Education Statistics, 2006.

18. Judson, T. J., A. S. Detsky, and M. J. Press. "Encouraging Patients to Ask Questions: How to Overcome 'White-Coat Silence,'" *Journal of the American Medical Association* 309 (2013): 2325–2326.

19. Cooper-Patrick, L. et al. "Race, Gender, and Partnership in the Patient-Physician Relationship," *JAMA* 282 (August 11, 1999): 583–589.

Chapter 15

1. A number of studies in recent years have pointed to the association between hierarchy, stress, and health. These include: Tung, J. et al. "Social Environment Is Associated with Gene Regulatory Variation in the Rhesus Macaque Immune System," *Proceedings of the National Academy of Sciences of the United States of America* 109, no. 17 (Apr 2012): 6490–6495; Snyder-Mackler, N. et al. "Social Status Alters Immune Regulation and Response to Infection in Macaques," *Science* 354, no. 6315 (Nov 25, 2016): 1041–1045; Sapolsky, R. M. "The Influence of Social Hierarchy on Primate Health," *Science* 308, no. 5722 (April 29, 2005): 648–652; Cundiff, J. M. et al. "Hierarchy and Health: Physiological Effects of Interpersonal Experiences Associated with Socioeconomic Position," *Health Psychology* 35, no. 4 (April 2016): 356–365; Marmot, M. G. et al. "Health Inequalities among British Civil Servants: The Whitehall II Study," *The Lancet* 337, no. 8754 (June 08, 1991): 1387–1393; Wilkinson, R. G. *Mind the Gap—Hierarchies, Health, and Human Evolution.* London: Weiderfeld and Nicolson, 2000.

2. Tsao, K., and M. Browne. "Culture of Safety: A Foundation for Patient Care," *Seminars in Pediatric Surgery* 24, no. 6 (December 2015): 283–287.

3. Angoff, N. et al. "Power Day: Addressing the Use and Abuse of Power in Medical Training," *Journal of Bioethical Inquiry* 13, no. 2 (June 2016): 203–213.
4. For further details on building a just culture, the following references can be helpful: Boysen, P. G., 2nd. "Just Culture: A Foundation for Balanced Accountability and Patient Safety," *Ochsner Journal* 13, no. 3 (September 2013): 400–406; Marx, D. "Patient Safety and the 'Just Culture': A Primer for Health Care Executives" (2001). http://www.chpso.org/sites/main/files/file -attachments/marx_primer.pdf; Pepe, J., and P. J. Cataldo. "Manage Risk, Build a Just Culture," *Health Progress* 92, no. 4 (July–August 2011): 56–60.

Chapter 16

1. Berkhof, M. et al. "Effective Training Strategies for Teaching Communication Skills to Physicians: an Overview of Systematic Reviews," *Patient Education and Counseling* 84 (2011): 152–162.

Chapter 17

1. Chou, C. et al. "The Impact of a Faculty Learning Community on Professional and Personal Development: the Facilitator Training Program of the American Academy on Communication in Healthcare," *Academic Medicine* 89 (2014): 1051–1056.
2. Ferguson, K. J. et al. "Defining and Describing Medical Learning Communities: Results of a National Survey," *Academic Medicine* 84 (2009): 1549–1556.
3. Kotter, J. P. "Leading Change: Why Transformation Efforts Fail," *Harvard Business Review* 73 (1995): 59–67.
4. Chou, C. L. et al. "Enhancing Patient Experience by Training Local Trainers in Fundamental Communication Skills," *Patient Experience Journal* 1(2) (2014): 36–45.
5. Berkhof, M. et al. "Effective Training Strategies for Teaching Communication Skills to Physicians: an Overview of Systematic Reviews," *Patient Education and Counseling* 84 (2011): 152–162.
6. Ericsson, K. A. "Deliberate Practice and the Acquisition and Maintenance of Expert Performance in Medicine and Related Domains," *Academic Medicine* 79, no.10 Suppl (2004): S70–81.
7. Frankel, R. M., and T. Stein. "Getting the Most Out of the Clinical Encounter: the Four Habits Model," *Permanente Journal* 3 (1999): 79–88.
8. Chou, C. L. et al. "Enhancing Patient Experience by Training Local Trainers in Fundamental Communication Skills," *Patient Experience Journal* 1(2) (2014): 36–45.
9. U.S. News Health. Accessed August 12, 2017. http://health.usnews.com/best -hospitals/area/az/mayo-clinic-6860019

10. Kennedy, D. M., J. P. Fasolino, and D. J. Gullen. "Improving the Patient Experience Through Provider Communication Skills Building," *Patient Experience Journal* 1(1) (2014): 56–60.
11. Merlino, J. *Service Fanatics: How to Build Superior Patient Experience the Cleveland Clinic Way*. New York, NY: McGraw-Hill Education, 2014.
12. Frankel, M., and T. Stein, "Getting the Most Out of the Clinical Encounter: The Four Habits Model," *Journal of Medical Practice Management* 16 (2001): 184–191.
13. Windover, A. et al. "The REDE Model of Healthcare Communication: Optimizing Relationship as a Therapeutic Agent," *Journal of Patient Experience* (2014); 1(1): 8–13. Note that REDE stands for *Relationship: Establishment, Development, and Engagement*.
14. G. Makoul, "The SEGUE Framework for Teaching and Assessing Communication Skills," *Patient Education and Counseling* 45 (2001): 23–34.
15. Beach, M.C., and T. Inui, Relationship-Centered Care Research Network, "Relationship-Centered Care: A Constructive Reframing," *Journal of General Internal Medicine* 21, suppl. 1 (2006): S3–8.
16. Boissy, A., and T. Gilligan, eds. *Communication the Cleveland Clinic Way: How to Drive a Relationship-centered Strategy for Exceptional Patient Experience*. New York, NY: McGraw-Hill Education, 2016.
17. Boissy, A., et al. "Communication Skills Training for Physicians Improves Patient Satisfaction," *Journal of General Internal Medicine* 31(7): 755–761.
18. The CAHPS® Clinician & Group Survey (CG-CAHPS) assesses patients' experiences with health care providers and staff in doctors' offices. Accessed April 19, 2017. https://www.cahpsdatabase.ahrq.gov/default.aspx.
19. Boissy, A., and T. Gilligan, eds. *Communication the Cleveland Clinic Way: How to Drive a Relationship-centered Strategy for Exceptional Patient Experience*. New York, NY: McGraw-Hill Education, 2016.
20. University of Maryland School of Medicine. Accessed May 20, 2017. http://www.medschool.umaryland.edu/about/.
21. University of Maryland School of Medicine. "The Program for Excellence in Patient-Centered Communication." Accessed April 12, 2017. http://www.medschool.umaryland.edu/programs/pep/.
22. The CAHPS® Clinician & Group Survey (CG-CAHPS) assesses patients' experiences with healthcare providers and staff in doctors' offices. Accessed April 19, 2017. https://www.cahpsdatabase.ahrq.gov/default.aspx.
23. U.S. News Health. Accessed May 20, 2017. http://health.usnews.com/best-hospitals/area/ca/san-mateo-medical-center-6933310.
24. Wake Forest Baptist Health System. Accessed May 20, 2017. http://www.wakehealth.edu/About-Us/.
25. Texas Children's Hospital. Accessed May 26, 2017. http://www.texaschildrens.org/about-us/news/releases/texas-childrens-hospital-ranks-4th-nationally-among-all-childrens-hospitals.

26. University of California San Francisco. "The Center for Enhancement of Communication in Healthcare: Testimonials." Accessed April 12, 2017. http://cech.ucsf.edu/testimonials.
27. Based on internal evaluation surveys collected immediately after participants attended the one-day program.

INDEX

ABOUT THE EDITORS

Calvin Chou, MD, PhD, is Professor of Clinical Medicine at the University of California San Francisco (UCSF) and staff physician at the Veterans Administration (VA) Medical Center in San Francisco. As Vice President for External Education for the Academy of Communication in Healthcare (ACH), he is nationally recognized for his efforts in education and research to enhance communication between patients and physicians. He is also director of VALOR, an innovative longitudinal program based at the VA that emphasizes humanistic clinical skill development for medical students, and he holds the first endowed Academy Chair in the Scholarship of Teaching and Learning at UCSF. He has delivered communication skills curricula for providers at medical centers across the country, including Mayo Clinic, Cleveland Clinic, Stanford University, New York Presbyterian Hospital, Wake Forest University, and Texas Children's Hospital. His research interests include assessment of curricular developments in clinical skills and clinical skills remediation, influencing feedback in health sciences education, and enhancing communication for interprofessional trainees. He is coeditor of the book *Remediation in Medical Education: A Midcourse Correction*.

A graduate of Yale University, he received his PhD in microbiology and his MD at Columbia University, and completed residency training in internal medicine at UCSF.

Laura Cooley, PhD, is Senior Director of Education and Outreach for the Academy of Communication in Healthcare (ACH). She leads strategic efforts to support the ACH mission by collaborating with healthcare leaders to develop and deliver customized communication skills training programs. While earning her doctorate in health communication at Bowling Green State University, she examined organizational and interpersonal communication dynamics encountered across the healthcare context. Her research interests include the intersections between patient-centered care, interpersonal skills, mindfulness, empathy, and communication in the end-of-life context. She has led presentations at many notable U.S. healthcare centers and at national events hosted by organizations such as the Institute for Healthcare Improvement (IHI), the American Medical Group Association (AMGA), Planetree, the Medical Group Management Association (MGMA), the Beryl Institute, and Press Ganey.

ABOUT
THE ACADEMY OF COMMUNICATION
IN HEALTHCARE

The Academy of Communication in Healthcare (ACH) is the professional home for all those who are committed to improving communication and relationships in healthcare. ACH accomplishes this by welcoming researchers, educators, clinicians, patients, patient advocates, and all members of the healthcare team; providing opportunities for collaboration, support, and personal and professional development; identifying the strengths, resources, and needs of patients, their family members, and healthcare professionals, both as unique individuals and in relationship with one another; developing skills that integrate biological, psychological, and social domains; applying existing scholarship from multiple disciplines and developing new knowledge through research; promoting collaborative relationships among clinicians and patients, teachers and learners, and all members of the healthcare team; and incorporating the core values of respect, empathy, and genuineness in human relationships and the importance of self-awareness in all activities.

Visit www.ACHonline.org